Easy
Low-Fat
Cooking

Easy Low-Fat Cooking

by
Beverly Chesser

New Leaf Press

First printing: June 1992
Second printing: April 1993
Third printing: November 1994

Library of Congress Catalog Number: 92-60941
ISBN: 0-89221-226-8

Contents

DEDICATION

It is a great privilege for me to dedicate this book to my beloved husband, Ryland S. Chesser, and my precious daughter, Rachel Chesser, both of whom made many sacrifices to enable me to do my television show, "Beverly Exercise," and my radio programs, "Your Health Coach," and "Health Tip." Many times Ryland and Rachel had to prepare their own meals and do lots of other things for themselves because of my hectic schedule. Without them, I know I would not have been able to do all that God has allowed me to do. Thank you, Ryland and Rachel, for being such encouragers and supporters.

Also, a special dedication to my mother, Leah Gore Payne, who raised ten children. I shall always remember her telling me whenever I attempted to cook, "Beverly, I don't know if you will ever learn how to cook . . . but you sure do know how to make a mess." I always left every cabinet and drawer wide open while I was cooking. To this day, I still make quite a mess; but I do like to cook and I clean up the mess.

ACKNOWLEDGEMENTS

A special thank you to Dr. Howard Ausherman for his foreword to this book and for all the information he has furnished over the years for my television program, "Beverly Exercise," and radio programs, "Your Health Coach" and "Health Tip."

I would like to acknowledge and thank all of my television viewers who have sent in their favorite low-fat recipes. Many of the recipes have been submitted by viewers. They are acknowledged by viewer name, city, and state.

(Please note: Calculations regarding fat percentages are only approximate. Many recipes sent in by viewers already carried fat percentages. We have retained these, listing the information as it was given. Also, you will notice our fat percentages go no higher than 30%. Thus, you can be assured that all recipes are relatively low in fat. Several years ago, our nation's Surgeon General advised us to keep the fat calories per day to no more than a maximum of 30%. Less than 30% is even better. When using a recipe that lists calories from fat at 30%, eat less of that particular food and fill up on fruits and vegetables instead.)

FOREWORD

As a retired anesthesiologist, I can say that an overweight patient is not only a greater problem to his physicians but also is at much greater risk than a normal-sized patient undergoing anesthesia and surgery. Sixty percent of Americans are overweight. The fact is that 90 percent of strokes, heart attacks, high blood pressure, and diseases related to the cardiovascular system are preventable. They are caused not by heredity or age but by all the ill effects of improper diet, lack of exercise, stress, and cigarette smoking. The individual impact of the life style choices are cumulative and interconnected.

The National Academy of Sciences concluded that one half of the ten leading causes of death in the U.S. are primarily related to life style habits that can work for good health or against it. The choice is ours to make. The American way of life has come to dictate the American way of death.

One does not have to be a nutritionist to understand that simple foods without added fat, sugar, sodium, dyes, and preservatives are generally preferable. You don't have to be a physiologist to understand that regular moderate exercise is preferable to no exercise.

Our shelves are already covered with a great variety of cookbooks filled with gourmet foods, rich dainties, and cholesterol-laden recipes. Today, we see more Americans beginning to realize the benefits of proper diet and exercise. Beverly has gleaned from numerous health publications valuable information with nutritious diets avoiding the pitfalls of the modern American diet. In her exercise program, viewed throughout the country on TV, she emphasizes a healthful diet with exercise.

My wife and I have been exercising with her and following her nutrition tapes for over five years. I am sure you will find this nutrition book valuable as a guide to healthful, everyday eating.

— Howard M. Ausherman, M.D.

INTRODUCTION

Reaping What We Sow —

Today you might be in a garden of briars and weeds in your life. Friend, it is time to plant seeds — seeds of health. Often we pray or ask others to pray that we might regain health. However, we cannot reap where we have not sown. We need to plant seeds of health today.

Please don't think I am talking down to you. You see, when I was twenty-seven years old, I found myself totally in a weed garden as far as my health and emotional self was concerned. I had gone through a divorce, lost a lot of weight (I weighed seventy-nine pounds at my lowest point) and had developed allergies to almost everything. At this low point, I discovered exercise and learned what changing my eating habits would do for me. I began to exercise daily and learned to eat the low-fat way. In a matter of weeks, I could feel my strength returning and I wasn't nearly as sick as I had been. I knew then that exercise and a healthy way of eating would be my choice for life. Today, at fifty years of age, I praise God for opening my eyes and showing me a better way.

I was sick in my body and God healed me through lifestyle changes of eating and exercising. If you are having trouble committing to exercise and right eating, perhaps you need to check your heart and spirit first.

Don't look in the mirror and just see a set of ugly thighs looking back at you or a potbelly. Look at your whole self and realize that you are a unique creation of God — maybe one that needs a little exercise and a better eating program — but still a unique creation of God!

Discipline is a gift from God. We may not like applying it to our lives, but boy, do we love the results! Discipline sets us free. It does not enslave. Bad habits such as not eating right and not exercising are what enslave and destroy a person.

I remember a pastor who told me about a king who did not like the message nor the messenger, so he threw him in jail. Please don't let that be your feelings toward me as I share with you the benefits of exercise and low-fat eating.

Fit For Service —

God does not want you worn-out and plugging along. For much too long we, as Christians, have just forgotten about our physical selves. Oh yes, we work on the spiritual self and that is good, but our physical selves have to be nurtured as well. Christians, we are hurting because of our neglect of our bodies. We are not all that God wants us to be because of this. Now is the time to recognize what we have done to ourselves and start anew. Today is a new day and a new beginning. God means for us to care for our bodies which are His holy temples. God shows us the things He wants us to do through our hearts and minds, but it is with our physical bodies that we have to carry these things out.

What? Know ye not that your body is the temple of the Holy Ghost which is in you, which you have of God and you are not your own? For ye are bought with a price: Therefore glorify God in your body, and in your spirit, which are God's (1 Cor. 6:19-20).

Tell yourself this: "Just for today I will take care of my body. I will exercise it, care for it and nourish it. I will not abuse it nor neglect it so it may become a more perfect machine for my Master's bidding."

Now some Christians just will not exercise because they think exercise is carnal. Overeating and laziness are carnal. Self-discipline and effort, when done to be fit and healthy for the glory of the Lord, are holy sacrifices. Carnal pertains to passions and appetites. I think neglect and self-destruction are carnal.

Romans 12:1 states that we are to present our bodies a living sacrifice, holy, acceptable unto God. We are also told this is our reasonable service. God is telling us that it is right and natural that we should care for and present our bodies as living sacrifices.

I believe when you become fit through the right motive — that of pleasing the Lord — you will be able to see the needs of others more clearly. When you are sick and feel bad, you tend to get caught up in self-pity and lack the energy to help yourself or others.

Maybe today God has your heart and your good deeds, but what about your body? Is it in sad shape? You belong to the Lord. All of us must train ourselves toward godliness in every area of our lives including our bodies.

Physical exercise is not a waste of time when we do it for God's glory. God designed our bodies to be physical. The Lord Jesus needs to be at the center of our exercise program. Friend, have we given God the right to be Lord over our physical health? Have we taken time to dedicate ourselves to God as healthy, fit people?

I spoke for a holiness church one evening. The pastor's wife told me that God had brought her under conviction about herself. She said, "Beverly, I am ten years younger that you, but I look ten years older because I have not taken care of my body."

She told me she had been taught to always do for others. She was spending hours and hours caring for her husband, her family, and everyone that needed help in her church. She said, "My doctor told me I was very obese and sick and I had to start taking care of myself or I wouldn't be around long to take care of anyone."

This lady started exercising daily and began following a low-fat diet. She was reclaiming her health for God's glory. She wanted to be around to help others and if she did not care for herself, this would be impossible. Understand, your health is your responsibility, not someone else's.

So, remember you don't have to be sick, overweight, tired, or blue. You can be free of vanity and pride when your program is dedicated to Jesus. You are in the Lord's army. Now, if you were in the regular army you would have to be fit. So why not be fit for the Lord's army?

Pray this prayer with me right now: "Yes, Lord, I choose to exercise myself, eat right unto godliness, and glorify God with my body, soul, and spirit."

1

Breads, Pancakes, & Waffles

INTRODUCTION TO BREADS

Many times people simply find it hard to believe that a low-fat diet coupled with regular exercise will bring about all the claimed benefits. The idea that a person can actually WANT to get up at 5 or 6 a.m. to exercise is totally absurd to some. The assertion that low-fat food can taste good seems an impossibility. But exercise can become such an uplifting, refreshing time that you will find yourself eagerly looking forward to it — even at 6 a.m. And low-fat food can taste just as good or better than the fat-laden meals of days past. Below is a poem written by one of my viewers who found exercise to be the perfect way to start the day — even better than a cup of coffee.

BEVERLY EXERCISE

One morning as I rose out of bed,
I reached for my coffee to clear up my head.
I turned on the TV for the morning news.
And soon found I was getting the blues.
I picked up the control and flipped through
    the stations.
But what I saw led to frustration.
Just when I was losing control,
Up came a lady I didn't know.
"Beverly Exercise" was her show.

"Beverly Exercise?" What is that?
I started to listen to this little lady;
Then I tuned-in to her show daily.
She gave me exercise to do,
And told me to drink water too.
Now I don't need black coffee to clear my
    head.
When six o'clock comes, I spring out of bed,
Turn on my TV and exercise instead.
        —*Geri Lynn Gates, Winter Haven, FL*

Do you need to feel good about yourself today and know that you are appreciated? Proverbs 19:14 states, "Houses and riches are the inheritance of fathers: and a prudent wife is from the Lord." So is a good husband.

Dear one, you are truly special and worthwhile. Think of yourself that way as you prepare healthy meals for yourself and your family. You are a treasure from the Lord. Honor God in shopping for meals, in preparation of meals, and in the care of yourself and your family.

Inseparable duo — exercise and low-fat eating

Do you think you can eat anything you like as long as you follow a good exercise program? I hope not.

Some runners think they can get by with eating a high-fat diet if they exercise enough. Even the famous Jim Fixx, who wrote *The Complete Book of Running,* thought he could. Once, in an interview with a London newspaper, he revealed he was not very concerned about his diet because a running program of ten miles a day would sufficiently stoke his furnace to burn whatever he ate. He added that for his breakfast he often had fried eggs, sausage, fried potatoes, butter, and cream.

My friend, such eating is cardiac disaster! As you may recall, Jim Fixx died suddenly while on a daily run.

On the other hand, some folks watch their diets religiously but rarely exercise. They eat grains, fruits, and vegetables, and as Jane Brody once said, ". . . sprinkle on wheat germ like it was holy water." But they don't move their bodies. This approach doesn't work either. What does work is a balanced, healthy life style which includes low-fat eating and regular exercise.

Why is fiber so important?

The Recommended Daily Allowance (RDA) is the National Research Council's official statement on how much of certain vitamins and minerals your body needs to be healthy. There is no such official recommendation for fiber, but the National Cancer Institute believes we need 20 to 30 grams of a fiber a day.

Of course, most of us want fiber in our diets, but too many of us tend to pick just one source, such as wheat bran, thinking we have done enough. This alone is not the answer.

There are two kinds of fiber. One is soluble fiber found in oat bran, barley, chick-peas, beans (kidney, pinto, navy, and lentils) and in some fruits such as pears, apples, citrus fruits, and prunes. Soluble fiber helps lower cholesterol in the bloodstream.

The other type of fiber is insoluble fiber found in wheat bran, corn bran, dried peas, nuts, seeds, popcorn, and the peelings of most fruits and vegetables. This fiber moves the food through the digestive system, promoting regularity and helping prevent colon cancer.

Fiber, the portion of food that your body cannot digest, is measured in grams. Most products containing fiber now list their fiber content per average serving.

Health experts urge that we keep score of our daily fiber intake. Look for fiber counts on food labels and record how much we eat. For example, if you are now eating 5 grams a day, increase the amount slowly, 2 to 3 grams daily each week, until you reach 25 grams per day. Slowly increasing fiber intake gives your body time to adjust.

As you increase your fiber, it is absolutely essential that you increase the amount of water you are drinking. Drink six to eight glasses a day to move the fiber through your system.

The following foods have medium fiber content (3 to 5 grams per serving): avocado, prunes, raisins, raspberries, broccoli, corn, potatoes, sweet potatoes, many cereals, and red kidney beans.

These foods are high in fiber (more than 5 grams per serving): figs, pears, all-bran and other bran cereals, baked beans, chick peas, lentils, lima beans, and pinto beans.

BREADS
— Beverly's Nonfat Corn Bread —
(6 to 8 servings)

Spray a nonstick skillet with nonstick cooking spray. Heat oven to 450 degrees. Preheat skillet in oven.

In the meantime, mix the following together:

2 c. self-rising corn meal (do not use corn meal mix)

1/4 c. egg substitute or 1 egg

Add buttermilk and stir. Add enough buttermilk to achieve a smooth consistency.

Remove skillet from oven and pour mixture in.

Bake at 450 degrees for about 25 minutes or until golden brown on top. (Note: A little extra buttermilk will make the bread more moist. And if you don't have buttermilk, you can make your own by adding 2 tablespoons of vinegar to one cup of skim milk. Set aside for a few minutes and then use in place of buttermilk.) (Fat: less than 25% calories from fat)

— Beverly Chesser, Anderson, SC

— Corny Corn Bread —
(8 servings)

1 T. plus 1 tsp. margarine

1 c. plain, yellow corn meal

1 tsp. baking soda

1/2 tsp. baking powder

1/4 tsp. salt

1-1/2 c. sour milk (Add 4 tsp. of lemon juice
to 1-1/2 c. of skim milk.)

2 T. honey

1 tsp. vanilla extract

1 egg or egg substitute

1 c. drained, canned corn

2 tsp. all-purpose flour

Preheat oven to 425 degrees. Place margarine in an 8-inch square baking pan and set aside.

In a large bowl, combine corn meal, baking soda, baking powder, and salt.

In a separate container combine milk, honey, vanilla, and egg. Blend until smooth.

Place pan in oven and preheat for 3 minutes.

Stir liquid mixture into dry ingredients. Toss corn with flour and stir into batter.

Place batter in preheated pan. Bake 20 to 22 minutes until firm and golden brown. (Fat: less than 20% calories from fat)

— Low-Fat Hush Puppies —
(makes 8)

1/4 c. yellow cornmeal

1/4 c. all-purpose flour

3/4 tsp. baking powder

1/4 tsp. salt

1/4 tsp. sugar

1/4 tsp. garlic powder

1/4 tsp. celery flakes

1/8 tsp. ground red pepper

1 egg white (beaten)

2 T. skim milk

2 tsp. canola or safflower oil

2 T. minced green onions

Nonstick cooking spray

(Continued)

Place first 8 ingredients in a large bowl, stirring well. Combine beaten egg white, milk, and oil in a small bowl. Mix well. Add liquid ingredients to dry ingredients, stirring just until blended. Gently stir in green onions.

Spoon 1 tablespoon batter into each of eight miniature muffin pans that have been sprayed with cooking spray. Bake at 425 degrees for 15 to 20 minutes, until golden brown. Remove from pan and serve warm. (Fat: 25% calories from fat)

— Whole-Wheat Zucchini Bread —
(8 servings)

3/4 c. whole-wheat flour
3/4 c. all-purpose flour
1-1/2 tsp. baking powder
1/2 tsp. baking soda
1 tsp. ground cinnamon
1/2 tsp. ground nutmeg
1 egg

1/4 c. sugar (or sweetener equivalent to 12 tsp. sugar)
1 tsp. vanilla extract
2 T. plus 2 tsp. margarine, melted
1-1/2 c. finely shredded, unpeeled zucchini
1/2 c. raisins

Preheat oven to 350 degrees. In a large bowl, combine both flours, baking powder, baking soda, and spices.

In a medium bowl, combine egg, sugar, vanilla, and margarine. Beat with a fork or wire whisk until blended. Add zucchini.

Stir zucchini mixture and raisins into dry ingredients until well-moistened.

Place batter in a 4x8-inch nonstick, loaf pan or one sprayed with a nonstick cooking spray.

Bake 50 minutes or until a toothpick inserted in the center comes out clean. Cool in pan 10 minutes; then invert onto a rack. (Fat: less than 30% calories from fat)

— No-Excuse Bread —
(makes 2 loaves or 3-4 dozen rolls)

2 packages yeast
2 tsp. lite salt
1/3 c. canola oil
1/3 c. honey
1 quart envelope nonfat dry milk powder

2 eggs
1/4 c. wheat germ or cooking oats
2 c. warm water
7 c. unbleached flour

Mix all ingredients, except half the flour, with electric mixer for 5 minutes.

Add remaining flour and knead on floured surface for 5-10 minutes. (Dough will be sticky, so spread margarine lightly on palms of your hands and keep flouring the surface while kneading.)

Place dough in a bowl sprayed with nonstick cooking spray. Cover with a dish towel and let rise 20 minutes.

Knead a few more times and then form loaves or rolls, placing them in sprayed loaf or muffin pans. Cover pans with dish towels and let rise again for one hour (or 2 hours to overnight in refrigerator).

Bake at 325 degrees for 40-50 minutes for 2 loaves or 15 to 20 minutes for 3-4 dozen rolls. Freezes well. (Fat: less than 30% calories from fat)

— *Janet Hardy, Mauldin, SC*

— Raisin Bread with Anise —
(10 servings)

2 c. minus 2 T. all-purpose flour
2-1/2 tsp. baking powder
3 T. plus 1 tsp. reduced-calorie margarine
1/2 c. skim milk
1/4 c. sugar (or sweetener equivalent to 12 tsp. sugar)

1 T. anise seeds, crushed
1/4 tsp. anise extract
1/2 tsp. lemon extract
1 egg
1/4 c. plus 1 T. raisins

Preheat over 350 degrees. In a large bowl, combine flour and baking powder. Add margarine and blend with a fork until mixture resembles coarse crumbs.

In a medium bowl, combine remaining ingredients, except raisins. Beat with a fork or wire whisk until blended.

Add this mixture and raisins to dry ingredients until well moistened.

Place in a 4x8-inch nonstick loaf pan or one sprayed with nonstick cooking spray. Pat dough down gently with slightly wet fingertips.

Bake 30 minutes or until a toothpick inserted in the center comes out clean. Cool in pan 10 minutes; then invert onto rack for further cooling. (Fat: less than 20% calories from fat)

— Three-Grain Bread —
(makes 3 small or 2 large loaves)

1 package rapid-rise yeast
2-1/4 c. very warm water
1/4 c. oil
1/4 c. brown sugar, honey, or combination
1 T. salt

1/2 c. nonfat powdered milk
1/2 c. rolled oats (old-fashioned or quick)
1/2 c. corn meal
1-1/2 c. whole-wheat flour
2-1/2 c. bread flour (more if needed)

Heat water and oil. Stir in salt and sugar (make sure it's not too hot or you will kill the yeast.)

Measure 1 cup of bread flour, the powdered milk, oats, cornmeal, 1 cup whole-wheat flour, and the yeast into a bowl. Stir in liquids. Mix well. Add remaining whole-wheat flour and enough bread flour to make a stiff dough. Knead about 10 minutes. Cover, let rest 15 minutes. Shape into loaves and place in greased pans. Cover and let rise until almost doubled in bulk. Preheat oven to 375 degrees (reduce to 350 degrees if bread is browning too quickly). Bake 30 minutes. (Fat: less than 30% calories from fat)
— *Sally Smith, Manassas, VA*

— Nut 'N Cranberry Bread —
(10 servings)

3/4 c. whole-wheat flour
1/2 c. plus 1T. all-purpose flour
2 tsp. baking powder
1/2 tsp. baking soda
2-1/4 ounces wheat germ
1 tsp. ground cinnamon
1 egg
1 c. buttermilk

1 T. plus 2 tsp. vegetable oil
1 tsp. vanilla extract
1/4 tsp. orange extract
3 T. honey
1 c. cranberries
1/2 c. raisins
1 ounce chopped walnuts

(Continued)

Preheat over to 350 degrees. In a large bowl, combine dry ingredients.

In a medium bowl, combine egg, buttermilk, oil, extracts, and honey. Beat with a fork or wire whisk until blended.

Place cranberries and raisins in a blender or food processor. Turn on and off a few times so fruit is chopped, not pureed.

Add cranberry mixture and nuts to buttermilk mixture. Stir in dry ingredients until well moistened.

Place batter in a 4x8-inch nonstick loaf pan or one that has been sprayed with a nonstick cooking spray.

Bake 35 minutes until golden brown. Cool 5 minutes; then invert onto rack for further cooling. (Fat: less than 30% calories from fat)

— Honey-Sweet Bread —
(20 slices)

This dark, whole-grain bread is a good breakfast food and also makes a delicious dessert bread served with fresh fruit.

2-1/2 c. whole-wheat flour	1 tsp. baking soda
1 c. honey	1 tsp. salt
1 c. skim milk	1 egg (beaten)
3 T. oil or melted low-calorie margarine	Nonstick cooking spray

Combine all ingredients in an electric mixer bowl. Beat 2 minutes.

Coat a 4-1/2x8-1/2-inch loaf pan with nonstick cooking spray. Transfer bread mixture to pan and bake 1 hour or until toothpick or knife comes out clean. (Fat: 30% calories from fat)

— Brown Bread 'N Molasses —
(12 servings)

1-1/2 c. plus 3 T. whole-wheat flour	1 egg (slightly beaten)
2-1/4 ounces wheat germ	1/4 c. water
1 tsp. baking soda	1 tsp. vanilla extract
1 tsp. ground cinnamon	1/4 c. plus 2 T. molasses
1/3 c. nonfat dry milk	2 T. vegetable oil
1 c. plain, low-fat yogurt	1/4 c. plus 2 T. raisins

Preheat oven to 350 degrees. In a large bowl combine flour, wheat germ, baking soda, cinnamon, and dry milk. Mix well.

In a medium bowl, combine remaining ingredients, except raisins. Beat with fork or wire whisk until blended. Add to dry mixture, along with raisins, and stir until well moistened.

Place in a 5x9-inch nonstick loaf pan or one that has been sprayed with nonstick cooking spray. Bake 40 minutes or until a toothpick inserted in the center comes out clean. Cool in pan 10 minutes; then invert on rack for further cooling. (Fat: less than 30% calories from fat)

— Quick 'N Easy Rolls —
(makes 1 dozen rolls)

2 c. self-rising flour
1/4 c. plus 2 T. nonfat mayonnaise

1/4 c. nonfat buttermilk
Vegetable cooking spray

Combine first 3 ingredients, stirring just until moistened. Spoon batter into muffin pans coated with cooking spray. Bake at 375 degrees for 12 to 15 minutes or until golden brown. (Fat: less than 20% calories from fat)

— No-Fat Biscuits —
(makes 10-12)

2 c. flour
4 tsp. baking powder
1/4 tsp. salt

Dash of sugar if desired
1/3 c. applesauce
2/3 c. skim milk

Mix dry ingredients. Add wet ingredients. Blend well. Drop onto cookie sheet sprayed with nonstick cooking spray. Bake at 425 degrees for 8 to 10 minutes. (Fat: less than 30% calories from fat)

— June Andrews, Mt. Vernon, OH

— Italian French Bread —
(6 servings)

6 slices (1-ounce) French bread (toasted)
2 T. commercial reduced-calorie Italian
    dressing

1/2 c. (2 ounces) shredded part-skim
    mozzarella cheese
1 T. minced fresh parsley
2 tsp. minced fresh basil

Place bread slices on a broiler rack. Brush top side of each bread slice lightly with salad dressing. Sprinkle cheese, parsley, and basil evenly over bread slices. Broil 6 inches from heat until cheese melts. Serve immediately. (Fat: 30% calories from fat)

— Lite 'N Fluffy Biscuits —
(makes 1 dozen)

1 package dry yeast
2 T. warm water
1 c. nonfat buttermilk
2-1/2 c. all-purpose flour
1-1/2 tsp. sugar

1 tsp. baking powder
1/2 tsp. salt
1/4 tsp. baking soda
3 T. shortening
Nonstick cooking spray

Dissolve yeast in warm water; let stand 5 minutes. Stir buttermilk into yeast mixture. Set aside. Combine flour and next 4 ingredients in a large bowl. Cut in shortening with a pastry blender until mixture resembles coarse meal. Add buttermilk mixture, stirring with a fork until dry ingredients are moistened. Turn dough out onto a lightly floured surface and knead lightly 3 or 4 times. Roll dough to 1/2-inch thickness, cut into rounds with a 2-1/2-inch biscuit cutter. Place biscuits on a baking sheet that has been coated with cooking spray. Cover and let rise in a warm place (85 degrees), away from drafts, for 10 to 15 minutes. Bake at 400 degrees for 10 to 12 minutes or until golden. (Fat: 30% calories from fat)

— Oat 'N Bran Bread —
(8 servings)

1/2 c. minus 1 T. all-purpose flour
1/2 c. whole-wheat flour
1-1/2 ounces bran
3/4 ounce quick-cooking oats (uncooked)
1 tsp. baking soda
1/2 tsp. ground cinnamon
2 T. plus 2 tsp. margarine (melted)

3 T. firmly-packed brown sugar (or sweetener equivalent to 9 tsp. brown sugar)
1/4 c. skim milk
1 tsp. vanilla extract
1 egg (slightly beaten) or egg substitute
1 c. applesauce (unsweetened)
1 tsp. freshly grated orange peel
1/4 c. raisins

Preheat oven to 350 degrees. In a large bowl, combine both flours, bran, oats, baking soda, and cinnamon. Mix well.

In a medium bowl, combine remaining ingredients, except raisins. Beat with a wire whisk until blended. Add to dry mixture with raisins. Stir until all ingredients are moistened.

Place in a 4x8-inch nonstick loaf pan. Bake 40 minutes or until a toothpick inserted in the center comes out clean. Cool in a pan 10 minutes; then invert onto rack for further cooling. (Fat: less than 30% calories from fat)

— Low-Fat Gingerbread —
(serves 9)

2 c. whole-wheat flour
1/2 tsp. salt
1 tsp. baking soda
2 tsp. baking powder
1-2 tsp. powdered ginger

2 eggs (beaten)
2 T. safflower or canola oil
1 c. light molasses
1 carton (8 ounces) low-fat vanilla yogurt
Nonstick cooking spray

Preheat oven to 325 degrees. In a large mixing bowl, stir flour, salt, baking soda, baking powder, and ginger together. In a medium bowl, stir beaten eggs, oil, molasses, and 3/4 cup hot tap water together. Stir liquid ingredients into dry until just blended.

Spray 8-inch round or square baking pan with nonstick cooking spray. Pour in batter. Bake 30 to 35 minutes or until a toothpick inserted near the center comes out clean. Cut and serve warm with a dollop of yogurt. (Fat: less than 30% calories from fat)

— Bran Muffins —
(makes 12 large or 24 small muffins)

3/4 c. All-Bran
1 c. skim milk
3 T. corn or canola oil
1 egg (well beaten)

1 c. sifted plain flour
3 tsp. baking powder
1/2 tsp. salt
3 T. sugar

Combine All-Bran and milk. Let stand until mostly absorbed. Add egg and oil. Beat well. Sift dry ingredients together. Add these to the wet ingredients and stir just until combined.

Fill large muffin tins sprayed with nonstick cooking oil to about 2/3 capacity. Bake at 400 degrees for 20 minutes. This yields 12 large muffins. If using small tart or muffin tins, bake at 375 degrees for only 15 minutes for a yield of 24 muffins. (Fat: 30% calories from fat)

— *Harriet Cottingham, Charleston, SC*

— Pear 'N Ginger Bran Muffins —
(makes 12 muffins)

1-1/2 c. bran-nugget cereal
1/2 c. pear or apple juice
1 pear, coarsely shredded
2 tsp. finely grated fresh ginger
1/2 c. nonfat yogurt
1/4 c. all-fruit pear or apple butter

1/4 c. maple syrup
2 egg whites or 1 egg, (lightly beaten)
1 T. canola or safflower oil
1-1/4 c. unbleached flour
2 tsp. baking soda
1 tsp. ground cinnamon

In a medium bowl, combine cereal, juice, pear, and ginger. Let soak for 10 minutes. Stir in the yogurt, pear or apple butter, maple syrup, egg, and oil.

In a large bowl, combine the flour, baking soda, and cinnamon. Pour liquid ingredients over flour mixture. Stir with a rubber spatula to moisten the flour; do not overmix.

Coat 12 muffin cups with nonstick spray or line them with foil liners. Divide the batter among the cups. Bake at 400 degrees for 18 to 20 minutes. (Fat: less than 20% calories from fat)

— Honey Oat Bran Muffins —
(12 servings)

2 c. oat bran cereal
1/4 c. brown sugar
1/4 c. honey
2 tsp. baking powder
1/2 tsp. lite salt (optional)
1-1/4 c. flour

1 c. buttermilk or nonfat milk
2 egg whites
2 T. canola oil
1 small apple, peeled and chopped
1 tsp. cinnamon

Preheat oven to 425 degrees. Spray 12 muffin tins with nonstick cooking spray or line them with cups.

Combine first 6 ingredients. Add next 3. Mix only until dry ingredients are moistened. Stir in apple and cinnamon.

Fill muffin cups 3/4 full. Bake 15 minutes or until golden brown. (Fat: 30% calories from fat)
— *Martha Elson, Anchorage, AK*

— No-Fat Angel Rolls —

1 package yeast in 1/4 c. warm water
4 egg whites or 2 whole eggs (beaten) —
   Note: if using whole eggs, fat content will
   be higher)
1/2 c. applesauce

4 c. flour
1/4 c. sugar (can use 1/4 c. more if desired)
1 c. warm water
1 tsp. salt

Mix dissolved yeast, sugar, eggs, and warm water. Add applesauce, salt, and flour. Mix and let stand 8 hours (or overnight) covered.

Put dough on floured board. Turn over several times. Divide into 3 parts. (Do not work flour into the dough.) Roll each part round like a pie and cut into pie-shaped sections and roll (wide edge first). Place on baking sheet sprayed with nonstick cooking spray. Let rise, uncovered, about six hours. Bake at 350 degrees for 12 minutes or until lightly brown. Can be frozen after baking. (Fat: 25% calories from fat)

— Oat Bran Muffins —

2-1/3 c. oat bran
1-1/3 c. whole-wheat flour
1-1/2 tsp. baking soda
1-1/2 tsp. baking powder
3 egg whites

1 c. unsweetened applesauce
1 c. nonfat milk mixed with 1 tsp. lemon juice
1/2 c. frozen apple juice concentrate
1/3 c. blueberries or cherries (fresh or frozen)

Preheat oven to 375 degrees. In a large bowl, combine oat bran, flour, baking soda, and powder.

In a medium bowl, using an electric mixer, beat egg whites until foamy. Set aside.

In a small bowl stir together applesauce, soured milk, apple juice concentrate, and blueberries or cherries. Pour this mixture into the dry mixture and stir just until moistened. Do not overstir. Fold in egg whites.

Divide batter into muffin tins and bake for 20 minutes or until a toothpick inserted in center of muffin comes out clean and dry. (Fat: less than 20% calories from fat)

— *Dolly Denman, Columbus, OH*

— Low-Fat Peppery Biscuits —
(makes 25)

1 c. unbleached flour
1/2 c. whole-wheat flour
1 T. baking powder
1/2 tsp. ground black pepper

2 T. minced lean ham
1/2 c. buttermilk (approx.)
1-1/2 T. olive oil

In a large bowl, mix together the unbleached flour, whole-wheat flour, baking powder, and pepper. Stir in ham.

In a cup, whisk together the buttermilk and oil. Pour over the dry ingredients. Toss together with a fork just until the mixture begins to form a mass. If it's too dry, add 1 or 2 tablespoons more buttermilk.

Turn the dough out onto a lightly floured board and press into a 7-inch square pan. Using a thin knife, divide into 25 biscuits (5 across and 5 down).

Spray a baking sheet with nonstick spray. Transfer the biscuits to the sheet with about 1 inch space between them. Bake at 400 degrees for 15 minutes or until golden. Best served warm. (May be made ahead and reheated.) (Fat: less than 30% calories from fat)

— Apple-Raisin Bran Muffins —
(makes 12 muffins)

1-1/2 c. shreds of wheat bran cereal
1 c. skim milk
1/4 c. margarine spread (melted)
1/2 c. honey
1 large cooking apple (peeled, cored, and
   grated) OR 1-1/2 c. applesauce

3/4 c. raisins
1 large egg (beaten)
1 tsp. cinnamon
1-1/4 c. all-purpose flour
2 tsp. baking powder
1/2 tsp. baking soda

(Continued)

Preheat oven to 400 degrees. Lightly grease 12 muffin cups.

In a large bowl, soak cereal in milk for 5 minutes. Stir in margarine, honey, apple, raisins, egg, and cinnamon.

In another bowl, combine remaining ingredients. With a rubber spatula, fold flour into mixture just enough to moisten. Do not overmix.

Evenly distribute among muffin cups. Bake 20 minutes or until done. (Fat: less than 30% calories from fat)

— Margie Bolton, Toccoa, GA

— Raisin 'N Oat-Bran Muffins —
(makes 18 muffins)

1/4 c. safflower or canola oil
3/4 c. brown sugar
1 c. unbleached white flour
2 tsp. baking powder
1/4 tsp. salt

1 c. buttermilk
2 egg whites or 1 egg
1 tsp. baking soda
1 c. oat bran
1 c. raisins

In a mixing bowl and with a wire whisk, combine oil, brown sugar, flour, baking powder, and salt. Add remaining ingredients and stir just until moistened.

Fill paper-lined muffin cups 3/4 full with batter. Bake at 400 degrees for 20 minutes, or until toothpick inserted into center comes out dry. Remove muffins from tins and cool on wire racks. (Fat per muffin: 25% calories from fat)

— Bananas 'N Oat Bran Muffins —
(8 servings)

3/4 c. all-purpose flour
1-1/2 tsp. baking powder
3 ounces quick-cooking oats (uncooked)
2 egg whites or 1 egg
1/2 tsp. vanilla butternut flavor

1/2 tsp. almond extract
1/4 c. skim milk
2 T. plus 2 tsp. canola or safflower oil
2 medium, ripe bananas (mashed)

Preheat oven to 400 degrees. In a small bowl combine flour, baking powder, and oats.

In a large bowl combine remaining ingredients. Beat with a fork or wire whisk until well blended. Add dry ingredients to banana mixture, stirring until well moistened.

Divide evenly into 8 nonstick muffin cups or ones that have been sprayed with a nonstick cooking spray. Bake 15 minutes until firm and lightly browned. Cool in pan 5 minutes; then transfer to rack for further cooling. (Fat: less than 30% calories from fat)

— Pineapple Carrot Muffins —

1-1/2 c. whole-wheat flour
1 c. unbleached flour
1 tsp. baking powder
1 tsp. soda
1 tsp. salt
1-1/2 tsp. cinnamon
4 egg whites (beaten)

1 c. nonfat yogurt
1/2 c. honey
1 small can crushed pineapple (unsweetened, undrained)
2 c. finely shredded carrots (or 2 large jars junior baby food)
1 c. raisins

Beat egg whites (slightly). Add honey, yogurt, and raisins. Mix dry ingredients together and add to first mixture. Mix well and add remaining ingredients. Fill paper muffin liners approximately 2/3 full and bake 20 minutes at 350 degrees. (Fat: less than 20% calories from fat)

— *Debitha Harrelson, Elba, AL*

— Pumpkin 'N Raisin Bran Muffins —
(6 servings)

3/4 c. whole-wheat flour
1/2 tsp. baking soda
1 tsp. each of baking powder and ground cinnamon
1/4 tsp. each of ground ginger, cloves, and nutmeg
1-1/2 ounces bran cereal flakes (slightly crushed)

2 egg whites or 1 egg
2 T. canola or safflower oil
1 tsp. vanilla extract
1 c. canned pumpkin
1/4 c. sugar (or sweetener equivalent to 12 tsp. sugar)
1/4 c. plus 2 T. raisins

Preheat oven to 375 degrees. In large bowl, combine flour, baking soda, baking powder, and spices. Stir in cereal.

In a medium bowl, combine remaining ingredients, except raisins. Beat with a fork or wire whisk until blended.

Add wet mixture and raisins to dry ingredients, stirring until well moistened.

Divide batter evenly among 6 nonstick muffin cups or ones that have been sprayed with nonstick cooking spray. Bake 20 minutes or until a toothpick inserted in the center comes out clean. Remove to rack for further cooling. (Fat: less than 30% calories from fat)

— Corn Muffins —
(makes 12)

4 egg whites or 2 whole eggs (beaten) - Note: using whole eggs increases fat content
1 c. skim milk
1/4 c. applesauce

1-1/2 c. yellow, self-rising corn meal mix
1 c. flour
1/4 c. to 1/2 c. sugar (depending on desired sweetness)

Mix in order listed and pour into baking tins. Bake at 425 degrees for 10 to 15 minutes. (Fat: less than 25% calories from fat)

— *June Andrews, Mt. Vernon, OH*

— Muffins with Blueberries —
(8 servings)

1-1/2 c. all-purpose flour
1-1/2 tsp. baking powder
1 egg or egg substitute
1/4 c. sugar (or sweetener equivalent to
    12 tsp. sugar)
2 T. plus 2 tsp. reduced-calorie margarine
    (melted)

3/4 c. skim milk
2 tsp. vanilla extract
1/4 tsp. lemon extract
1 c. fresh or frozen blueberries (unsweetened).
    (If using frozen berries, thaw and drain
    well.)

Preheat oven to 375 degrees. In a medium bowl, combine flour and baking powder.

In a large bowl, combine remaining ingredients, except blueberries. Beat on low speed of an electric mixer until smooth. Stir in dry ingredients until well moistened. Add blueberries.

Divide mixture evenly into 8 nonstick muffin cups or ones sprayed with nonstick cooking spray. Bake 20 minutes until firm and lightly browned. Cool in pan 5 minutes; then transfer to rack for further cooling. (Fat: less than 30% calories from fat)

— Banana Tea Bread —
(makes 1 loaf — 9x5x3)

1-3/4 c. sifted, all-purpose flour
2 tsp. baking powder
1/4 tsp. baking soda
1/2 tsp. salt
1/3 c. (scant) applesauce

2/3 c. granulated sugar
4 egg whites or 2 whole eggs (well beaten) —
    Note: whole eggs mean higher fat content.
1 c. ripe bananas (mashed)

Sift together flour, baking powder, soda, salt, and sugar.

In separate bowl, combine applesauce, bananas, and eggs. Stir this mixture into dry ingredients. Mix well.

Pour into loaf pan sprayed with nonstick cooking spray and coated with flour. Bake at 350 degrees for approximately 50 minutes. Use toothpick to check for doneness. (Fat: less than 20% calories from fat)

— June Andrews, Mt. Vernon, OH

PANCAKES

— Ravenel's Oatmeal 'N Whole-Wheat Pancakes —

3/4 c. oatmeal (whole, rolled oats)
1/4 c. wheat bran (or wheat flour)
3 T. corn starch
2 tsp. baking soda

1 tsp. yeast
1 T. apple concentrate (sugar free)
2 T. no-sugar fruit spread
Skim milk or water

Mix all the above in a blender, adding skim milk or water to achieve desired consistency. Pour into a nonstick frying pan sprayed with nonstick cooking spray or wiped with canola oil. Cook each pancake on both sides until done to taste.

(Continued)

Sauce for pancakes:

1 banana (peeled and cut up)
1 apple (chopped with peel)

2 T. apple concentrate (sugar free)
2 T. no-sugar fruit spread

Place all the above in blender. Add skim milk or water and blend until smooth in texture. Heat in small saucepan and spread on pancakes instead of syrup. (Fat: less than 25% calories from fat)

— Ravenel Scott, Greenville, SC

— Country Morning Pancakes —
(makes 20 pancakes)

2 c. sifted unbleached white flour
1/2 tsp. salt
1-1/4 tsp. baking soda
3/4 tsp. baking powder

2 egg whites or 1 egg
2-1/4 c. buttermilk
2 tsp. skim milk
1 T. safflower or canola oil

In a mixing bowl, blend ingredients with a wire whisk, just enough to moisten. Dip up batter with a large serving spoon. Bake on a preheated nonstick griddle or frying pan. Turn pancakes when top side is full of bubbles. Flip only once. (Fat: 19% calories from fat per pancake)

— Blender Pancakes —
(makes 4 pancakes)

1/2 c. low-fat or nonfat cottage cheese
4 egg whites

1-1/2 tsp. all-purpose flour
Vegetable cooking spray

Combine all ingredients, except cooking spray, in blender; process until smooth.
For each pancake, pour 1/4 of batter onto a hot nonstick skillet coated with cooking spray.
Cook over medium heat, turning pancakes when tops bubble. (Fat: less than 10% calories from fat)

— Family-Style Pancakes —

The Mix:
4 c. whole-wheat flour
4 c. all-purpose flour
2 c. wheat germ
1 c. nonfat dry milk
1/3 c. baking powder
1 tsp. salt

The Pancakes:
(makes 12 pancakes)
1-1/2 c. dry mix
1 egg (beaten) or egg substitute
1-1/4 c. skim milk or water
1 T. canola or safflower oil
Nonstick cooking spray

Combine the mix with the egg, milk and oil. Do not overmix. Batter will be slightly lumpy.
Heat a nonstick skillet or pan sprayed with nonstick cooking spray, over medium heat. Pour about 1/4 cup of batter per pancake onto heated pan. When cakes bubble well on top and brown on bottom, flip and brown on other side. (Fat: Less than 30% calories from fat per serving)

— Cottage Cheese Pancakes —
(4 servings)

1 c. low-fat cottage cheese
1/2 c. skim milk
1 egg
1 egg white

1 T. sugar (optional)
1/2 tsp. low-sodium baking powder
1/2 c. whole-wheat flour

Separate eggs, discard one yolk, save other. Beat egg whites until soft peaks form.

Thoroughly blend all ingredients except beaten egg whites. Fold egg whites into blended ingredients.

Heat nonstick frying pan to medium-hot and use about 2 Tablespoons of batter to form each pancake. Brown quickly on one side, turn, and brown quickly on other side.

Suggested serving ideas: Top with low-fat yogurt and sliced fruit. Or mix a teaspoon of low-calorie jam with 2 tablespoons plain yogurt. (Fat: 1 gram of fat per serving)

— Buttermilk Pancakes —
(makes 20 pancakes)

2 c. sifted unbleached white flour
1/2 tsp. salt
1-1/4 tsp. baking soda
3/4 tsp. baking powder

2 egg whites or 1 egg
2-1/4 c. of 1% buttermilk
2 tsp. skim milk
1 T. of canola or safflower oil

Blend ingredients with fork or wire whisk just enough to moisten. Cook on a preheated, nonstick griddle or pan. Turn pancakes when top bubbles well. Flip only once. (Fat: 19% calories from fat)

— Oat 'N Apple Pancakes —
(makes 14, 4-inch pancakes)

3/4 c. quick-cooking oats (uncooked)
1-1/2 c. skim milk
4 egg whites or 2 eggs (beaten)
3/4 c. unsweetened applesauce
1 T. safflower or canola oil
1-1/4 c. all-purpose flour

1 T. baking powder
1 T. sugar
1/2 tsp. salt
1/2 tsp. ground cinnamon
Nonstick cooking spray

Combine oats and milk in a medium bowl; let stand 5 minutes. Add eggs, applesauce, and oil to oat mixture, stirring well.

Combine flour, baking powder, sugar, salt, and cinnamon in a large bowl; add oat mixture to dry ingredients, stirring until moistened.

For each pancake, pour 1/4 cup batter onto a hot griddle or skillet that has been coated with cooking spray. Turn pancakes when tops are covered with bubbles and edges look cooked. (Fat: 30% calories from fat)

— Cornmeal Griddle Cakes with Fruit Sauce —
(makes 16, 4-inch cakes)

1-1/2 c. cornmeal
1/4 c. whole-wheat flour
1 tsp. baking soda
1 tsp. salt
2 c. buttermilk

2 T. safflower or canola oil
1 egg (separated)
1 tsp. honey
Nonstick cooking spray

Sift all dry ingredients together in a medium bowl. Add buttermilk, oil, egg yolk, and honey to dry ingredients. Mix well.

Beat the egg white until stiff and fold it into cornmeal mixture. Let batter stand 10 minutes while griddle heats. Cook on hot griddle sprayed with nonstick cooking spray or in a nonstick frying pan. (Fat: less than 25% calories from fat)

Top with the following Fruit Sauce:
(makes 1 quart)
4 peaches or fruit of choice
1/4 c. water

1/2 c. honey
1 tsp. lemon
1 tsp. reduced-calorie margarine

Quarter fruit and steam until soft. Puree fruit in blender. Add remaining ingredients. Blend. Pour unused sauce in jar and keep chilled in refrigerator. Reheat in microwave as needed. (Fat: less than 10% calories from fat)

WAFFLES

— Buttermilk Waffles —
(makes 4 large waffles)

3 egg whites
1 egg yolk
2 c. of 1% buttermilk
1-1/4 c. unbleached white flour
3/4 c. whole-wheat flour

2 tsp. granulated sugar
2 tsp. baking powder
1 tsp. baking soda
1/4 tsp. salt
2 T. canola or safflower oil

Beat egg whites and yolk lightly. Add buttermilk. Beat with fork or wire whisk. Add remaining ingredients. Beat until smooth. Bake in nonstick waffle iron until golden brown.

Serving suggestions: Instead of syrup, top with pureed fresh or frozen strawberries, raspberries, blueberries, or blackberries. (Fat: 25% calories from fat)

2

Breakfast

INTRODUCTION TO BREAKFAST RECIPES

May we be teachable

I know you would not have this book if you were not teachable and eager to learn right eating. Perhaps weight gain or sickness have brought you to this point or maybe you have always sought a low-fat diet. Whatever the case, you are on the right track if you are determined to eat low-fat.

Weight gain or sickness can be warnings that we are not making time for ourselves. We may not be taking enough "mini-vacations" from stress and setting aside time for exercise and personal devotions with God.

I hope you have begun to value yourself enough to eat for nourishment's sake, to exercise for your mental and physical well being, and to seek God for your spiritual health. Our bodies, minds and spirits warn us when we are getting off track.

I am reminded of the lady who told me that she never weighs herself. She simply tries on her favorite blue jeans occasionally. If they fit nicely she knows she is keeping her weight under control. If they do not, she knows she needs to cut back on fat and exercise more.

"Oh, Lord, may we always be alert to the warnings you give us and the warnings our bodies give us. Help us be sensitive first to You, then to others, and then to our own selves. May we have teachable spirits."

> Son of man, I have made thee a watchman unto the house of Israel: therefore,
> hear the word at my mouth and give them warning from me (Ezek. 3:17).

Breakfast — absolute necessity

I know you've heard it before, but breakfast IS the most important meal of the day. A good breakfast helps you avoid overeating the remainder of the day. A FIBER-RICH breakfast keeps your metabolism rate up. Calories consumed at morning are easily burned off. As I stated in my book, *Your Health Coach*, the old saying that we should "eat breakfast like a king, lunch like a prince, and dinner like a pauper," is quite true.

Whether you have read *Your Health Coach* or not, let me repeat some of what I said about breakfast in that book.

Breakfast should be your biggest meal. After going without food all night, your body is in dire need of complete nourishment to supply you with maximum energy and strength for the day ... USDA studies have shown that a lifetime of regular breakfasts is associated with vigorous old age in men and women. Other studies show that breakfast eaters have a faster reaction time throughout the morning and less midday fatigue ..."

Breakfast eaters are known to perform better on the job. Children who eat a balanced breakfast do better in school.

Some people think that eating a big breakfast will cause them to gain weight. Just the opposite is true. Going without food for long periods of time will trigger the body's starvation mechanisms, slowing your metabolism, and hindering use of stored fat. Not eating breakfast is known to cause a rise in blood cholesterol as well.

Common sense tells you that eating a good breakfast will cut back on the amount of food you will desire the remainder of the day. Having no breakfast makes you feel so famished you will tend to overeat at lunch and even dinner.

As I said in *Health Coach*, the best breakfast consists mainly of a good whole grain cereal, fresh fruit, and skim milk. Of course, there are other healthy, tasty alternatives and we have put them in this section just for you.

Breakfast tips

— Since carbohydrates are our bodies' main source of fuel, an ideal breakfast should concentrate on whole grains and fresh fruit.

— Read labels on cereal boxes. Avoid those showing added fat, sugar, and salt.

— Choose cereals made from whole grains, such as whole-wheat or oats.

— Use skim milk on cereal or for a delicious alternative, try unsweetened fruit juice.

— For toast, use whole grain breads.

— Instead of butter, choose a reduced-calorie margarine high in polyunsaturated fats. Or better yet, skip the margarine and use only a little no-fat jam or jelly when possible.

— Watching your cholesterol? Try egg substitutes or egg whites instead of whole eggs.

— Beware of sausage and bacon, both of which are very high in saturated fats.

— Bagels and English muffins are generally low in fat and are a good choice.

— Try some of the delicious muffin recipes under the breads section of this book. Most can be made ahead of time, frozen, and quickly reheated as needed.

— Mix left-over rice with part-skim ricotta cheese and add cinnamon, vanilla, and raisins for a delicious breakfast.

— Combine plain, low-fat yogurt with your choice of fresh fruit. Sweeten lightly and add your favorite cereal.

— Before going to bed, fill a crockpot with oats, rice, grits, millet, or any grain combination. Add water, raisins, cinnamon, and vanilla. You'll wake up to a delicious breakfast. (Approximately 3 cups water to 1 cup grains)

— Top a baked potato with yogurt or a little margarine for a quick, nutritious breakfast. Bake ahead of time and warm in toaster oven or bake quickly in microwave.

— A baked sweet potato topped with cinnamon and a little margarine makes a tasty breakfast.

— Try a breakfast milkshake of skim milk, fruit, and ice mixed in a blender.

— Top a rice cake with low-fat cottage cheese, unsweetened apple butter, and a sprinkling of sunflower seeds.

Giving Eggs a Break —

Since the U.S. Department of Agriculture announced new measurements revealing that eggs contain less cholesterol than originally thought, the American Heart Association revised its position on eggs too. Now the AHA recommends a limit of 300 milligrams of cholesterol a day, meaning a healthy adult can eat up to four, rather than three, egg yolks per week.

Even though new guidelines are more lenient, never forget that the egg yolk is still a concentrated source of cholesterol. So it is best to learn how to make use of the egg's good qualities without use of its cholesterol.

Here are some options for enjoying eggs:

— Use egg whites. Substitute two egg whites for each whole egg called for in a recipe. An egg's cholesterol is entirely in the yolk. The egg white has protein but no cholesterol. Egg whites are fat free as well. Some recipes, such as those for muffins, omelets, and scrambled eggs, work better if you substitute egg whites for only half the total eggs. For example, if a muffin recipe calls for 2 eggs, use 1 egg plus 2 egg whites.

— Don't be afraid to use commercial egg substitutes. It is not always convenient nor frugal to throw away egg yolks and just use the whites. This is where egg substitutes come in handy. There are several varieties of frozen or refrigerated egg substitutes. To use them, use 1/4 cup of liquid egg substitute for one whole egg. These products contain little or no cholesterol because they consist mainly of egg whites. Color is added to make them resemble whole eggs.

Whatever your choice, egg whites or egg substitutes, remember that you will often pay more for the substitute than for the real eggs, but you will not have the waste with egg substitutes that you have when using egg whites and discarding the yolk.

BREAKFAST RECIPES
(See Breads section also)

— Ravenel's Oatmeal —

1 c. 100% natural rolled oats
1 tsp. cinnamon
1 dozen raisins
3 prunes

1 T. apple concentrate (sugar-free)
1 tsp. honey (optional)
1 apple (chopped with peel)
Skim milk

For smoothness, blend cinnamon, apple, raisins, prunes, and apple concentrate in blender. Add this mixture to oatmeal and water or skim milk in saucepan. Cook over medium heat until done to your taste. (Fat: less than 20%)
— *Ravenel Scott, Greenville, SC*

— Fruity Breakfast Rice —
(4 servings)

This is a great idea for leftover rice.

2 c. cooked brown rice (heated)

1 c. plain, nonfat yogurt

1 T. honey or brown sugar

1 tsp. cinnamon

1 medium apple (chopped) or fruit of choice

3 T. raisins

Combine rice, yogurt, honey or brown sugar, and cinnamon in a bowl. Stir in chopped apple and raisins. Reheat. (Fat: less than 20% calories from fat)

— Apple-Spice Oatmeal —
(6 servings)

1/4 c. light brown sugar

1 tsp. cinnamon

1 medium-large apple, room temperature, cut into small chunks

3 c. hot cooked oatmeal

1/3 c. raisins

2 T. walnuts or pecans (chopped)

Stir brown sugar and cinnamon into cooked oatmeal. Add apple chunks, raisins and chopped nuts. Serve hot. (Fat: less than 30% calories from fat)

— Oatmeal 'N Cinnamon-Raisins —
(4 servings)

1-1/2 c. water

1/4 tsp. salt

2 T. raisins

2/3 c. uncooked, quick-cooking oats

1 tsp. ground cinnamon

Combine water, salt, and raisins in a small saucepan. Bring to boil. Stir in oats and cinnamon. Reduce heat and simmer 1 minute or until water is absorbed. Serve warm. (Fat: less than 10% calories from fat)

— Apple Coffee Cake —
(12 servings)

2-1/2 c. peeled and coarsely chopped apples

1-1/4 c. unbleached white flour

3/4 c. whole-wheat flour

1/2 c. plus 1 T. brown sugar

2 tsp. baking powder

1/4 tsp. salt

1/2 tsp. cinnamon

1/4 c. safflower or canola oil

1/2 c. skim milk

2 egg whites or 1 egg

In a small bowl, toss apples with 1/2 cup of unbleached white flour. Set aside.

In a mixing bowl, combine remaining unbleached, white flour, whole-wheat flour, 1/2 cup brown sugar, baking powder, salt, and 1/4 teaspoon of cinnamon. Add oil, milk, and egg. Stir with fork or wire whisk until well moistened. Add apples.

Pour batter into a 10-inch, round, nonstick baking pan. Combine remaining 1 tablespoon brown sugar and 1/4 teaspoon cinnamon. Sprinkle over coffee cake. Bake at 400 degrees for 30 minutes or until toothpick inserted in center comes out clean. (Fat: 26% calories from fat)

— Just Peachy Coffee Cake —
(8 servings)

3/4 c. all-purpose flour
1 tsp. baking powder
2 T. plus 2 tsp. reduced-calorie margarine
4 egg whites or 2 eggs (further reduce fat by using egg whites)
2/3 c. low-fat cottage cheese
2 tsp. vanilla extract

3 T. plus 1 tsp. sugar (or sweetener equivalent to 10 tsp. sugar)
4 medium, ripe peaches (peeled and sliced)
Topping:
2-1/2 tsp. sugar (or equivalent amount of sweetener)
1/2 tsp. ground cinnamon

Preheat oven to 375 degrees. In a medium bowl, combine flour and baking powder. Add margarine and mix with fork or pastry blender until crumbs form.

Combine eggs, cottage cheese, vanilla, and sugar. Beat with a fork or wire whisk until blended. Mixture will be lumpy. Add cottage cheese mixture to dry ingredients, stirring until all ingredients are moistened. Spoon batter into a 10-inch glass pie pan that has been sprayed with a nonstick cooking spray.

Arrange peach slices evenly over batter. Press them down slightly into the batter.

Combine topping ingredients and sprinkle evenly over peaches. Bake 25 minutes. Cool in pan on wire rack. Serve warm or cold. (Fat: less than 30% calories from fat)

— French Toast —
(9 servings)

1/2 c. skim milk
1 whole egg plus 3 egg whites (slightly beaten)
1/4 tsp. vanilla

1/4 tsp. cinnamon
9 slices of bread

Combine milk, eggs, vanilla, and cinnamon. Dip bread into egg mixture. Fry in nonstick skillet until brown. (Fat: 13% calories from fat)

— Coffee Cake —
(12 servings)

3 c. low-fat whole-wheat pancake mix
1/2 c. sugar
2 egg whites or 1 egg (beaten with fork)
1/4 c. canola or safflower oil
1 c. water
2 c. blueberries

Topping:
1/4 c. low-fat margarine
1-1/2 c. raw quick-cooking oatmeal
1/3 c. brown sugar
1 tsp. cinnamon
1 tsp. vanilla

Preheat oven to 375 degrees (350 degrees for glass pan). Spray a 7-1/2x11-3/4 inch pan with nonstick cooking spray. In a mixing bowl, combine pancake mix and sugar. In a small bowl, mix together egg, oil, and water. Add wet mixture to dry mixture, and stir in blueberries; mixture will be thick. Spread into prepared pan.

For topping, melt margarine in a small bowl in microwave oven or in pan on top of stove. Add oatmeal, brown sugar, cinnamon, and vanilla to melted margarine and mix well. Spread evenly over coffee cake mixture in pan. Bake for 30 minutes in conventional oven or until a toothpick comes out clean. (Fat: 30% calories from fat)

— Egg 'N Muffin —
(1 serving)

1/4 c. nonfat egg substitute
Nonstick cooking spray
1-ounce slice Canadian bacon or lean ham
1 English muffin

1/4 to 1/2 c. Alpine Lace Fat-Free Cheese (grated)
Salt and pepper to taste

Scramble the egg substitute in a nonstick skillet sprayed with nonstick cooking spray. Heat the bacon or ham slice.

Meanwhile, toast the English muffin. Top with scrambled egg and Canadian bacon or ham slice. Sprinkle on Alpine Lace Fat-Free Cheese. Season with salt and pepper. (Fat: less than 30% calories from fat)

— Fantasy Danish —
(4 servings)

2 English muffins (split and toasted)
1 c. nonfat cottage cheese
1 tsp. cinnamon

1 T. sugar
1/2 c. applesauce

Spread 1/4 cup cottage cheese on each toasted muffin half. Combine the cinnamon and sugar; sprinkle over the cottage cheese.

Top each muffin with 2 tablespoons of applesauce. Place on a cookie sheet or in toaster oven and broil until bubbly.

Additional serving suggestions: Top with sliced peaches, banana, or apples instead of applesauce. (Fat: less than 30% calories from fat)

— French Toast for Two —
(2 servings)

1/2 c. egg substitute
1 egg white
2 T. skim milk
1/4 tsp. cinnamon

Dash salt
2 slices whole-grain bread
Nonstick cooking spray

Beat egg substitute, egg white, and milk with cinnamon and salt until foamy. Dip bread in egg mixture, coating both sides.

Heat a skillet or griddle and spray with nonstick cooking spray. Cook the bread in the heated skillet, turning once, until golden brown on both sides.

Serving Suggestions: Top with a fruit spread, fresh fruit, applesauce, or a tablespoon or two of real maple syrup. (Fat: less than 20% calories from fat per serving)

— Breakfast Shake —
(4 servings)

2 c. skim milk
1 T. honey or to taste

1 c. sliced strawberries
1 c. sliced peaches

Place all ingredients in a blender and puree until smooth. (Fat: less than 10% calories from fat)

— Spicy Apple Rice —
(8 servings)

1-1/3 c. water
1 c. unsweetened apple juice
1 c. uncooked long grain rice
1 c. cooking apple (peeled and chopped)

1/2 tsp. salt
1/4 tsp. apple pie spice
Cinnamon to taste

Combine water and apple juice in a medium saucepan. Bring to boil. Stir in rice and remaining ingredients. Cover, reduce heat, and simmer 20 to 25 minutes or until rice is tender and liquid is absorbed. (Fat: less than 10% calories from fat)

— Eye-Opener Grits —
(9 servings)

Nonstick cooking spray
1 tsp. unsalted, reduced-calorie margarine
2 T. minced onion
1 small green pepper (seeded and finely chopped)
2 drops of hot sauce

2 medium tomatoes (peeled and coarsely chopped)
3 T. chopped lean cooked ham
3 c. water
1/2 tsp. salt
3/4 c. quick-cooking grits

Coat a medium-sized nonstick skillet with cooking spray. Add margarine. Place over medium-high heat until hot. Add onion and green pepper. Saute until tender. Stir in tomatoes and hot sauce. Reduce heat and simmer uncovered for 20 minutes or until thickened. Set aside.

Coat a small nonstick skillet with cooking spray. Place over medium-high heat until hot. Add ham and saute 2 minutes or until ham is browned. Set aside.

Combine water and salt in a medium saucepan. Bring to boil and stir in grits. Cover. Reduce heat and simmer 5 minutes or until thickened, stirring occasionally. Remove from heat. Stir in reserved tomato mixture. Top each serving with 1 teaspoon reserved ham. Serve immediately. (Fat: less than 25% calories from fat)

— Low-Fat Breakfast Danish —

Partially toast 1/2 English muffin, then top with about 2 tablespoons of low-fat cottage cheese that has been mixed with about 2 tablespoons of mashed banana, peach, or fruit of choice.

Re-toast to heat topping.

This is also delicious when done with green peppers, red peppers, tomatoes, shredded carrots, etc., for lunch; or with shrimp and compatible vegetables for dinner. (Fat: less than 20% calories from fat)

— Anne Watson, Anchorage, AK

— Ravenel's Stir-Fry Omelet —
Ravenel's Stir-Fry Recipe

2 egg whites
2 T. skim milk

Beat egg whites and skim milk together. When vegetable stir-fry is ready to serve and most of the juices have evaporated, pour beaten egg whites mixed with skim milk over entire stir-fry and allow to cook on medium heat until firm on bottom. To eliminate burning the bottom of the omelet and still get the top done, place the frying pan under the oven broiler for a few minutes until top is firm as well. The omelet can then be rolled up or served flat, looking like a pizza and tasting just as good but without fat and cholesterol.

— Homemade Granola —

4 c. oatmeal   1/2 c. wheat germ   1/2 c. sunflower seeds

Mix equal parts of water, honey, and vegetable oil to make 1 cup of liquid. Pour this over dry ingredients and lightly mix. Or just 1 cup of water.

Bake at 350 degrees for 30 minutes. Remove and stir in desired amounts of raisins or chopped dates and nuts of choice.

This may be eaten as a snack or as a cereal. When eaten as a cereal, you may top with a small banana and skim milk. (Fat: 30% calories from fat)   — *Sue Prisciella, Orlando, FL*

— Low-Fat Syrup —
(makes 3/4 cup)

1/4 c. firmly-packed brown sugar   1/2 c. plus 2 T. skim milk
1 tsp. cornstarch   1 T. reduced-calorie margarine
1/4 tsp. ground cinnamon   1/4 tsp. maple flavoring

Combine sugar, cornstarch, and cinnamon in small saucepan. Blend well. Gradually stir in milk. Bring to boil. Reduce heat and simmer until slightly thickened, stirring constantly. Remove from heat. Add margarine and maple flavoring, stirring until margarine melts. Serve warm over pancakes. (Fat: 0.6 grams or 27 calories per tablespoon)

— Banana Breakfast Bars —
(4 servings)

3 ounces quick-cooking oats (uncooked)   1 tsp. vanilla extract
2/3 c. nonfat dry milk   1/2 tsp. vanilla butternut flavor
1/2 tsp. ground cinnamon   1/4 tsp. banana extract (optional)
1/2 tsp. baking soda   2 T. plus 2 tsp. sugar (or sweetener equivalent
1/2 tsp. baking powder   to 8 tsp. sugar)
2 medium, ripe bananas (mashed)

Preheat oven to 350 degrees. In a medium bowl, mix dry ingredients. In another bowl, combine remaining ingredients. Add to dry mixture, mixing until well moistened.

Spread mixture in an 8-inch square baking pan sprayed with a nonstick cooking spray. Bake 20 minutes until lightly browned. Cool in pan on wire rack. Cut into squares to serve. (Fat: less than 10% calories from fat)

— Orange Cinnamon Rolls —
(10 servings)

1 T. plus 2 tsp. reduced-calorie margarine   and unsweetened)
    (melted)   1/2 tsp. ground cinnamon
3 T. sugar (or sweetener equal to 9 tsp. sugar)   1 package (10-ounce) refrigerator biscuits
1 T. frozen orange juice concentrate (thawed   (10 biscuits)

Preheat oven to 350 degrees. In a 9-inch pie pan, combine margarine, sugar, orange juice concentrate, and cinnamon. Spread evenly over bottom of pan.

Arrange biscuits evenly in pan. Bake 20 to 25 minutes until golden. Cool in pan 1 minute then invert onto serving plate. Serve warm for best flavor. (Fat: less than 30% calories from fat)

Ravenel's Breakfast Stir-Fry

Try these energy-building alternatives to traditional breakfast. These are original recipes by Ravenel Scott of Greenville, South Carolina, a dear friend who is dedicated to healthy eating and regular exercise.

Ravenel suggests you pick your favorite vegetables fresh from your market or use frozen Chinese stir-fry vegetables. Learn to use and like many varieties to include yellow, reds, and green vegetables in order to benefit from their varied nutrients.

Using peppers and herbs for seasoning, Ravenel uses little or no salt. Like me, he uses oils that are highly monunsaturated and cholesterol free.

— Vegetable Stir-Fry —

Several fresh or frozen vegetables (thinly sliced or cubed)

Seasoning Sauce (see recipe below)

Have vegetables chopped, cubed, or sliced ahead of time. Also prepare seasoning sauce before you start.

Place your choice of vegetables such as squash, broccoli, mushrooms, cabbage, spinach, tomatoes, eggplant, okra, and green onions in one bowl. These particular vegetables require less cooking time and are very good just steamed. In a different bowl place your choice of such vegetables as celery, carrots, irish potatoes, radishes, turnips and turnip greens, green beans, or beets. These vegetables take longer than others to cook in a stir-fry.

Seasoning Sauce:

1/2 c. hot water
2 T. Mexican salsa (hot, medium, or mild)
Pinch of basil
Pinch of marjoram
Pinch of no-salt seasoning

1 to 2 tsp. low-salt soy sauce
1 T. corn starch
1 tsp. Worcestershire sauce
1 clove of garlic (minced)
1 T. canola or olive oil

Mix the above, except for the garlic. (Dissolve cornstarch in hot water before mixing in with other ingredients.)

Then begin your stir-fry by sauteing a small, thinly sliced onion in 1 tablespoon of canola oil or olive oil. When onions become transparent, add slow-cooking vegetables and stir-fry for about 5 minutes on high heat. Then add quick-cooking vegetables. Stir-fry on high heat for another 3 minutes. Then add 1/2 cup of sauce and cover with tight lid. Let steam on medium heat until most of the water has evaporated. (You may add water as needed to make vegetables more tender.) Sauce should be thickened, not watery. At this point, stir in garlic. Heat briefly and serve hot on a bed of grits, rice, or whole-wheat toast.

If serving with whole-wheat toast, cut toasted bread in pieces and stir in with sauce and vegetables in pan, before serving.

Alternatives for stir-fry:

Beef, ham, chicken, fish or salmon (sliced in thin strips or diced).

When using meats, begin by sauteing onion in oil. Then add diced or sliced lean beef, ham, chicken (skinless), fish, or canned salmon. Saute until mostly done, then add vegetables and sauces as described above.

3

Desserts

INTRODUCTION TO DESSERTS

Controlling Your Appetite —

Don't tell me — you have an incurable sweet tooth and just have to have your chocolate fix every day!

I realize some folks are truly addicted to chocolate and have to completely get it out of their systems before they can stop craving it. If you are like this, remember you will have to abstain from chocolate for at least two weeks before the craving will ease. And you will need to avoid it from then on. An addict cannot stop with just a bite of chocolate. One bite and she is off on a binge, much like an alcoholic. So if you are truly addicted to chocolate, just avoid it altogether.

> The Lord knoweth how to deliver the godly out of temptations (2 Pet. 2:9).

Memorize this Scripture and call upon it in times of temptation and need. The Lord desires you to be well, healthy, and fit for Him.

> Dearly beloved, I beseech you as strangers and pilgrims, abstain from fleshly lusts, which war against the soul (1 Pet. 2:11).

Yes, food is one of the most common of fleshly lusts. Did you ever think that lusting after food can be a kind of sin? Lusting can lead to binges and gluttonous acts. I believe this grieves the Lord.

Since lusting often leads to overeating and binging, many fall into the trap of anorexia or bulemia in an effort to stay thin. In other words, rather than face a lustful appetite and control it with God's help, many people will try to control it through the destructive behavior associated with anorexia or bulemia. To learn more about this, read my book, *Your Health Coach.*

Let's approach our food as "fuel" for our bodies and desire to honor God with our life styles.

Perhaps you need healing in your body or in your life style today. The greatest promise of healing is found in 1 Peter 2:24, "By whose stripes you were healed."

Christ paid the penalty for our sins at Calvary. When we confess our sins and ask Him into our hearts to be our Lord and Savior, we have access to God's healing, sustaining power. We are new creations in Christ Jesus. Has there been a time in your life when you have done this? Accepting Christ is the beginning of all healing.

Calorie-cutting dessert tips —

For so many people, desserts are an important part of a "special" meal. And do keep them for special meals. However, we all need nutrients in order to be healthy; and it is so much better when we reach for a piece of fresh fruit for dessert.

When having dessert, serve very small portions. Desserts, as a rule, contain few nutrients and are high in calories. Be especially careful of having large servings of desserts containing cooking oil or margarine.

Always remember, any recipe will be lower in fat if you use egg whites or egg substitute instead of the whole egg. Now, here are some tips to help lower fat and calories in your desserts:

— In most dessert recipes, the amount of sugar used can be cut in half without adversely affecting the texture or taste of the dessert. Sugar has been reduced in all my dessert recipes.

— While artificial sweeteners work fine in pies and puddings, they often adversely alter the texture of cakes, cookies, and pastries. If you use a sweetener, for best results use half sugar and half sweetener.

— Don't use NutraSweet in cooked desserts because prolonged exposure to heat breaks this sweetener down and it is lost. However, you can add NutraSweet after cooking.

— Honey can be used as sweetener in most pies and puddings but may alter the texture of cakes and cookies. Honey, by the way, has as many calories as sugar.

— Adding or increasing required amounts of vanilla extract can make foods taste sweeter than they really are.

— Add fiber, vitamins, iron, and protein to desserts by replacing half the white flour with whole-wheat flour. In making this substitution, always add a little more liquid to the recipe.

— Reduce cholesterol in a recipe by either using an egg substitute or 2 egg whites in place of each egg.

— Always use a vegetable oil that is high in polyunsaturates such as safflower, canola, sunflower, corn, or soybean oils.

— Beware of oils containing coconut or palm oils. These are high in saturated fats that your body stores as cholesterol.

— Avoid butter, lard, and suet for the same reasons as those above.

— Using margarine instead of butter means lower saturated fat in your recipe and lower cholesterol. Calories, however, are about the same.

— As with oil, choose a margarine high in polyunsaturated fats.

— Reduced-calorie, tub margarines usually have a high water content and may alter the texture of your recipes. Be careful when using them.

— Grease pans always with nonstick cooking spray.

— Use low-fat cottage cheese and part-skim ricotta cheese in cheesecakes and other recipes that call for higher fat varieties. Taste is the same.

— Instead of regular sour cream, use the new nonfat sour cream or substitute plain low or nonfat yogurt.

— Replace all milks and creams in recipes with skim milk. Vanilla can be added for a richer taste.

— Go easy with whipped toppings. Read the labels. Most contain coconut oil.

— Forget two-crust pies. Deleting one crust saves a lot of calories.

— You can reduce the amounts of coconut or nuts in recipes by as much as 1/2 to 3/4 without affecting taste.

— When a recipe calls for ground nuts, substitute wheat germ.

— Using cocoa instead of solid chocolate saves calories. Use 3 tablespoons of cocoa to 1 ounce of solid chocolate.

— When using canned or frozen fruits in a recipe, or anytime, choose the unsweetened varieties.

— When a dessert calls for fruit, choose those that are naturally the sweetest in order to cut back on sugar.

— Fruit purees such as applesauce, bananas, and cooked prunes add moistness that will compensate for the lower fat content of a recipe.

— Graham cracker crusts, moistened with 2 Tablespoons of oil or fruit juice (enough to make the crust stick together) are much lower in fat that pastry crusts that call for shortening or butter.

— Use applesauce, lightened with 2 tablespoons per cup of vanilla or lemon yogurt, to sandwich cake layers.

— Instead of butter frostings, use a decorative glaze made of confectioners sugar with enough fruit juice or skim milk for a thick pouring consistency.

— Refrigerate or freeze all uneaten low-fat baked goods. Lowered fat and sugar contents mean they will not keep as well as other baked goods.

— Some desserts have always been low-fat and are definitely acceptable. They are: sponge cakes, meringues, and honey and spice cakes and cookies.

PUDDINGS

— Sweet Potato Pudding —
(4 servings)

12 ounces peeled raw sweet potatoes (grated)
1 c. carrots (grated)
1 small, sweet apple (grated)
1 tsp. vanilla extract
1 tsp. ground cinnamon

1/2 c. orange juice (unsweetened)
1 T. plus 1 tsp. maple syrup
1/4 c. raisins
1/2 ounce chopped walnuts

Preheat oven to 350 degrees. In a large bowl, combine all ingredients. Mix well. Place in a 1-quart casserole that has been sprayed with a nonstick cooking spray. Bake, uncovered, for 50 minutes. (Fat: 20% calories from fat)

— Happy Rice Pudding —
(8 servings)

1-1/4 c. water
1/2 c. uncooked brown rice
1 can (8-ounce) unsweetened, crushed
    pineapple (undrained)
1-1/2 c. skim milk
1/4 c. raisins

1/4 c. firmly-packed brown sugar
1/2 tsp. ground cinnamon
3 T. whole-wheat flour
1 tsp. vanilla extract
1/4 c. slivered almonds (toasted)

Bring water to a boil in a medium saucepan. Add rice; cover, reduce heat, and simmer 45 minutes.

Drain pineapple, reserving juice; set pineapple juice aside. Add pineapple and milk to rice, stirring well. Place over medium-low heat; cover and cook 15 minutes. Stir in raisins, sugar, and cinnamon.

Combine reserved pineapple juice and flour. Blend well. Gradually add flour mixture to rice mixture. Cook over medium heat until thick and bubbly. Remove from heat; stir in vanilla. Spoon into individual dessert dishes; top each with 1-1/2 teaspoons slivered almonds. Serve warm or chilled. (Fat: 3.2 grams or 157 calories per 1/2-cup serving)

— Microwave Lemon Pudding —
(6 servings)

1/4 c. plus 2 T. sugar
1/3 c. all-purpose flour
1/4 tsp. salt
2 eggs (separated)

3/4 c. skim milk
2 T. lemon juice
1 T. lemon rind
Nonstick cooking spray

Combine first 3 ingredients in a medium bowl. Set aside.

Beat egg yolks at high speed until thick and lemon colored. Add milk and lemon juice, beating well. Combine this mixture with dry ingredients. Beat well. Beat egg whites (at room temperature) at high speed until soft peaks form. Gently fold egg whites and lemon rind into milk mixture.

Pour batter evenly into 6 (6-ounce) custard cups that have been coated with cooking spray. Place 3 custard cups in microwave oven. Microwave, uncovered, at medium-high (70% power) for 2 to 2-1/2 minutes, rotating a half-turn after 1 minute. Let stand 2 minutes. Repeat for remaining custard cups. Best served warm. (Fat: 2.2 grams or 116 calories per serving)

— No-Bake Bread Pudding —
(8 servings)

4 slices whole-wheat bread (cubed)
1/2 c. orange juice (unsweetened)
1/4 tsp. ground cinnamon
1 medium, ripe banana (sliced)
1 small orange (peeled and sectioned)
1 envelope unflavored gelatin

3/4 c. water
2/3 c. nonfat dry milk
1-1/3 c. nonfat cottage cheese
1 T. vanilla extract
3 T. sugar (or sweetener equivalent to 9 tsp.)
10 small ice cubes (approx. 1 cup)

(Continued)

Place bread cubes in a large bowl. Pour orange juice over bread, sprinkle with cinnamon. Add banana and orange and toss.

In a small saucepan, sprinkle gelatin over water. Heat over low heat, stirring frequently until gelatin is completely dissolved. In a blender, combine gelatin mixture with remaining ingredients. Blend until ice cubes are completely dissolved.

Pour mixture over bread. Mix well. Place in an 8-inch square casserole dish. Press bread and fruit down gently in liquid. Chill until firm. (Fat: less than 10% calories from fat)

— Banana-Bread Pudding —
(4 servings)

2 eggs or 1/2 c. egg substitute	1/4 tsp. grated nutmeg
2 egg whites	1/4 tsp. ground cinnamon
1 c. skim milk	3 slices whole-wheat bread (diced)
4 T. brown sugar or honey	4 bananas (very ripe, mashed)

In a large bowl, whisk together the eggs and egg whites until well blended. Add milk, sugar (or honey), nutmeg, and cinnamon. Add bread. Let stand 5 minutes. Add bananas.

Coat a 1-to 1-1/2-quart casserole with nonstick cooking spray. Add bread mixture. Place the dish in a larger baking pan and add enough hot water to come halfway up the sides of the inside pan.

Bake at 350 degrees for 50 minutes. Remove casserole dish from water and allow to cool on a wire rack for 10 to 15 minutes. (Fat: less than 20% calories from fat)

— Creamy Banana Pudding —
(10 servings)

3 T. unbleached white flour	2 eggs (beaten) or egg substitute
3 c. skim milk	1 tsp. vanilla extract
1/3 c. granulated sugar	3 large bananas (sliced)
1 egg white (slightly beaten)	Fresh lemon juice

In a covered jar, shake flour and 1/2 cup skim milk. Set aside. In top of double boiler, combine remaining milk, sugar, and eggs. Place over boiling water. Gradually add floured milk. Cook, stirring frequently, 20 to 25 minutes until mixture thickens. Remove from heat. Stir in vanilla extract.

Line bottom and sides of a 9-inch pie plate with sliced bananas. Pour pudding over bananas. (Brush bananas with lemon juice to keep them from darkening.) Chill 2 to 3 hours. (Fat: less than 20% calories from fat per serving)

— Quick 'N Easy Chocolate Pudding —
(5 servings)

1/4 c. unsweetened cocoa powder
1/2 c. granulated sugar
2 T. cornstarch
1/8 tsp. salt

2 c. skim milk
1 egg (beaten) or egg substitute
1/2 tsp. vanilla extract

In a medium saucepan, blend cocoa, sugar, cornstarch, salt, and milk. Cook over medium heat, stirring constantly, until mixture comes to a boil and begins to thicken. Remove from heat.

Mix 1/4 cup of the mixture with beaten egg. Gradually stir egg mixture into hot mixture. Cook over low heat, stirring constantly, 5-10 minutes, or until mixture comes to a boil. Remove from heat. Stir in vanilla extract. Pour into custard cups. Chill. (Fat: less than 20% calories from fat per 1/2 cup serving)

— Banana Pudding 'N Meringue —
(8 servings)

1 package (7-ounce) vanilla pudding mix
   (instant or regular)
3 c. skim milk
32 vanilla wafers
3-4 bananas (sliced)

3 egg whites (at room temperature)
1/8 tsp. cream of tartar
1/2 tsp. vanilla
1/4 c. sugar

Prepare pudding with milk according to package directions.

In bottom of an 8x8-inch baking dish, arrange half the vanilla wafers. Top with a generous layer of sliced bananas and then half the pudding. Repeat with a layer of remaining vanilla wafers, bananas, and pudding.

Beat egg whites, cream of tartar, and vanilla using highest speed on electric mixer until soft peaks form. Gradually add sugar, beating until stiff peaks form. Spread meringue evenly over pudding mixture, sealing to edge of dish.

Bake at 350 degrees for about 10 minutes or until golden brown. (Fat: less than 10% calories from fat per serving)

— Delicious Raspberry Tapioca —
(4 servings)

2 c. fresh or frozen (thawed) raspberries
   (unsweetened)
3 T. quick-cooking tapioca (uncooked)

2 T. plus 2 tsp. sugar (or sweetener equivalent
   to 8 tsp. sugar)

Place berries in a blender container. Blend until smooth. Pour through a strainer. In a small saucepan, combine pureed berries with enough water to equal 2 cups. Stir in tapioca and sugar. (If using NutraSweet as a sweetener, add it after cooking.) Let mixture stand 5 minutes.

Bring to boil over medium heat, stirring frequently. Remove from heat. Cool in pan 20 minutes. Then stir and place in 4 custard cups. Chill. (Fat: less than 10% calories from fat)

— Tapioca Dessert with Apples —
(4 servings)

4 small, sweet apples (peeled, coarsely shredded)
1 c. water
2 T. plus 2 tsp. quick-cooking tapioca (uncooked)

1 tsp. vanilla extract
1/2 tsp. ground cinnamon
1/4 tsp. ground nutmeg
1 T. plus 1 tsp. sugar (or sweetener equivalent to 4 tsp. sugar)

Preheat oven to 350 degrees. Combine all ingredients in a large bowl and mix well.

Place in a 1-quart baking dish sprayed with nonstick cooking spray. Let stand 10 minutes. Smooth the top of the pudding with the back of a spoon. Bake, uncovered, 40 minutes until tapioca granules are clear. Serve hot or cold. (Fat: less than 10% calories from fat)

COBBLERS AND FRUIT DESSERTS

— Fat-Free Fruit Cobbler —

1/2 c. flour
1/2 c. sugar

1 tsp. baking powder
1/2 c. skim milk

Stir all ingredients together to make a batter. Pour into greased 9x9 pan. Top with 1-1/2 cups fresh, frozen, or canned fruit of choice. Cherries, blueberries, raspberries, and sliced peaches work well. Bake 30-40 minutes in preheated 350-degree oven. If using sweetened or naturally sweet fruit, sugar in batter can be reduced somewhat. — *Sally Smith, Manassas, VA*

— Sugarless Apple Dessert —
(5 servings, 1/2 cup each)

3 envelopes unflavored gelatin
1 (12-ounce) can unsweetened frozen apple juice concentrate (diluted)
1 tsp. ground cinnamon

1/2 tsp. ground nutmeg
5 c. peeled, sliced apples
1 T. reduced-calorie margarine

Combine gelatin, diluted apple juice concentrate, cinnamon, and nutmeg in a large skillet, stirring well; let stand 1 minute. Cook over low heat 1 minute or until gelatin dissolves. Add apples. Cover and continue to cook over low heat 15 to 20 minutes or until tender.

Stir apples gently and baste with pan juice several times during cooking process. Add margarine; stir gently until margarine melts. Remove from heat. Cover and refrigerate until thoroughly chilled. Spoon mixture into dessert dishes to serve. (Fat: less than 20% calories from fat)

— Crumb Peach Bake —
(4 servings, 1/2 cup each)

2 c. sliced fresh peaches
Nonstick cooking spray
1/3 c. graham cracker crumbs

1/2 tsp. ground cinnamon
1/8 tsp. ground nutmeg
2 tsp. reduced-calorie margarine (melted)

Layer sliced peaches in bottom of an 8-inch square dish coated with nonstick cooking spray. Combine graham cracker crumbs, cinnamon, and nutmeg in bowl, stirring well. Add margarine and blend well.

Sprinkle graham cracker crumb mixture over peaches. Bake at 350 degrees for 30 minutes. Serve warm. (Fat: 20% calories from fat)

— Spicy Fruit —
(8 servings, 3/4 cup each)

1 medium-size orange
1 can (15,1/4-ounces) unsweetened pineapple chunks (undrained)
2 cans (16-ounces) unsweetened pear halves (drained)

1 can (16-ounce) unsweetened apricot halves (drained)
2 sticks (2-inch) of cinnamon
6 whole cloves

Peel orange, reserving rind. Section orange and remove seeds. Drain pineapple, reserving juice.

Combine orange sections, pineapple chunks, pear halves, and apricot halves in a large bowl. Set aside.

Combine orange rind, pineapple juice, cinnamon, and cloves in a small saucepan, stirring well. Bring to a boil; reduce heat and simmer 5 minutes. Remove from heat.

Strain mixture, discarding rind and whole spices. Pour juice over fruit, tossing gently to combine. Cover and refrigerate until thoroughly chilled. (Fat: Only trace)

— Peach Dessert —
(3 servings)

1 can (16-ounce) unsweetened peach halves (undrained)
1/2 tsp. cornstarch
1/8 tsp. ground cinnamon

1/8 tsp. ground nutmeg
1/8 tsp. ground cloves
1/8 tsp. grated orange rind

Drain peaches, reserving juice; set peaches aside.

Combine cornstarch and spices in a medium saucepan; stir in peach juice and rind.

Add peaches to mixture in saucepan; bring to a boil, stirring constantly. Reduce heat and simmer 2 minutes, stirring occasionally. Remove from heat and serve warm. (Fat: Only trace)

— Peaches with Yogurt —
(4 servings)

1 can (1-lb. diet peaches, drained)
1/2 container (8-ounce) plain yogurt

1 T. sugar
Dash almond extract

Arrange peaches in small, glass serving bowl.

Combine yogurt, sugar, and almond extract, blend well with rubber spatula. Pour over peaches. Refrigerate at least 2 hours. (Fat: 88 calories per serving)

— *Ruby L. Campbell, Danville, VA*

— Apple Strudel —
(2 servings)

2 slices thin-sliced whole-wheat bread
2 tsp. reduced-calorie margarine
Filling:
1/4 c. applesauce (unsweetened)
2 tsp. reduced-calorie orange marmalade
1/4 tsp. coconut extract
1/4 tsp. ground cinnamon

1 tsp. sugar (or equivalent amount of sweetener)
Topping:
1/4 tsp. ground cinnamon
1 tsp. sugar (sweeteners do not work well here)

Preheat oven to 350 degrees. Place bread between 2 sheets of wax paper and flatten with a rolling pin. Spread 1 side of each slice with margarine. Place margarine-side down on a sheet of wax paper.

In a small bowl, combine all filling ingredients. Divide evenly onto the bread. Spread filling, staying 1 inch away from the edges.

Gently roll each piece of bread like a small jelly roll. Sprinkle with the combined remaining sugar and cinnamon. Place rolls in a shallow baking pan. Bake 10 minutes until lightly browned. Remove from pan and serve warm. (Fat: less than 20% calories from fat)

— Apples and Cream —
(4 servings)

2 small, sweet apples (peeled and chopped into 1/4-inch pieces)
2 eggs or egg substitute
2 T. sugar (or sweetener equivalent to 6 tsp. sugar)

1 tsp. vanilla extract
1 c. evaporated skim milk
Topping:
1/4 tsp. ground cinnamon
1 tsp. sugar

Preheat oven to 350 degrees. Divide apple pieces evenly into 4 custard cups. In a small bowl, beat eggs, vanilla, and sugar with a fork or wire whisk. Gradually whisk in milk. Pour mixture over apples.

Place custard cups in an 8-inch square baking dish. Pour 1 cup of boiling water into bottom of pan. Bake 30 minutes until set.

Combine cinnamon and sugar. When custard comes out of the oven, sprinkle each with the topping and place on a rack to cool. Serve warm or chill and serve cold. (Fat: less than 20% calories from fat)

— Apples and Blueberry Delight —
(12, 1/2-c. servings)

8 c. sweet apples (peeled, sliced 1/4-inch thick)
4 c. fresh or frozen blueberries (unsweetened)
1-1/2 c. water
1 tsp. lemon juice
1/2 tsp. ground cinnamon
1 T. plus 1 tsp. cornstarch
3 T. sugar (or sweetener equivalent to 9 tsp. sugar)

In a large saucepan, combine all ingredients. (If using NutraSweet as sweetener, add it after cooking.) Cook over medium heat, stirring occasionally, until mixture comes to a boil.

Reduce heat to low and cook, stirring frequently, until apples are tender.

Serve warm or chill and serve cold. (Fat: less than 10% calories from fat)

— Baked Pears 'N Cinnamon —
(4 servings)

4 small pears
2 T. firmly-packed brown sugar (or sweetener equivalent to 6 tsp. brown sugar)
1/2 c. water
1 T. lemon juice
1/4 tsp. ground cinnamon

Cream Sauce
1/2 c. plain low-fat yogurt
1/2 tsp. ground cinnamon
1/2 tsp. vanilla extract
1 T. firmly-packed brown sugar (or sweetener equivalent to 3 tsp. brown sugar)

Prepare cream sauce ahead of time. In a small bowl, combine all ingredients in cream sauce. Chill to blend flavors.

Preheat oven to 350 degrees. Peel pears, cut in half lengthwise, and scoop out core. Place, flat side down, in a small shallow baking dish. Combine brown sugar, water, lemon juice, and cinnamon. Pour over pears.

Cover and bake 45 minutes or until pears are tender. Baste occasionally with pan juices while baking.

To serve, place 2 pear halves in each of 4 individual serving bowls. Spoon pan juices over pears; then top each serving with a dollop of cream sauce. Serve right away. (Fat: less than 10% calories from fat)

— Rhubarb Crisp —

4 c. rhubarb
3/4 c. sugar (or 1/2 cup of Sugar Twin)
1/4 c. low-fat margarine
1/2 c. skim milk
1 egg (or two egg whites) — Note: whole eggs increase fat content.
1 c. flour
1 tsp. salt
1 c. sugar (or equivalent in Sugar Twin)
2 tsp. dry strawberry jello
1 T. cornstarch
1 c. boiling water

Put rhubarb in 9x13 baking dish. Cream 3/4 cup sugar and margarine. Put in beaten egg, milk, 1 cup flour, and salt. Mix well and pour over rhubarb. Mix together 1 cup sugar, jello, and cornstarch. Sprinkle evenly over first mixture. Pour 1 cup boiling water over all. Bake 45 minutes at 350 degrees. (Fat: 30% calories from fat)

— Elegant Berries Romanoff —
(2 servings)

1 c. plain low-fat yogurt
1 T. plus 1 tsp. sugar (or sweetener equivalent
  to 4 tsp. sugar)

1 tsp. vanilla extract
1/2 tsp. orange extract
2 c. fresh strawberries

In a small bowl, combine all ingredients, except strawberries. Mix well.

Chill to blend flavors. To serve, divide berries into individual serving bowls. Stir yogurt mixture and spoon over berries. (Fat: less than 10% calories from fat)

— Elegant Ambrosia —
(8 servings)

2 c. applesauce (unsweetened)
2 medium, ripe bananas (sliced)
1 c. canned mandarin oranges (unsweetened)

1 ounce slivered toasted almonds
2 T. shredded coconut (unsweetened)

Combine all ingredients. Chill. (Fat: less than 30% calories from fat)

— Baked Apples —
(4 servings)

4 apples (cored)
1/2 c. raisins
2 T. brown sugar

1 tsp. cinnamon
1/2 c. apple juice (or water)

Place apples in a shallow baking dish.

Combine the raisins, brown sugar, and cinnamon. Spoon into centers of apples. Pour apple juice over apples.

Bake at 350 degrees for 45 minutes or until apples are tender, basting occasionally. Serve warm with frozen yogurt. (Fat: less than 10% calories from fat)

— Fruit Dessert —
(4 servings)

1 peach
1/2 c. mandarin orange or tangerine sections
1/2 c. grapefruit sections

1/2 c. blueberries
1/2 c. grapefruit juice
1/2 c. orange juice

Divide the peach equally among 4 glasses. Divide the additional fruits and juice among the 4 glasses. Mix and chill. (Fat: less than 10% calories from fat)

— Apple-Pear Dumpling —
(8 servings)

3 T. brown sugar
1 T. cornstarch
1/4 tsp. ground cinnamon
1/4 tsp. ground nutmeg
1 c. water
3 medium-size fresh pears (peeled, cored, chopped)
2 large cooking apples (peeled, cored, sliced)
1/4 c. raisins

Nonstick cooking spray
1/2 c. plus 1 T. all-purpose flour
1 T. sugar
1 tsp. baking powder
1/4 c. skim milk
1 T. chopped, blanched almonds
2 tsp. sugar
1/8 tsp. ground cinnamon

Combine first 4 ingredients in medium saucepan, stirring well. Add water, stirring well. Bring to a boil over medium heat. Cook 1 minute, stirring constantly. Remove from heat. Gently stir in pears, apples, and raisins. Spoon mixture into an 8-inch square baking dish that has been coated with cooking spray.

Combine flour, 1 tablespoon sugar, and baking powder in a medium bowl. Add skim milk, stirring just until dry ingredients are moistened. Drop dumpling mixture by level tablespoons over apple-pear mixture. Combine almonds, 2 teaspoons sugar, and cinnamon. Stir well. Sprinkle cinnamon mixture over dumplings. Bake at 400 degrees for 25 to 30 minutes or until dumplings are lightly browned. (Fat: 30% calories from fat)

— Watermelon Basket —

1 long (15-inch) watermelon (approx. 15 lb.)
1 cantaloupe
1 pint fresh strawberries

1 honeydew melon
1/4 pound seedless grapes

On top of watermelon, insert wooden picks to mark 2 diagonal, 1-1/2-inch wide bands, making an "x" cut about 4 inches into watermelon on outer side of marking, leaving uncut diamond in center. Cut in from sides being careful not to cut through bands. Remove 4 pieces from top of watermelon.

Cut watermelon meat from under bands with melon ball scoop. Scoop out about 2 cups of watermelon balls from extracted pieces and from watermelon.

Scoop 2 cups each from honeydew melon and cantaloupe.

Wash and hull strawberries. Wash grapes and snip stems to make small bunches.

Pile fruits in watermelon. Wrap with plastic film to hold fruits in place. Refrigerate until well chilled. At serving time, let guests serve themselves.

— Mr. Campbell, Danville, VA

PIES

— Microwave Raspberry Pie —
(8 servings)

2 T. reduced-calorie margarine
1 c. vanilla wafers (crushed)
2 c. fresh raspberries
1/3 c. sugar
1/3 c. skim milk
2 egg yolks
1 envelope unflavored gelatin

1/2 tsp. vanilla extract
1/4 tsp. salt
2 egg whites
1/4 tsp. cream of tartar
2 T. sugar
Fresh raspberries for garnish (optional)

Place margarine in a 9-inch pie plate. Microwave, uncovered, on HIGH for 30 seconds or until melted. Add crushed wafers, stirring well. Press mixture evenly over bottom and up sides of pie plate. Microwave, uncovered, on HIGH for 1-2 minutes or until firm, rotating pie plate a half-turn every 30 seconds. Set aside. Let cool.

Place raspberries in container of an electric blender. Cover and process until smooth. Strain puree, discarding seeds. Combine puree, sugar and next 5 ingredients in a 1-1/2-quart baking dish. Microwave, uncovered, at MEDIUM (50% power) for 4-6 minutes or until mixture boils, stirring every 2 minutes. Let stand 30 to 40 minutes or until mixture thickens slightly.

Beat egg whites (at room temperature) and cream of tartar at high speed using an electric mixer just until foamy. Gradually add 2 tablespoons sugar, 1 tablespoon at a time, beating until stiff peaks form and sugar dissolves (2-4 minutes). Gently fold raspberry mixture into meringue. Pour mixture into crust. Chill 2 hours or until firm. If desired, garnish with fresh raspberries. (Fat: 30% calories from fat)

— Fresh Peach Pie —

2 low-fat pie crusts (baked and cooled) —
   (See this section for recipe)
8 ounces "lite" cream cheese
2/3 c. confectioners sugar
4 or 5 medium peaches

1 c. water
1 c. sugar
4 T. cornstarch
4 T. sugar-free peach gelatin
Non or low-fat dessert topping

Mix cream cheese with confectioners sugar and spread into cooled pie crusts. Quarter peaches and place on top of cream cheese mixture. Mix water, sugar, and cornstarch. Cook on medium heat until thickened. Add gelatin to mixture and pour over peaches. Place pies in refrigerator for about 1 hour before serving. Top with dessert topping. (Fat: 30% calories from fat)

— Cherlyn Sanders, Taylors, SC

— Fluffy Chocolate Pie —
(6 or more servings)

3/4 c. graham cracker crumbs
3 T. melted margarine
1 package of reduced-calorie chocolate
   pudding (cooking kind)

1 envelope of reduced-calorie whipped
   topping mix
1 T. vanilla

Crust: Combine crumbs and margarine. Press into pie pan. Bake 8 minutes at 350 degrees. Cool.

Filling: Prepare 1 package reduced-calorie pudding mix as directed for pie. After cooling 5 minutes, measure 1 cup; cover and chill. Pour remaining filling into pie crust. Chill.

Prepare 1 envelope whipped topping as directed. Beat chilled measured filling until smooth; blend in 1-1/3 cups prepared whipped topping, along with the vanilla. Spread over filling in crust. Chill 2 hours. Garnish with remaining topping. Makes one, 7 or 8-inch pie. (Fat: 30% calories from fat)

— Fluffy Peach Pie —
(8 servings)

16 (2x2-inch) graham crackers
2 T. reduced-calorie margarine
1 c. sugar
2 egg whites
1 tsp. vanilla

1 tsp. lemon juice
1 c. reduced-calorie whipped topping
4 fresh peaches (peeled and finely chopped)
Pinch of salt

Crush crackers in a blender or with rolling pin and transfer to pie plate. Melt margarine and stir into cracker crumbs, pressing mixture evenly over bottom and up sides of pan.

In medium mixing bowl, combine sugar, egg whites, vanilla, and lemon juice. Beat at medium speed for 15 minutes or until stiff. Fold in whipped topping and peaches. Pile lightly into prepared crumb shell. Chill 1-1/2 hours and serve. (Fat: less than 25% calories from fat)

— Low-Fat Pumpkin Pie —
(8 servings)

1 can (16-ounce) solid-pack pumpkin
1 can (13-ounce) evaporated skim milk
1 egg
2 egg whites
1/2 c. biscuit mix
2 T. sugar

8 packets sugar substitute (heat stable —
   Sunette or Sweet One are brands
   recommended for cooking)
2 tsp. pumpkin pie spice
2 tsp. vanilla

Heat oven to 350 degrees. Lightly spray 9-inch pie pan with nonstick cooking spray.
Place all ingredients in blender or mixing bowl. Blend 1 minute or beat 2 minutes with mixer.
Pour into pie pan and bake for 50 minutes or until center is puffed. (Fat: 30% calories from fat)

— Gelatin Lemon Pie —
(6 servings)

1 package (3-ounce) lemon-flavored gelatin
1 small carton low-fat, small curd cottage
   cheese

2 T. fresh lemon juice (optional — if use this
   count it as part of your liquid)

Mix gelatin in bowl using 3/4 cup hot water and pouring a little at a time until mixed thoroughly. Add 3/4 cup cold water with some ice in the water. Stir until ice melts. Stir in cottage cheese with gelatin. Place in blender and blend until real creamy. Pour into prepared graham cracker crust (see our crust recipes) and refrigerate 3-4 hours. (Fat: less than 10% calories from fat)

— Mary Richardson, The Rock, GA

— Meringue Rhubarb Pie —
(8 servings)

1 c. all-purpose flour
1/4 tsp. salt
1/4 c. reduced-calorie margarine
3 T. cold water
3 c. chopped fresh rhubarb
1/4 c. unsweetened orange juice

1/3 c. sugar
2 T. cornstarch
2 T. water
3 egg whites (at room temperature)
1/4 tsp. cream of tartar
2 T. sugar

Combine flour and salt; cut in margarine with a pastry blender until mixture resembles coarse meal. Sprinkle cold water evenly over surface of flour mixture; stir with a fork until dry ingredients are moistened. Shape dough into a ball and chill. Roll dough to 1/8-inch thickness. Place in a 9-inch pie plate; fold edges under. Prick bottom and sides with a fork. Bake at 425 degrees for 12 to 15 minutes. Cool.

Combine chopped rhubarb, orange juice, and sugar in a medium saucepan. Place over medium heat and cook until mixture is thickened. Dissolve cornstarch in water; stir cornstarch mixture into rhubarb mixture. Pour into baked pie shell. Set aside.

Beat egg whites and cream of tartar at high speed with an electric mixer for 1 minute. Gradually add sugar, 1 tablespoon at a time, beating until stiff peaks from and sugar dissolves (2 to 4 minutes). Spread meringue over hot filling, sealing to edge of pastry. Bake at 425 degrees for 5 minutes or until meringue is golden brown. (Fat: 30% calories from fat)

— Walnut Apple Pie —
(8 servings)

1 c. whole-wheat pastry flour
1 c. sugar
1/2 tsp. vanilla
4 egg whites

1/2 c. chopped walnuts
2 tsp. baking powder
2 c. chopped apple

Preheat oven to 350 degrees. In a large bowl, mix first six ingredients. Mixture will be thick. Stir in chopped apples. Grease pie pan with nonstick cooking spray. Place mixture in pan. Bake about 35 minutes. (Fat: 18% calories from fat)

— Easy Pie Crust —

Instead of mixing graham cracker crumbs with margarine for a pie crust, line the pie plate with the actual graham crackers. To line sides, place the 1/4-size pieces of a graham cracker against the side of the pie plate and press. They will break and lay flat against the sides.

— Harriet Cottingham, Charleston Hgts., SC

— Pastry Shell —
(makes 1, 8- or 9-inch pie crust)

1 c. sifted all-purpose flour
3/4 tsp. salt
3/4 tsp. sugar (optional)

1/4 c. canola or safflower oil
2 T. skim milk

Preheat oven to 475 degrees (or according to recipe for filling). Mix flour, salt, and sugar in a bowl. Combine oil and milk in a measuring cup and pour all at once over flour mixture. Stir with fork until mixed. Shape into a ball, place on sheet of waxed paper, flatten and cover with another sheet of waxed paper. Roll out with a rolling pin and peel off top paper. Turn dough upside down over pie pan, peel off bottom paper, and fit dough into pan. Trim. If dough tears, mend without moistening. Flute edge. If crust is to be baked before filling is added, prick pastry all over with a fork and bake about 10 minutes. Cool before adding filling. If filling is to be baked with pie, do not prick crust and follow directions of your recipe. (Fat: 30% calories from fat)

— Coconut Custard Pie —
(8 servings)

2 c. skim milk
8 egg whites or 4 eggs (further reduce fat by
   using egg whites)
2 T. plus 2 tsp. reduced-calorie margarine
1/2 tsp. vanilla butternut flavor
1 tsp. coconut extract
1 tsp. vanilla extract

1/4 c. plus 2 T. all-purpose flour
2 tsp. baking powder
1/4 c. plus 1 T. sugar (or sweetener equivalent
   to 15 tsp. sugar)
1 c. carrots (finely shredded)
Ground nutmeg

Preheat oven to 350 degrees. In a blender, combine all ingredients, except carrots and nutmeg. Blend 1 minute. Stir in carrots. Pour mixture into a 9-inch glass pie pan sprayed with nonstick cooking spray. Sprinkle lightly with nutmeg. Let stand 5 minutes.

Bake 40 minutes until set. Cool slightly, than chill. (Fat: less than 30% calories from fat)

— Pumpkin Pie —

Empty 1 can of pumpkin puree into bowl. Do not use a mix.

Add: 1/3 c. powdered milk (dry) and 1/2 box of vanilla, sugar-free instant pudding.

Add water to consistency desired or add part fruit juice (unsweetened) and part water. Add a dash of cinnamon. Mix.

Use as filling for a pie crust or put about 1/3 in a bowl and top with cottage cheese (low-fat) and fruit. Keeps well in covered bowl in refrigerator. (Fat: less than 30% calories from fat)

— Mary Alice Stevens, Springhill, LA

GELATIN DESSERTS

— Pineapple Cloud —
(8 servings)

1 can (8-ounce) crushed pineapple (undrained)
1 envelope unflavored gelatin
4 eggs (separated)

1/2 c. sugar (divided)
2 T. lemon juice
1/4 c. vanilla wafer crumbs

Drain pineapple, reserving juice. Set pineapple aside. Add enough cold water to juice to equal 1/2 cup. Sprinkle gelatin over pineapple juice mixture; set aside.

Beat egg yolks in small saucepan until smooth. Add 1/4 cup sugar, reserved drained pineapple and lemon juice. Stir until well blended. Cook over medium-low heat, stirring constantly for 5 minutes or until mixture thickens. Remove from heat; add gelatin mixture, stirring until gelatin dissolves. Cool to room temperature. Chill thoroughly.

Beat egg whites (at room temperature) in a large mixing bowl at high speed with an electric mixer until foamy. Gradually add remaining 1/4 cup sugar, 1 tablespoon at a time, beating until stiff peaks form. Fold into pineapple mixture.

Sprinkle vanilla wafer crumbs evenly over bottom of an 8-inch square pan. Spoon filling over crumbs. Chill until firm. Cut into squares to serve. (Fat: 3.0 grams or 117 calories per serving)

— Rhubarb Salad —

10 c. rhubarb (add no water)
2 small packages jello dissolved in 2 c. hot water and 1 c. cold

2 packages vanilla instant pudding (can use sugar-free)
Sugar to taste (or sugar substitute)

Cook rhubarb at a low temperature for 20 minutes. Remove from stove. Add sugar and prepared jello. Add dry pudding. Chill and serve. (Fat: less than 25% calories from fat)

— *Ann Buel, Fairfax, VA*

— Apple Gelatin Dessert —
(4 servings)

2 c. low-calorie cranapple juice
1 envelope low-calorie strawberry gelatin
1/4 tsp. salt

1 c. chopped apple
1/2 c. chopped celery

Bring 1 cup juice to boil. Stir in gelatin until dissolved. Add remaining juice and salt. Chill until partially set, stir in apples and celery gently. Pour into desired mold. Chill until set. (Fat: less than 20% calories from fat)

— Fruity Fluff —
(6 servings)

1 package of lime or strawberry flavored gelatin
1 c. hot water

1 c. canned pineapple juice
1/8 tsp. salt
1 egg white

Dissolve gelatin in hot water. Add pineapple juice and salt. Chill until slightly thickened. Place in bowl of ice and water. Add the egg white and whip with egg beater until fluffy and thick. Pile lightly in sherbet glasses. Chill until firm. (Fat: less than 20% calories from fat)

— Gelatin Favorite —

2 boxes (3-ounce) sugar-free jello
2 c. boiling water
1 c. pineapple juice
1 No. 2 can crushed pineapple (sugarless and
   drained)
1 c. cold water
2 serving size tablespoons of fat-free
   "Miracle Whip"
1/2 c. chopped celery
1/2 c. nuts (optional)

Stir Miracle Whip into dry jello. Add boiling water to dissolve. Then add cold water and pineapple juice. Beat with hand beater until smooth. Chill until thick but not firm. Whip with electric mixer until light. Add pineapple and celery. Pour into 8- or 9-inch square dish. Chill. Serve on lettuce.

May use orange, cherry, lemon, or lime gelatin. (Fat: less than 30% calories from fat)

— Mrs. Darl Hetrick, New Bethlehem, PA

— Light Citrus Fluff —
(4 servings)

1 envelope unflavored gelatin
1/2 c. water
1/4 c. frozen orange juice concentrate
   (unsweetened and thawed)
1/4 tsp. lemon extract
15 small ice cubes (approx. 1-1/2 cups)
3 T. sugar (or sweetener equivalent to 9 tsp.
   sugar)
2 egg whites
1/4 tsp. cream of tartar

In a small saucepan, sprinkle gelatin over combined water and orange juice concentrate. Heat over low heat, stirring frequently until gelatin is completely dissolved.

Remove from heat. Add sugar and extracts, stirring until sugar is dissolved.

Add ice. Stir until mixture thickens. Discard any remaining pieces of ice.

Beat egg whites and cream of tartar using high speed on electric mixer until stiff. Fold orange mixture into egg whites gently and thoroughly. Chill 1 hour before serving. (Fat: less than 10% calories from fat)

— Orange Gelatin —
(4 servings)

Sprinkle one envelope unflavored gelatin over 1 cup of orange, or any flavor, juice in a small saucepan. Let soften a few minutes. Heat, stirring frequently, over low heat, until gelatin is completely dissolved. Remove from heat. Stir in one more cup of juice. Pour mixture into desired serving bowl. Chill. (Fat: less than 10% calories from fat)

DESSERT TOPPINGS, ICES, ICE CREAM

— Chilly Cantaloupe Sherbet —
(6 servings)

1 bottle (10-ounce) lemon-lime flavored
   sparkling mineral water (chilled)
2 c. lime sherbet
3 c. cubed cantaloupe

Combine cantaloupe and water in a bowl. Toss gently. Spoon 1/2 cup cantaloupe into individual dessert dishes using a slotted spoon. Reserve water. Top each serving with 1/3 cup of sherbet. Spoon remaining mineral water evenly over sherbet. Serve immediately. (Fat: 0.8 grams or 98 calories per serving)

— Grapefruit Sorbet —
(6 cups)

4 c. unsweetened pink grapefruit juice
  (divided)
1/4 c. plus 2 T. honey

1 envelope unflavored gelatin
1/4 c. lemon juice

Combine 1/2 cup grapefruit juice and honey in a small saucepan. Cook over low heat until honey melts.

Sprinkle gelatin over honey mixture in saucepan. Let stand 5 minutes. Cook over low heat, stirring constantly until gelatin dissolves. Combine gelatin mixture, remaining 3-1/2 cups grapefruit juice, and lemon juice in a large bowl. Stir well. Cover and freeze until firm. Remove from freezer. Let stand 10 minutes.

With knife blade in food processor, process frozen mixture until smooth. Serve in individual dessert bowls immediately. (Fat: 0.1 grams or 67 calories per 1/2-cup serving)

— Tangy Fruit Sherbet —
(makes 7 cups)

2-1/4 c. nonfat buttermilk
1 c. peeled, cubed mango
3 medium kiwifruit (peeled and quartered)
1 can (6-ounce) frozen orange juice
  concentrate (thawed and undiluted)

1 medium banana (peeled and sliced)
1/4 c. lime juice
3 T. honey
1/4 tsp. coconut extract

Combine all ingredients in blender or food processor and blend until smooth.

Pour mixture into freezer can of a 1-gallon hand-turned or electric freezer. Freeze according to appliance instructions. Serve immediately. (Fat: 0.4 grams or 73 calories per 1/2-cup serving)

— Strawberry Ice Cream —

1/2 c. skim milk
Sweetener to taste

1 c. frozen strawberries (can use other fruits)

Place in blender and blend for about 30 seconds. Add more milk if shake consistency is desired. (Fat: less than 20% calories from fat)
                 — *Ann Buel, Fairfax, VA*

— Cantaloupe Ice —
(4 cups)

3/4 c. unsweetened orange juice
3 T. sugar

3 c. coarsely chopped cantaloupe
1 tsp. lime juice

Combine orange juice and sugar in a non-aluminum saucepan. Bring to boil and boil for 1 minute. Remove from heat and cool.

Place cantaloupe in blender or food processor. Add 1/4 cup of cooled juice mixture and process until smooth. Combine pureed cantaloupe, remaining juice mixture, and lime juice. Stir well.

Pour cantaloupe mixture into freezer can of a hand-turned or electric ice-cream freezer. Follow appliance instructions for freezing. When frozen, serve in individual dessert dishes. (Fat: 0.2 grams or 50 calories per 1/2-cup serving)

— Lemon Ice —

Since reading Beverly's recommendation in *Your Health Coach* to put lemon in water to make it more enjoyable, I began squeezing juice from fresh lemons, mixing it with water (half water and half lemon juice), and freezing it in ice cube trays. Then when I have a glass of water, I put one or two cubes of lemon ice in the glass. Juice from three or four lemons, mixed half and half with water, will fill two ice trays. (Fat: None)

— Mary Richardson, The Rock, GA

— Chocolate-Lover's Ice Milk —
(7 cups)

1 envelope unflavored gelatin
4 c. 1% low-fat chocolate milk (divided)
3 eggs

1/3 c. sugar
1/4 c. semisweet chocolate mini-morsels

Combine gelatin and 1 cup milk in a small saucepan. Let stand 1 minute. Cook over medium heat, stirring constantly about 1 minute or until gelatin is dissolved. Set aside.

Combine eggs and sugar in a large bowl. Beat at high speed with an electric mixer, 4 to 5 minutes or until thickened and doubled in volume. Stir in gelatin mixture, remaining 3 cups milk, and mini-morsels.

Pour mixture into freezer can of hand-turned or electric ice-cream freezer and follow appliance directions for freezing. Serve when frozen to ice cream consistency. (Fat: approx. 30% calories from fat)

— Peachy Lean Ice Cream —
(8 servings)

2 c. fresh peaches (peeled and crushed)
1 c. sugar
1-1/2 T. lemon juice
1 tsp. ascorbic acid powder

1/2 tsp. vanilla
1/4 tsp. almond extract (optional)
1 c. instant nonfat dry milk
1 c. ice water

Crush peaches smooth. Add sugar, lemon juice, ascorbic acid powder, and vanilla. Stir to dissolve sugar. Whip instant milk and water in a 2-quart bowl with rotary beater or electric mixer until soft peaks form. Fold whipped milk into peach mixture. Pour into 2 ice trays (1 quart each). Freeze. When frozen, turn mixture into a 2-quart bowl and beat until smooth and creamy, but not melted. Return to ice trays and refreeze. (Fat: 160 calories per serving)

— Strawberry Shake —
(6 servings)

Juice of 1 orange
2 pints strawberries (washed and hulled)
1/2 tsp. vanilla extract

1 c. plain nonfat yogurt
2-3 ice cubes

Puree orange juice and berries in a blender or food processor. Add vanilla and yogurt. Blend 1 minute. Add ice cubes, one at a time, and crush. Serve immediately. (Fat: 7% calories from fat)

— Grape Juice Sherbet —

1-1/2 c. boiling water
1 c. sugar
1/2 c. cold water
2 c. grape juice

1 T. unflavored gelatin
4 T. lemon juice
1/3 c. orange juice
Dash of salt

Make a syrup of boiling water and sugar for 10 minutes. Add gelatin which has been soaked in cold water for 5 minutes. Cool. Add fruit juices and freeze until partially frozen. Beat and return to freezer. Beat once again when partially frozen. This beating process prevents ice from forming and results in smooth sherbet. (Fat: fat free)   — *Jan Pietrosewicz, Springfield, VA*

— Strawberry 'N Fruit Sherbet —
(2 servings)

1 c. frozen strawberries (unsweetened — do
   not thaw)
1/2 medium, ripe banana

1/4 c. orange juice (unsweetened)
1 tsp. honey

Combine all ingredients in a blender. Mix until smooth, stopping blender several times to stir mixture.

Spoon into sherbet glasses and enjoy. Or add more juice and make a cold drink. (Fat: less than 10% calories from fat)

— Cloud Topping —
(8 servings)

1/2 tsp. unflavored gelatin
1/4 c. cold water
1/4 c. granulated sugar

3 egg whites
1/4 tsp. cream of tartar
1 tsp. vanilla extract

In a small saucepan, soften gelatin in cold water. Stir in sugar. Cook over low heat, stirring constantly, 2-3 minutes, or until mixture is hot. Do not boil.

In top of double boiler, using an electric mixer, beat egg whites to stiff peaks. Put pan over boiling water. Add cream of tartar; beat 2 minutes. Rewarm gelatin and pour in a steady stream into egg whites, beating at high speed to stiff peaks, about 1 minute.

Pour hot water out of the double-boiler bottom. Fill with ice water. Put top of double boiler over ice water. Add vanilla extract, beat 3 minutes. Serve. (Fat: None)

— Poly-Whipped Topping —
(2 cups)

This polyunsaturated substitute has a taste and consistency very similar to whipped cream without the saturated fat.

1 tsp. unflavored gelatin
2 tsp. cold water
3 T. boiling water
1/2 c. ice water

1/2 c. nonfat dry milk
3 T. sugar
3 T. canola oil

(Continued)

Chill a small mixing bowl. Soften gelatin with 2 teaspoons cold water. Add boiling water, stirring until gelatin is completely dissolved. Cool until tepid. Place ice water and nonfat dry milk in the chilled mixing bowl. Beat at high speed until the mixture forms stiff peaks. Add sugar, still beating, followed by oil and gelatin. Place in freezer for about 15 minutes, then transfer to refrigerator until ready for use. Stir before use. (Fat: less than 30% calories from fat)

— *Mrs. Hazel McConnell, Alma, MI*

— Merry-Berry Fruit Salad Dressing —
(1-3/4 cups)

1 c. plain skim milk yogurt
1 c. fresh or frozen unsweetened berries of choice

1/4 tsp. ground cinnamon
1-2 drops vanilla

Blend all ingredients in blender until berries are pureed. Chill well before serving over fruit salad. (Fat: none)

— *Ann Buel, Fairfax, VA*

— Delight Sauce —
(1 cup)

1/3 c. miniature marshmallows
1 T. plus 2 teaspoons unsweetened cocoa
1 T. cornstarch
1 c. skim milk
1 T. light corn syrup

1 tsp. vanilla extract
1/4 tsp. ground cinnamon
1/4 c. miniature marshmallows
1 T. chopped pecans

Combine 1/3 cup marshmallows, cocoa, and cornstarch in a small saucepan. Gradually stir in milk and corn syrup. Cook over medium heat, stirring constantly, until thickened. Remove from heat; stir in vanilla and cinnamon. Let cool. Stir in 1/4 cup marshmallows and pecans. Serve over ice milk, angel food cake, or fresh fruit. (Fat: 0.4 grams or 23 calories per tablespoon)

— Vanilla Sauce —
(2 cups)

3 T. sugar
2 T. plus 1/2 tsp. cornstarch

1-1/4 c. skim milk
1-1/2 tsp. vanilla extract

Combine first 3 ingredients in a medium saucepan, stirring well. Cook over medium heat, stirring constantly, until mixture comes to a boil. Cook an additional 2 minutes. Remove from heat. Stir in vanilla. Cover and chill. Serve over fresh or baked fruit, baked puddings or custards. (Fat: None)

FOR THE COOKIE JAR

— Raspberry Brownies —
(32 brownies)

1/4 c. plus 2 T. margarine
1/4 c. plus 2 T. unsweetened cocoa
2/3 c. sugar
4 egg whites or 2 eggs (beaten) — (further reduce calories by using egg whites)
1/2 tsp. vanilla extract

1/2 c. all-purpose flour
1/8 tsp. salt
Nonstick cooking spray
1 package (10-ounce) frozen raspberries in light syrup (thawed undrained)

Drain raspberries, reserving 3 tablespoons of juice. Set raspberries and juice aside.

Combine margarine and cocoa in a large saucepan. Cook over low heat, stirring constantly until margarine melts and mixture is smooth. Remove from heat. Cool slightly. Add sugar, eggs, and vanilla to cocoa mixture. Blend well. Stir in 3 tablespoons reserved raspberry juice. Combine flour and salt; add this to cocoa mixture. Blend well. Gently fold raspberries into cocoa mixture.

Spoon batter into 8-inch square baking pan coated with nonstick cooking spray. Bake at 350 degrees for 20 minutes or until a wooden pick inserted in center comes out clean. Cool brownies completely. Cut and serve. (Fat: 2.6 grams or 61 calories per serving)

— Dressed-Up Brownies —
(makes 2 dozen)

1/4 c. plus 2 T. reduced-calorie margarine (softened)
1/3 c. "lite" cream cheese (softened)
2/3 c. sugar
4 egg whites or 2 eggs (beaten)
1 tsp. vanilla extract

3/4 c. all-purpose flour
1/2 tsp. baking powder
1/4 tsp. salt
3 T. unsweetened cocoa
Nonstick cooking spray

Cream margarine and cheese. Gradually add sugar, beating at medium speed with an electric mixer until light and fluffy. Add eggs and vanilla. Beat well.

Combine flour, baking powder, and salt. Add to creamed mixture, beating well. Divide batter in half. Sift cocoa over half of batter and fold in gently. Spoon cocoa mixture into an 8-inch square baking pan that has been coated with cooking spray. Pour remaining half of batter into pan. Cut through mixture in pan with a knife to create a marbled effect.

Bake at 350 degrees for 25 minutes or until a wooden pick inserted in center comes out clean. Cool, cut, and serve. (Fat: 3.1 grams or 70 calories)

— Spicy Fruit Squares —
(16 squares)

1/2 c. sugar
1/4 c. oil (corn, safflower, or canola)
1/4 c. buttermilk
3 egg whites
1 c. unsweetened applesauce
1-3/4 c. all-purpose, unbleached flour

1 tsp. cinnamon
1 tsp. baking powder
1/2 tsp. ground cloves
1/4 tsp. ground nutmeg
3/4 c. golden raisins, chopped dates, or finely chopped, unpeeled tart apple

Preheat oven to 350 degrees. Coat 9x9-inch baking pan with nonstick cooking spray.

In a medium bowl, beat sugar, oil, buttermilk, and egg whites with a wire whisk until smooth. Blend in applesauce. Mixture will look curdled.

In another medium bowl, stir together flour, cinnamon, baking powder, cloves, nutmeg, and 1/4 teaspoon salt. Add this to applesauce mixture just until blended. Mix in raisins, dates, or chopped apple. Spread batter in pan and smooth.

Bake 40 to 50 minutes, until top springs back when lightly pressed. Cool completely in pan on wire rack. Cut into squares. (Fat: 23% of calories from fat)

— Pumpkin Squares —
(5 dozen)

1 c. canola oil
2 c. plain flour
1-1/4 c. sugar
2 c. canned pumpkin
2 eggs (beaten slightly)

4 egg whites (beaten slightly)
2 tsp. cinnamon
2 tsp. baking powder
1 tsp. baking soda
Nonstick cooking spray

Mix all ingredients thoroughly. Pour into sprayed and floured 15x10 jelly roll pan. Bake at 350 degrees for 20 to 25 minutes. Cool thoroughly and frost.

FROSTING:
3 ounces of "lite" cream cheese
3/4 stick of low-calorie margarine

1 tsp. vanilla
1 T. skim milk
1-1/4 c. powdered sugar

Mix thoroughly and spread on cooled cake. (Fat: 30% calories from fat)

— Strudel Bars —
(6 servings)

1/2 c. water
1/2 c. canned crushed pineapple (unsweetened, drained)
2 T. juice from pineapple
1-1/2 envelopes unflavored gelatin
2 T. sugar (or sweetener equivalent to 6 tsp. sugar)

1/4 tsp. orange extract
1/4 tsp. coconut extract
1/4 tsp. ground cinnamon
1/2 c. plus 2 T. raisins
1 T. shredded coconut (unsweetened)
4-1/2 ounces nut-like cereal nuggets

(Continued)

In a medium saucepan, combine water and pineapple juice. Sprinkle with gelatin and let stand a few minutes. Heat over low heat, stirring frequently, until gelatin is completely dissolved.

Add sugar. Stir until dissolved. Add remaining ingredients, except cereal. Mix well. Stir in cereal. Mix until cereal is moistened. Place mixture in a 6x11 inch baking pan that has been sprayed with a nonstick cooking spray. Press firmly in pan. Chill. Cut into squares and serve. (Fat: less than 10% calories from fat)

— Molasses Bars —
(20 bars)

1/3 c. reduced-calorie margarine	1/4 c. whole-wheat flour
1/2 c. nut-like cereal nuggets	1/3 c. quick-cooking oats (uncooked)
1/3 c. firmly packed brown sugar	1/2 tsp. baking powder
2 T. molasses	1/8 tsp. baking soda
1 tsp. vanilla extract	Nonstick cooking spray
2 egg whites or 1 egg (beaten)	2 tsp. powdered sugar
1/2 c. all-purpose flour	

Melt margarine in a medium saucepan over medium heat. Add cereal. Cook 2 minutes, stirring constantly. Remove from heat; add brown sugar, molasses, vanilla, and egg, stirring until well blended.

Combine flours and next 3 ingredients in a medium bowl. Add to cereal mixture. Stir well. Spread into an 8-inch square pan sprayed with nonstick cooking spray. Bake at 350 degrees for 18 minutes. Cool. Sprinkle with powdered sugar. (Fat: 2.5 grams or 79 calories per bar)

— Spiced Oatmeal Cookies —

Mix the following dry ingredients together:

3/4 c. plain flour	1/2 tsp. ground cinnamon
1/2 tsp. baking powder	1/4 tsp. ground nutmeg
1/8 tsp. ground cloves	1/2 c. brown sugar
1/4 tsp. salt	1/2 c. white sugar

In a separate bowl, mix wet ingredients:

2 egg whites or 1 whole egg (beaten)	1/2 c. applesauce
Note: whole eggs increase fat content.	1/2 tsp. vanilla

Add dry ingredients to wet. Mix well. Then add 1-1/2 c. of oats. Mix well. Place by spoonful on cookie sheet sprayed with nonstick cooking spray. Bake at 350 degrees for 12 minutes (approximately). (Fat: less than 25% calories from fat)

— June Andrews, Mt. Vernon, OH

— Fudge Surprise Oatmeal Cookies —
(45 cookies)

1/2 c. low-calorie margarine (softened)
3/4 c. brown sugar
3/4 c. white sugar
4 egg whites or 2 eggs
1 tsp. pure vanilla extract
1 c. applesauce (unsweetened)

2 c. fine whole-wheat flour or unbleached flour
1 tsp. salt
1 tsp. baking soda
1 tsp. cinnamon
2 c. quick-cooking or old-fashioned rolled oats

Fudge Frosting:
1/4 c. low-calorie margarine (softened)
2 T. cocoa powder

3 T. skim milk
1-3/4 c. powdered sugar
1/2 tsp. pure vanilla extract

Preheat oven to 350 degrees. In a mixing bowl, cream together butter and sugars. Add eggs, vanilla, and applesauce. Mix well. In a separate mixing bowl, stir together flour, salt, baking soda, and cinnamon. Add this to creamed mixture, blending well. Stir in rolled oats and mix well. Drop by spoonfuls onto nonstick cookie sheets. Bake for about 8 minutes. Remove from pan and cool on rack.

When cookies are cooled, prepare frosting as follows: Bring margarine, cocoa, and skim milk to a boil. Remove from heat. Add powdered sugar and vanilla. Stir until smooth. Frost cookies immediately. (Fat: less than 29% calories from fat)

— Oatmeal-Raisin Cookies —
(small batch)

1/2 c. regular oats (uncooked)
1/2 c. all-purpose flour
1/4 c. packed brown sugar
1/4 tsp. ground cinnamon
1/8 tsp. baking soda

1/8 tsp. salt
3 T. applesauce (level)
2 T. skim milk
1/3 c. raisins or nuts (or a little of both)

Place oats on baking sheet. Bake at 350 degrees for 10 minutes. Remove from oven. Set aside. Combine flour, sugar, cinnamon, soda, and salt in a medium bowl. Combine applesauce and milk and pour into flour mixture. Add oats and raisins. Drop batter by teaspoonful, 2 inches apart, onto pans sprayed with nonstick cooking spray. Bake at 350 degrees for 10-12 minutes. Cool 1 minute on cookie sheet. Remove and continue to cool on racks. (Fat: less than 25% calories from fat)

— June Andrews, Mt. Vernon, OH

— Old-Fashioned Oatmeal Cookies —
(4 dozen)

1-1/2 c. sifted, unbleached white flour
1/2 tsp. baking powder
3/4 tsp. baking soda
1/2 tsp. salt
1 tsp. cinnamon
1/2 tsp. ginger
1/4 c. brown sugar

1/4 c. granulated sugar
1/3 c. safflower or canola oil
1/2 c. molasses
2 eggs or egg substitute
1-1/2 c. rolled oats
1 c. raisins

In a mixing bowl, combine flour, baking powder, baking soda, salt, cinnamon, ginger, and sugars. Add oil, molasses, eggs, and rolled oats; mix with a wooden spoon until blended. Stir in raisins. (Dough will be soft.) Drop batter by heaping teaspoons onto nonstick baking sheet. Bake at 350 degrees for 12-15 minutes. Remove from oven. Let stand 1 minute. Remove from baking sheet. Cool on wire racks. (Fat: 26% calories from fat per cookie)

— Old-Fashioned Spice Cookies —
(about 5 dozen)

1/3 c. low-calorie margarine (softened)
2/3 c. brown sugar (firmly packed)
1 egg (beaten)
1/2 tsp. lemon extract
1/4 tsp. vanilla extract
1-1/2 c. all-purpose flour
1-1/2 tsp. baking powder

1/2 tsp. ground allspice
1/2 tsp. ground cinnamon
1/4 tsp. ground cloves
1/4 tsp. ground nutmeg
1/4 c. unsweetened apple juice
Nonstick cooking spray
Raisins

Cream margarine. Gradually add brown sugar, beating at medium speed with an electric mixer until light and fluffy. Add beaten egg and flavorings. Mix well.

Combine flour and next 5 ingredients, mixing well. Add this to creamed mixture alternately with apple juice, beginning and ending with flour mixture and mixing well after each addition.

Drop dough by rounded teaspoonfuls, 2 inches apart, onto cookie sheet coated with nonstick cooking spray. Press a raisin in center of each cookie. Bake at 325 degrees for 15 to 20 minutes. Cool slightly on cookie sheet then remove to wire racks to finish cooling. (Fat: 1.2 grams or 37 calories each)

— Nutty Sour Cream Balls —
(3 dozen)

1/4 c. low-calorie margarine
1/4 c. plus 2 T. sifted powdered sugar
1/4 c. nonfat sour cream
1 tsp. vanilla extract

1-1/4 c. all-purpose flour
1/3 c. ground pecans
Nonstick cooking spray
2 tsp. powdered sugar

(Continued)

Cream margarine. Gradually add 1/4 cup plus 2 tablespoons sugar, beating at medium speed with an electric mixer until light and fluffy. Add sour cream and vanilla. Blend well. Stir in flour and pecans. Shape into a ball. Chill.

Shape dough into 1-inch balls. Place on a cookie sheet sprayed with nonstick cooking spray. Bake at 350 degrees for 14 minutes or until lightly browned. Cool on wire racks. Sift remaining 2 teaspoons of powdered sugar over cookies. (Fat: 2.3 grams or 45 calories per cookie)

— Sugar Cookies —
(about 5 dozen)

2 c. all-purpose flour (sifted)	4 egg whites plus 2 T. oil
2 tsp. baking powder	2/3 c. canola or safflower oil
1/4 tsp. nutmeg	1 tsp. vanilla
1/2 tsp. salt	3/4 c. sugar

Preheat oven to 400 degrees. Sift together flour, baking powder, salt, and nutmeg. In a large bowl, beat egg whites. Stir in oil and vanilla. Blend in sugar. Stir flour mixture into egg mixture. Drop by teaspoonfuls, 2 inches apart, on an ungreased cookie sheet. Flatten each cookie with oiled glass bottom dipped in sugar. Bake 8 to 10 minutes until a light brown. Remove immediately from baking sheet. (Fat: 30% calories from fat)

— Lemon Delights —
(2-1/2 dozen)

1/4 c. plus 2 T. reduced-calorie margarine (softened)	1 tsp. grated lemon rind
2/3 c. sugar	3/4 tsp. cream of tartar
2 egg whites or 1 egg (further reduce calories by using egg whites)	1/2 tsp. baking soda
1/2 tsp. lemon extract	1/8 tsp. salt
1-3/4 c. all-purpose flour	Nonstick cooking spray
	2 T. sugar

Cream margarine. Gradually add 2/3 cup sugar, beating well at medium speed with an electric mixer. Add egg and lemon extract. Blend well. Combine flour, lemon rind, cream of tartar, soda, and salt. Gradually add to creamed mixture until well blended. Cover and freeze dough for 1 hour.

Shape dough into 1-inch balls. Place on cookie sheets that have been sprayed with nonstick cooking spray. Flatten cookies slightly. Sprinkle cookies evenly with 2 tablespoons sugar. Bake at 375 degrees for 8 minutes or until lightly browned. Cool on wire racks. (Fat: 1.7 grams or 65 calories each)

— Chewy Peanut Butter Cookies —
(8 servings — 2 cookies per serving)

1/4 c. peanut butter
1/2 c. evaporated skim milk
1/2 tsp. vanilla extract
1 T. plus 2 tsp. sugar (or sweetener
   equivalent to 5 tsp. sugar)

2 tsp. shredded coconut (unsweetened)
1/4 c. raisins
3 ounces corn or oat flakes cereal
   (unsweetened)

Preheat oven to 375 degrees. In a medium bowl, combine all ingredients except cereal. Mix well. Stir in cereal. Mix well, crushing cereal lightly with the back of a spoon.

Drop mixture by rounded teaspoonfuls onto a nonstick cookie sheet or one that has been sprayed with nonstick cooking spray. Bake 12 minutes or until lightly browned. Remove to rack for cooling. (Fat: less than 30% calories from fat)

— Filled Mocha Cookies —
(5-1/2 dozen)

1 T. plus 1 tsp. instant coffee granules
   (divided)
2-1/2 tsp. hot water (divided)
1/4 c. light cream cheese
2 tsp. powdered sugar
1/4 c. low-calorie margarine (softened)

1/2 c. sugar
2 egg whites or 1 egg
1/2 tsp. vanilla extract
1-1/2 c. plus 2 T. sifted cake flour
2 T. unsweetened cocoa
1/2 tsp. baking soda

Dissolve 1 teaspoon coffee granules in 1/2 teaspoon hot water. Add cream cheese and powdered sugar, beating until smooth. Set aside.

Dissolve remaining 1 tablespoon coffee granules in 2 teaspoons hot water. Set aside. Cream margarine. Gradually add sugar, beating at medium speed with an electric mixer until light and fluffy. Add egg and vanilla. Beat well. Combine flour, cocoa, and soda. Add to creamed mixture, mixing well. Chill dough at least 30 minutes.

Shape dough into 3/4-inch balls. Place 2 inches apart on ungreased cookie sheets. Press thumb into middle of each cookie, leaving indentation. Bake at 350 degrees for 8 minutes. Remove to wire racks. Spoon 1/4 teaspoon reserved cream cheese mixture into each cookie indentation and let cool. (Fat: 1.0 grams or 25 calories each)

— Macaroons 'N Almonds —
(10 servings)

1 egg white
1/4 c. sugar (sweeteners do not work well)

1 tsp. almond extract
1/4 c. wheat germ

Preheat oven to 325 degrees. In a deep bowl, beat egg white on low speed with an electric mixer until frothy. Beat on high speed until stiff.

Gradually beat in sugar and then almond extract. Fold in wheat germ. Drop mixture by 1/2 teaspoonfuls onto a cookie sheet sprayed with nonstick cooking spray and dusted lightly with flour. Place cookies in oven and immediately reduce heat to 200 degrees. Bake 1 hour. Turn off heat and leave cookies in oven to cool.

— Choco-Mint Meringue Bites —
(3-1/2 dozen)

2 egg whites (at room temperature)
1/3 c. sugar

1/2 c. semisweet chocolate mini-morsels
1/2 tsp. peppermint extract

Beat egg whites in a large bowl at high speed with an electric mixer for 1 minute. Gradually add sugar, 1 tablespoon at a time, beating until stiff peaks form and sugar dissolves (2-4 minutes). Gently fold in chocolate morsels and peppermint extract.

Drop by heaping teaspoonfuls onto cookie sheets lined with wax paper. Bake at 300 degrees for 35 minutes. Cool slightly on cookie sheets. Gently remove from wax paper and cool completely on wire racks. (Fat: 30% calories from fat)

— Ginger Bites —
(4-1/2 dozen)

6 T. reduced-calorie margarine (softened)
1 c. dark brown sugar (not packed)
1 tsp. lemon juice plus water to equal 1/4 cup
1 tsp. fresh ginger (grated)
1-3/4 c. flour

1 tsp. baking soda
1/2 tsp. salt
1 tsp. dry ginger
Pinch white pepper

Beat together the butter and brown sugar. Beat in the lemon-flavored water. Add the grated fresh ginger. Mix dry ingredients and stir into dough. Turn dough onto double sheet of wax paper and roll into a long log about 2 inches in diameter. Refrigerate at least 12 hours or freeze until needed.

Preheat oven to 400 degrees. Cut dough into 1/8-inch slices and set on greased cookie sheet or use nonstick baking paper. Bake 7 to 10 minutes or until the cookies have flattened and look dry. Cool. (Fat: 30% calories from fat)

— Ladyfingers —
(4 dozen)

2 eggs plus 1 extra egg white (separated and divided)
7 T. superfine sugar (divided)

1/2 tsp. vanilla extract
6 T. cake flour
Pinch of salt

Preheat oven to 300 degrees. Cover cookie sheets with nonstick baking paper.

Beat 3 egg whites to light peaks, then beat in 3 tablespoons of sugar gradually to form stiff meringue.

Beat yolks with 3 tablespoons sugar until light. Add vanilla, then stir in flour and salt. Stir in 1/4 of the meringue mixture to lighten the batter, then gently fold in remaining meringue to make a very light mixture. Turn batter into a piping bag fitted with a 1/2-inch tip. Pipe 3-inch strips onto baking paper. (Must use baking paper since cookies are so delicate.)

Sprinkle tops of cookies with remaining tablespoon of sugar. Bake for about 15 minutes or until ladyfingers are lightly browned and crisp. Allow to cool before peeling from paper. (Fat: 16% calories from fat)

— Orange Biscuit Cookie —
(about 4 dozen)

6 T. safflower or canola oil
8 egg whites or 4 eggs (use of egg whites
   reduces fat content)
2/3 c. sugar
1 tsp. grated orange rind

1 tsp. dried orange rind
3 c. flour
2 tsp. baking powder
1/2 tsp. salt

Preheat oven to 375 degrees. Grease a cookie sheet or spray with nonstick cooking spray.

Beat together oil, eggs, sugar, and rinds for 2 to 3 minutes. Meanwhile, stir together dry ingredients.

Stir flour mixture into oil mixture, blending until smooth. Divide batter into 2 equal parts and form logs 2 inches in diameter and 14 inches long on greased cookie sheet. Try to make the logs even. Bake for 20 minutes or until puffed, lightly browned, and dry. Remove from oven.

Reduce oven temperature to 350 degrees. Cut each log into 23 pieces. Place each cookie on its side. (Two cookie sheets will be needed.) Bake another 10 minutes. Turn the cookies over and bake 10 more minutes. The biscuit cookie should be golden brown and dry. Cool. (Fat: 30 to 34% calories from fat)

CAKES

— Fat-Free Chocolate Cake —
(16 servings)

Nonstick cooking spray
1-1/4 c. plain flour
1 c. sugar
1/2 c. unsweetened cocoa
1/4 c. cornstarch

1/2 tsp. baking soda
1/2 tsp. salt
4 egg whites
1 c. water
1/2 c. light or dark corn syrup

Preheat oven to 350 degrees. Spray 9-inch baking pan with cooking spray. In a large bowl combine dry ingredients until well mixed. In medium bowl whisk egg whites, water, and corn syrup. Stir into dry ingredients until smooth. Pour into prepared pan. Bake 30 minutes or until cake springs back when lightly touched. Cool on wire rack for 10 minutes. (Fat: none)

— *Tracy DeLoach, Greenwood, SC and Judy Looney, Belton, SC*

— Frosted Carrot Cake —
(9 servings)

2/3 c. whole-wheat flour
1/2 c. all-purpose flour
1 tsp. baking powder
1 tsp. ground cinnamon
1/4 tsp. ground allspice
2 egg whites or 1 egg
1/4 c. plus 2 T. firmly packed brown
   sugar
1/2 c. skim milk

1/4 c. reduced-calorie mayonnaise
1 tsp. vanilla extract
1 c. shredded carrots
1/4 c. unsweetened grated coconut
Nonstick cooking spray
3 ounces "lite" cream cheese (softened)
2 T. plus 1 tsp. powdered sugar
1/2 tsp. skim milk

Combine first 5 ingredients. Set aside. Combine egg and next 4 ingredients in a large bowl. Beat at medium speed with an electric mixer until well blended. Add dry ingredients, stirring just until dry ingredients are moistened. Stir in carrots and coconut.

Spoon batter into an 8-inch square baking dish sprayed with nonstick cooking spray. Batter will be thin. Bake at 350 degrees for 20-25 minutes or until toothpick inserted in center comes out clean. Cool in pan.

Topping: Combine cheese, sugar, and 1/2 teaspoon skim milk. Blend well. Spread mixture over top of cake. Cut in squares. (Fat: 6.4 grams or 178 calories per servings)

— Moist Chocolate Cake —
(24 pieces)

1-2/3 c. plain flour
1 c. sugar
1/2 c. cocoa
1 tsp. soda

1/2 tsp. salt
1 c. low-fat buttermilk
1/2 c. canola or safflower oil
1-1/2 tsp. vanilla

Preheat oven to 375 degrees. Sift together flour, sugar, cocoa, soda, and salt. Beat in buttermilk, vegetable oil, and vanilla. Stir until smooth. Spread in 9x12-inch pan which has been sprayed with nonstick cooking spray. Bake 30 minutes. (Fat: 30% calories from fat)

— Peach of a Puddingcake —
(15 pieces)

2 c. whole-wheat pastry flour
2 tsp. baking powder
1/2 tsp. salt
1 tsp. ground cinnamon
1/2 tsp. ground allspice

4 egg whites or 2 eggs (further reduce fat by
   using egg whites)
1/2 c. honey
1/2 tsp. vanilla extract
2 T. melted low-calorie margarine
3 c. sliced, fresh peaches (or frozen-thawed)

Preheat oven to 350 degrees. Sift together the flour, baking powder, salt, and spices.

In a separate bowl mix together with an electric beater the eggs, honey, vanilla, and margarine. Add this to the flour mixture and blend thoroughly. Fold in peaches.

Put the mixture into a buttered 12x8-inch baking pan. Bake 35 minutes. (Fat: less than 25% calories from fat)

— Apple Caramel Cake —

2 c. sugar
1 c. canola or safflower oil
6 egg whites plus 3 T. oil
3 c. self-rising flour
1 tsp. ground cinnamon

2 tsp. vanilla
3 c. peeled, chopped apples
1-1/2 c. chopped dates
1-1/2 c. chopped pecans

Preheat oven to 325 degrees. Spray a 9- or 10-inch tube pan with nonstick cooking spray. Lightly flour it.

Mix together sugar and oil. Add egg whites and beat well. Blend in flour, cinnamon and vanilla. Stir in apples, coconut, dates, and pecans. Spoon batter into prepared pan. Bake for 1-1/2 hours or until wooden pick inserted in cake comes out clean. Remove from oven and immediately pour hot caramel topping over hot cake and allow to soak in. Let cake cool completely before removing from pan. Chill for easier slicing.

Caramel Topping:
1 c. firmly packed brown sugar
1/2 c. low-calorie margarine
1/2 c. skim milk

Combine all ingredients in saucepan. Heat and stir until blended. Boil 2 minutes.

— Chocolate on Chocolate Cake —

(24 servings)

1 c. pineapple juice (unsweetened)
1 c. applesauce (unsweetened)
3/4 c. low-fat buttermilk
3 T. cocoa
2 c. plain flour

2 T. cinnamon
1-1/2 c. sugar
4 egg whites
1 tsp. baking soda
1/2 c. low-fat buttermilk

Frosting:
3/4 c. marshmallow creme
2 T. nonfat milk
4 T. cocoa

1 T. light corn syrup
2 tsp. vanilla
3/4 c. chopped pecans

Preheat oven to 350 degrees. Spray 13x9-inch baking pan with nonstick cooking spray.

In a medium saucepan, simmer pineapple juice until it is reduced in volume to 1/2 cup. Meanwhile, in a medium bowl, combine applesauce, 3/4 cup buttermilk, and cocoa powder. Set aside.

In a large bowl, combine flour, cinnamon, and sugar. Set aside.

When pineapple juice is reduced, add applesauce mixture to saucepan. Increase heat to medium and stir until mixture boils. Pour heated mixture into flour mixture and mix well with a spoon. Cool to lukewarm. Add egg whites to lukewarm batter and mix well.

Dissolve baking soda in 1/2 cup buttermilk. Add to batter and stir only until mixed. Do not overstir. Pour into pan. Bake for 35 to 45 minutes until inserted toothpick comes out clean.

Combine first four frosting ingredients in a small saucepan. Stir over medium heat until marshmallow creme is melted. Remove from heat, add vanilla. Stir in pecans. Spread on cool cake. (Fat: 17% calories from fat per serving)

— Lemon Lover's Cake —

1 package (3-ounce) lemon gelatin
3/4 c. boiling water
1-1/2 c. sugar
3/4 c. canola or safflower oil
8 egg whites plus 4 T. of oil
2-1/2 c. all-purpose flour
2-1/2 teaspoons baking powder
1 tsp. salt
2 T. lemon juice
1 T. grated lemon peel
1 T. lemon extract
1 can (6-ounce) frozen lemonade
3/4 c. powdered sugar

Preheat oven to 350 degrees. Dissolve gelatin in boiling water and set aside to cool. Mix together sugar and oil. Add egg whites, one at a time, beating well after each addition. In separate bowl mix together flour, baking powder, and salt. Add flour mixture alternately with gelatin mixture to egg mixture, beginning and ending with dry ingredients. Beat well after each addition. Stir in lemon juice, lemon peel, and lemon extract.

Pour batter into 10-inch tube pan sprayed with nonstick cooking spray and lightly floured. Bake for 1 hour without opening door. While cake is baking, thaw lemonade and stir in powdered sugar. Beat until smooth. Punch holes in top of cake and pour lemonade mixture over cake while still warm. Let cool in pan before removing. (Fat: 30% calories from fat)

— Citrus Surprise Cakes —

(8 servings)

3 eggs (separated)
1/2 c. sugar (divided)
1 T. plus 1-1/2 tsp. lemon juice
1 T. plus 1-1/2 tsp. unsweetened
   orange juice
1 tsp. grated lemon rind
1 tsp. grated orange rind
1/4 tsp. vanilla extract
1 c. sifted cake flour
1/4 tsp. cream of tartar
1/4 tsp. salt
Nonstick cooking spray
Glaze (recipe follows)
1 T. plus 1 tsp. powdered sugar
4 medium navel oranges (peeled, seeded, and
   sectioned)

Beat egg yolks at medium speed with an electric mixer for 5 minutes or until thick and lemon colored. Add 1/4 cup sugar, 1 tablespoon at a time. Beat well after each addition. Add lemon juice and next 4 ingredients. Mix well. Gradually add flour, mixing just until blended.

Beat egg whites (at room temperature), cream of tartar, and salt at high speed with an electric mixer for 1 minute. Gradually add remaining 1/4 cup sugar, 1 tablespoon at a time, beating until stiff peaks form and sugar dissolves (2-4 minutes).

Gently fold egg white mixture into yolk mixture. Spoon batter evenly into 8 sponge cake cups that have been coated with cooking spray. Bake at 350 degrees for 15 to 20 minutes or until cakes spring back when lightly touched. Carefully remove from pans. Cool completely on wire racks. To serve, place cakes on individual plates. Spoon 1 tablespoon glaze over each cake. Sift 1/2 teaspoon powdered sugar over each. Place orange sections alongside cakes.

Glaze (makes 1/2 cup):
2 tsp. sugar
1-1/2 tsp. cornstarch
1/3 c. plus 1 T. unsweetened orange juice
2 T. lemon juice

Combine sugar and cornstarch in a non-aluminum saucepan. Stir in juices. Cook over medium heat, stirring constantly, until thickened. Remove from heat. Cool. (Fat: 30% calories from fat)

— Cake Roll —

1 c. flour	1 c. sugar
1 tsp. baking powder	1/3 c. water
1/4 tsp. salt	1 tsp. vanilla
3 eggs or egg substitute (whole eggs add to fat content)	Powdered sugar

Spray jelly roll pan with nonstick cooking spray. Line with waxed paper. Blend flour, baking powder, and salt. Beat eggs until thick and lemon colored. Beat in sugar; gradually blend in water and vanilla on low speed. Mix in flour mixture until smooth. Pour into pan. Bake at 375 degrees for 12 minutes. Loosen edges; turn onto towel sprinkled with powdered sugar. Roll cake and towel from narrow end. Cool cake on wire rack. Unroll. Remove towel and paper. Fill with favorite filling. Roll again. (Fat: less than 30% calories from fat)

— *Harriet Cottingham, Charleston Heights, SC*

— Pound-Less Pound Cake —
(serves 16)

1/2 c. applesauce	2-3/4 c. flour
1/2 c. nonfat milk	2 tsp. baking powder
1 tsp. vanilla	8 egg whites
3-1/2 tsp. almond extract	1-1/2 c. sugar

Spray tube pan with nonstick cooking spray and flour lightly. In a mixing bowl, combine applesauce, milk, vanilla, and almond extract. Set aside. In a second bowl, combine flour and baking powder. Set aside. In a third bowl, beat egg whites until foamy. Gradually add sugar and beat until soft peaks form.

Alternately drizzle milk mixture and sprinkle flour mixture into egg foam and fold in. Pour batter into tube pan. Bake at 350 degrees for 50 to 55 minutes. Immediately invert cake, still in pan. Cool thoroughly. Gently loosen sides of cake and remove it from pan. (Fat: less than 20% calories from fat)

— Angel Cake with Berries 'N Yogurt —
(serves 12)

1-1/2 c. sifted powdered sugar	1/4 tsp. salt
1 c. sifted cake flour	1 c. granulated sugar
12 large egg whites	4 c. berries (recipe follows)
1-1/2 tsp. cream of tartar	1 c. sweetened yogurt (recipe follows)
1 tsp. vanilla	

Preheat oven to 350 degrees. Sift together powdered sugar and flour, repeating twice. Set aside. In a gallon bowl, place egg whites, cream of tartar, vanilla, and salt. Beat with large balloon whisk. As egg whites stiffen, gradually add granulated sugar, a sprinkle at a time. Continue beating until stiff peaks form. Sift about 1/4 of flour mixture over whites, folding in lightly with a large rubber spatula or with your flattened hand. Repeat until all flour mixture

(Continued)

is folded in. Turn into ungreased 10-inch tube pan and bake for 1 hour, or until done. Cake is done if surface springs back when touched. Invert cake pan on wire rack and cool completely. Loosen cake from pan with silver knife or metal spatula. Remove. Top each slice with berries and 2 teaspoons sweetened yogurt.

Berries:
4 c. berries (blueberries, blackberries, raspberries, sliced strawberries, or a combination of all)
1/2 c. superfine sugar
   Wash berries, drain, and toss lightly with sugar. Refrigerate about 30 minutes. Makes 4 cups berries.

Sweetened Yogurt: 1/2 tsp. vanilla
1 c. plain low-fat or nonfat yogurt   2 T. powdered sugar

   Stir all ingredients together. Makes 1 cup. (Fat: less than 30% calories from fat)

— Low-Fat Strawberry Shortcake —

   Bake yellow or white 94-95% fat-free cake mix. Mix fresh strawberries with a couple of envelopes of artificial sweetener. Let stand a few minutes for it to dissolve and some juice to form. Spoon on top of cake and top with reduced calorie whipped topping. (Fat: less than 30% calories from fat)

— Mrs. Darl Hetrick, New Bethlehem, PA

— Spicy Honey Cake —
(8 servings)

3/4 c. whole-wheat flour
1/2 tsp. baking soda
1 tsp. ground cinnamon
1/2 tsp. ground nutmeg
1/4 tsp. ground cloves
1/4 tsp. ground allspice
2 T. plus 2 tsp. reduced-calorie
   margarine

2 egg whites or 1 egg
1 tsp. vanilla extract
2 T. honey
1/2 c. plain low-fat yogurt
2 T. plus 2 tsp. sugar (or sweetener
   equivalent to 8 tsp. of sugar
1/4 c. raisins

   Preheat oven to 350 degrees. In a medium bowl, combine flour, baking soda, and spices. Mix well.
   Add margarine. Using a fork or pastry blender, mix until mixture resembles coarse crumbs.
   In a large bowl, combine remaining ingredients, except raisins. Beat on low speed with an electric mixer until smooth.
   Add dry ingredients. Beat 1 minute. Stir in raisins. Place batter in a 4x8-inch nonstick loaf pan or one sprayed with nonstick cooking spray.
   Bake 25 minutes. Cool in pan 10 minutes; then invert onto a rack to finish cooling. (Fat: less than 20% calories from fat)

— Upside-Down Pina Colada Cake —
(8 servings)

Topping:
2 c. canned crushed pineapple
   (unsweetened, drained)
1/4 c. juice from pineapple
2/3 c. nonfat dry milk
2 T. cornstarch
2 tsp. shredded coconut (unsweetened)
1 tsp. coconut extract
1 T. sugar (or sweetener equivalent to 3
   tsp. sugar)

Cake:
3/4 c. all-purpose flour
1 tsp. baking powder
2 T. plus 2 tsp. reduced-calorie margarine
2 eggs or egg substitute
2/3 c. nonfat cottage cheese
2 tsp. vanilla extract
3 T. sugar (or sweetener equivalent to 9
   tsp. sugar)

Preheat oven to 350 degrees. Spray a 9-inch glass pie pan with nonstick cooking spray. Line pan with wax paper and spray again.

In a small bowl, combine all topping ingredients, mixing well. Spread evenly in pan.

In a medium bowl, combine flour and baking powder. Add margarine and mix with a fork or pastry blender until mixture resembles coarse crumbs.

Combine eggs, cottage cheese, vanilla, and sugar. Beat with a fork or wire whisk until blended. Mixture will be lumpy. Add cottage cheese mixture to dry ingredients, stirring until all ingredients are moistened. Spoon batter evenly over topping in pan.

Bake 30 minutes until golden. Cool in pan on wire rack 15 minutes. Then loosen edges with knife and invert cake onto a plate. Peel off wax paper. (Fat: less than 20% calories from fat)

— Low-Fat Pineapple Cake —

One 94-95% fat-free yellow cake mix   2 c. crushed pineapple (unsweetened)

Mix according to directions. Bake in 9x13-inch pan for 30 minutes or until done. With large meat fork, make holes all over top of cake. Pour 2 cups of crushed, unsweetened pineapple (juice and all) over top of cake. Let cool completely. (May also use a Lemon Lite Cake mix instead of yellow.)

Topping:
1 package (3-4 ounces) of vanilla sugar free instant pudding.

Follow package directions using 1 cup of skim milk. Let thicken. Fold in 3/4 of a 10-ounce container of Lite Cool Whip. Spread on top of cake. Refrigerate several hours or overnight. (Fat: less than 30% calories from fat)

— Mrs. Darl Hetrick, New Bethlehem, PA

— No-Egg Pudding Cake —
(8 servings)

3/4 c. orange juice (unsweetened)
1-1/3 c. nonfat dry milk
1/2 medium, ripe banana
1 small orange (peeled and sectioned)
1/4 c. plus 2 T. sugar (or sweetener equivalent to 18 tsp. of sugar)
1 tsp. vanilla extract
1/2 tsp. each baking powder and baking soda
1 tsp. each grated orange peel and ground cinnamon

1 tsp. ground allspice
1/2 tsp. each ground cloves, nutmeg, and mace
8 slices white or whole-wheat raisin bread (crumbled)
1/2 c. canned crushed pineapple (unsweetened and drained)
1 c. fresh or frozen blueberries (unsweetened)
2 small, sweet apples (peeled and finely chopped)

Preheat oven to 350 degrees. In a blender combine orange juice, dry milk, banana, orange, sugar, vanilla, baking powder, baking soda, and spices. Blend until smooth. Add bread. Blend until combined, stopping blender occasionally to stir. Continue to blend 1 more minute.

Pour batter into a large bowl. Add remaining ingredients. Mix well. Place in 8-inch square baking pan sprayed with nonstick cooking spray. Bake 1 hour, until edges are brown and top is set. Cool on rack. (Fat: less than 10% calories from fat)

— Angel Food Ice Cream Cake Roll —

Mix Angel Food Cake Mix according to directions. Bake in ungreased 11x18 jelly roll pan at 375 degrees for 20 minutes. Turn onto powdered sugar dusted cloth. Roll up, cloth and all.

Prepare a filling of 1/2 gallon of strawberry, raspberry, or peach frozen yogurt, or any flavor of fat-free ice cream that has been softened. Carefully unroll cake, remove cloth, spread on filling. Carefully roll cake up once again. Place on cookie sheet. Place in freezer for about one hour. Slice with an electric knife. Serve immediately or wrap individually and freeze. (Fat: less than 30% calories from fat)

— Mrs. Darl Hetrick, New Bethlehem, PA

— Lemon Pudding Cake —
(4 servings)

2/3 c. nonfat cottage cheese
2 eggs (slightly beaten) or egg substitute
1/2 tsp. ground cinnamon
1 tsp. each baking powder and vanilla extract
1/2 tsp. lemon extract

2 T. plus 2 tsp. sugar (or sweetener equivalent to 8 tsp. sugar)
1-1/2 ounces bran cereal flakes (slightly crushed)

Lemon Sauce:
1 c. water
1-1/2 T. lemon juice
1 T. plus 1 tsp. cornstarch

2 drops yellow food color
2 T. plus 2 tsp. sugar (or sweetener equivalent to 8 tsp. sugar)

(Continued)

Preheat oven to 350 degrees. Combine all ingredients, except cereal, in a bowl. Mix well.

Stir in cereal. Place mixture in a 4x8-inch nonstick loaf pan. Smooth the top with the back of a spoon. Bake 20 to 25 minutes until set and lightly browned.

When cake is almost done, combine all sauce ingredients in a small saucepan. (If using Nutrasweet sweetener, add it after cooking.) Stir until cornstarch is dissolved. Cook, stirring over medium heat, until mixture comes to a boil. Continue to cook and stir 1 minute. Remove from heat.

To serve, cut hot cake into squares, place in individual serving bowls, and spoon hot sauce over cake. (Fat: less than 20% calories from fat)

— Lemon Jelly Roll —
(8 servings)

Lemon filling (see recipe below)	1/2 c. sugar (divided)
3/4 c. all-purpose flour	2 large egg yolks
1 tsp. baking powder	1 tsp. vanilla extract
1/2 tsp. salt	1 T. confectioners' sugar
4 large egg whites	Raspberries for garnish

At least 2 hours before serving, prepare lemon filling and cool to room temperature.

Meanwhile, spray 13x9 metal baking pan with nonstick cooking spray. Line pan with waxed paper. Spray waxed paper.

In small bowl, mix flour, baking powder, and salt. In another small bowl, with mixer at high speed, beat egg whites until soft peaks form. Gradually beat in 1/4 cup sugar until sugar dissolves and whites stand in stiff peaks.

Preheat oven to 375 degrees. In large bowl, at high speed, beat egg yolks, vanilla, and 1/4 cup sugar for 5 minutes. Fold in flour mixture and beaten whites. Spread batter in pan. Bake 8 to 10 minutes until top springs back when touched.

Sprinkle cloth towel with confectioners' sugar. Invert cake onto towel. Peel off waxed paper. Starting at long side, roll cake with towel, jelly-roll fashion. Cool on wire rack. Unroll cooled cake. Spread with filling. Roll up again without towel.

Cut jelly roll crosswise into 16 slices. Arrange slices on dessert plates and garnish with raspberries.

Lemon Filling:	
1/2 c. water	2 T. cornstarch
1/2 c. sugar	1 tsp. grated lemon peel
3 T. lemon juice	1/4 tsp. salt
	2 drops yellow food coloring

Combine all ingredients and bring to boil in 1-quart saucepan over medium heat, stirring constantly. Boil 1 minute. (Fat: 170 calories or 1 gram fat per serving —2 slices per serving)

— *Martha Jensen-Urey, Orlando, FL*

4

Salads, Dressings, & Sauces

INTRODUCTION TO SALADS

Why Exercise? —

If you had to guess what poses the single greatest risk for heart disease, what would you say? Smoking? High-fat diet? High blood pressure? Elevated cholesterol level or obesity? The answer is none of the above. What poses the greatest health risk today is the sedentary life styles of most people — living without a planned exercise program.

You are leading a sedentary life if you are getting less than 20 minutes of aerobic exercise three times a week. Aerobic exercise could be just taking a 20-minute walk three times a week. It is as easy as that.

Dr. Kenneth Cooper; of the Institute for Aerobics Research in Dallas; has found that even modest amounts of exercise, such as regular walking, greatly reduce the chances of dying from a heart attack.

Other research at the institute also points to the fact that the amount of exercise we have is much more important than what we eat. Mr. Steve Farrell, also of the institute, states that of all the risk factors, such as poor eating habits, smoking, or high blood pressure, lack of exercise is probably the most important risk factor of all. He adds that organizations such as the American Heart Association should put more emphasis on encouraging regular exercise than on eating a proper diet.

Why is exercise so important? Exercise strengthens the heart. As the heart becomes stronger, it pumps blood more efficiently and is less prone to weakness and heart attack.

Even though heart disease seems to be declining somewhat in recent years, it is still the Number One killer of Americans. The Center for Disease Control has stated new findings showing that heart disease could be considerably reduced if everyone became more physically active.

That Draggy Feeling —

Do you frequently find yourself lacking energy or feeling down in the dumps for no particular reason? Have you gone without exercise for awhile and then found that the more you lie around, the less you feel like doing anything? When we don't get enough exercise, our bodies and minds just cannot function properly.

Could such inactivity be a sin? Look at what Proverbs 19:15 says: "Slothfulness casteth into a deep sleep; and an idle soul shall suffer hunger."

Even though you may be constantly convicted about your poor eating habits and your failure to exercise, do you just shrug it off and put it off? Maybe you see a friend at church with whom you used to walk. She's your age, but she's still exercising and looks so good. Do you feel God's gentle chastening as you are reminded of the body you have neglected? If so, take heart.

Hebrews 12:11 reminds us, "Now no chastening for the present seemeth to be joyous, but grievous: nevertheless afterward it yieldeth the peaceable fruit of righteousness unto them which are exercised thereby."

God chastens us because He loves us. Today is the day of a new beginning. Start afresh with your exercise program and good, low-fat diet. Thank God for loving you and forgiving you. Thank God for new beginnings.

Time wasted can never be recalled. Idleness produces a deep stupor in the soul and an unhealthy body to go along with it. Idleness can make a person think he is hungry when he is not. What so many mistake as a physical hunger is actually a hunger of the mind and soul.

The person who keeps God's commandments, saves his soul from hunger. Meditate on God's Word each day and call on Jesus to sustain you. Then MOVE! Exercise regularly. Exercise creates endorphins or natural tranquilizers in the brain that make a person feel and think better.

> Every wise woman buildeth her house: but the foolish plucketh it down with her hands (Prov. 1:1).

Just put body in place of house in that verse above. Don't destroy your body, God's holy temple, by failing to exercise or by eating foods that are unhealthy. Be a good steward of your body

Something to remember: "Hardening of the heart ages people more quickly than hardening of the arteries."

When Making a Salad —

Salads can be high in fat. In fact, salads drowned in creamy, oily dressings can contain more fat than a piece of pie or cake. Following are some tips that should help you have a salad that is truly low in fat:

— Choose an oil low in saturated fat and high in polyunsaturated fat such as safflower or canola oil. Although the calories are the same as in saturated oils, polyunsaturated oils seem to lower blood cholesterol levels.

— Recent studies show that olive oil, a monounsaturated oil, may also have a cholesterol-lowering effect. This oil is good in salad dressings that are used with vegetables. It does not blend as well with fruit salads.

— When a recipe calls for oil, try using half the amount and substituting water for the other half.

— Reduced-calorie mayonnaise or no-fat salad dressings always work well. Just read labels carefully on bottled dressings. Some are high in saturated fat, calories, and sodium.

— Experiment with vinegar, lemon juice, and different spices on a tossed salad. Look in our section on dressings for some delicious low-fat dressing recipes.

— Dijon mustard adds a delicious spark to oil and vinegar dressings.

— When a recipe calls for sour cream, substitute nonfat sour cream or plain low-fat or nonfat yogurt.

— Some mayonnaise-type salads, such as cole slaw, can be made a day ahead, using less mayonnaise than the recipe calls for. You will be surprised at how much liquid is drawn out of the vegetables when they marinate overnight.

— If using canned fruit in a salad, always choose those packed in water, fruit juice, or sugarless.

Salads With Greens

— Cucumber Salad —
(6 servings)

2 cucumbers (peeled and thinly sliced)
1 medium onion (sliced thin)
1 tsp. salt substitute

1 tsp. sugar
1 tsp. dillweed
3/4 c. rice wine vinegar

Mix cucumbers and onion together in a ceramic or glass bowl. Add salt substitute, sugar, and dillweed to vinegar and pour over cucumbers and onions. Chill 1 hour before serving. (Fat: less than 10% calories from fat)

— Martha Elson, Anchorage, AK

— Fish Fry Cole Slaw —
(4 servings)

4 c. thinly sliced cabbage
1/2 c. thinly sliced red peppers
1/4 c. thinly sliced onions
2 T. pickle relish
1 T. Dijon mustard

1 tsp. vinegar
1 tsp. celery seed
2 T. nonfat yogurt
1/4 tsp. black pepper

In a large bowl toss together cabbage, red peppers, and onions.

In a small bowl whisk together relish, mustard, vinegar, and celery seed. Fold in yogurt. Pour over cabbage and toss well. Sprinkle with black pepper. Refrigerate for at least 30 minutes. (Fat: 15% calories from fat)

— Slaw 'N Fruit —
(8 servings)

4 firm, ripe pears (peeled and diced)
2 firm tart apples (peeled and diced)
2 T. lemon juice

3 c. shredded green cabbage
1/2 c. raisins

(Continued)

In a large bowl, toss diced pears and apples with lemon juice. Add cabbage and raisins. Mix well.

Dressing:

1 c. plain low-fat yogurt

1 tsp. grated lemon rind

1 tsp. lemon juice

1 tsp. honey

In a small bowl, whisk together all dressing ingredients. Add to slaw and toss. Chill for 30 minutes to 1 hour before serving. (Fat: less than 10% calories from fat)

— Greens 'N Garlic —
(10 servings)

1 c. nonfat buttermilk

3 cloves garlic (minced)

2 T. fresh parsley (minced)

2 T. reduced-calorie mayonnaise

1 tsp. or less cracked pepper

1 can (14-ounce) artichoke hearts (drained and quartered)

1 can (14-ounce) hearts of palm (drained and sliced into 1/2-inch pieces)

3 c. Boston lettuce (shredded)

2 c. fresh spinach (shredded)

1 c. curly endive (shredded)

1 c. fresh watercress (torn)

1/2 c. celery (chopped)

1 T. fresh chives (chopped)

Combine buttermilk, garlic, parsley, mayonnaise, and pepper in a jar. Cover and shake vigorously. Cover and chill 2 hours.

Combine artichoke hearts and remaining ingredients in a large serving bowl. Shake and pour chilled dressing over salad. Toss lightly. (Fat: 1.0 grams of fat per serving)

— Tart Slaw —
(6 to 8 servings)

1 medium-sized head cabbage (shredded)

1 green pepper (chopped)

1/2 c. celery stalk and leaves (chopped)

1/2 c. shredded carrots

1 tart apple (cubed)

1/2 c. of cooked cole slaw dressing (see dressings section)

In large bowl, combine all ingredients. Mix well. Chill 2 hours before serving. (Fat: less than 20% calories from fat)

— Spinach 'N Mushroom Salad —
(4 servings)

2 bunches fresh spinach

1 bunch radishes (sliced)

8 fresh mushrooms (sliced)

Your favorite low-fat vinaigrette

Wash and trim spinach. Chill. Tear into bite-size pieces. Put in a bowl and toss with radishes and mushrooms. Serve dressing on side. (Fat: trace)

— Creamy Cucumber Salad —

2 cucumbers (peeled, thinly sliced)
1/2 tsp. salt (optional)

3 or 4 green onions (finely chopped)
1 c. plain, low-fat yogurt

Combine all ingredients except yogurt. Mix well. Chill 1 hour to blend flavors. Stir in yogurt and serve. (Fat: less than 20% calories from fat)

— Northern Cole Slaw —

3 pounds cabbage (shredded)
1 large onion (thinly sliced)

1 green pepper (thinly sliced)

Combine and bring the following to a boil:
1 c. sugar (or substitute)
1 c. canola oil
1 c. vinegar

2 T. mustard seed
1 T. celery seed
1-1/2 tsp. salt (optional)

Cool and pour over cabbage mixture. Mix well. Refrigerate before serving. (Fat: 30% calories from fat)

— Italian Cucumber Salad —
(5 servings, 1/2-cup each)

1/2 c. commercial low-fat Italian dressing
1/8 tsp. pepper
1 medium cucumber (peeled and thinly sliced)

1/2 small onion (thinly sliced)
1/4 c. radishes (thinly sliced)
2 T. fresh parsley (chopped)

Combine Italian dressing and pepper in bowl. Mix well. Add cucumber, onion, radishes, and parsley. Toss gently.
Cover and marinate in refrigerator at least 4 hours. Use slotted spoon when serving. (Fat: less than 10% calories from fat)

— Italian Cole Slaw —
(12 servings, 1/2 cup each)

3 c. cabbage (shredded)
1 large green pepper (diced)
1 large onion (diced)
1/2 c. sugar

1-1/2 c. commercial low-calorie Italian
   dressing
1 T. dry mustard
1 T. celery seeds

Combine cabbage, green pepper, onion, and sugar. Mix well.
Combine Italian dressing, dry mustard, and celery seeds in small saucepan. Bring to a boil. Remove from heat.
Pour dressing mixture over vegetable mixture. Toss gently.
Cover and refrigerate 1 hour. Stir gently before serving. Use slotted spoon to serve. (Fat: less than 10% calories from fat)

— Western Coleslaw —
(8 servings)

1 c. cabbage (shredded)
1 c. red cabbage (shredded)
1/2 c. carrot (shredded)
1/2 c. green pepper (chopped)
1/2 c. sweet red pepper (chopped)
1/4 c. onion (chopped)
1 T. plus 1-1/2 tsp. fresh parsley (minced)

1/4 c. vinegar
1/4 c. commercial Italian low-calorie
   dressing
1/4 c. sugar
1/8 tsp. salt
1/8 tsp. pepper

Combine cabbages, carrot, green and red peppers, onion, and parsley in large bowl. Mix well. Set aside.

Combine vinegar, Italian dressing, sugar substitute, salt, and pepper in a jar. Cover and shake well.

Pour dressing mixture over vegetables. Toss gently.

Cover and refrigerate until chilled. Stir before serving and serve with slotted spoon. (Fat: less than 10% calories from fat)

— Spinach 'N Rice Salad —
(4 servings)

1-1/4 c. water
1/2 c. uncooked long-grain rice
2 T. reduced-sodium soy sauce
1 T. honey
1 T. rice wine vinegar
1/2 tsp. sweet red pepper flakes

1-1/2 c. fresh spinach leaves (cut in thin
   strips)
1-1/2 c. mushrooms (thinly sliced)
1/4 c. celery (thinly sliced)
1/4 c. green onions (thinly sliced)

Bring water to boil in small saucepan over medium heat. Add rice. Cover. Reduce heat and simmer 20 minutes. Rice should be tender and water absorbed. Transfer rice to large bowl. Cool slightly.

Combine soy sauce, honey, vinegar, and red pepper flakes in a jar. Cover and shake well. Pour soy sauce mixture over rice. Add spinach and remaining ingredients. Toss gently. Cover and chill 8 hours. (Fat: less than 20% calories from fat)

Vegetable and Bean Salads

— Carrot 'N Orange Salad —
(4 servings)

3 c. carrots (finely shredded)
2 small oranges (peeled and sectioned)
1/4 c. raisins
1/2 c. plain, low-fat yogurt

1/2 tsp. coconut extract
1/2 tsp. vanilla extract
1 T. honey

(Continued)

In large bowl, combine carrots, orange sections, and raisins.

In small bowl, combine remaining ingredients. Mix well. Spoon over carrot mixture. Toss. Chill, tossing gently occasionally while chilling. Serve on bed of lettuce with a scoop of nonfat cottage cheese. (Fat: less than 10% calories from fat)

— Tomato Salad —
(4 servings)

1-1/2 c. tomatoes (thinly sliced)
1/2 c. red onions (thinly sliced)
1-1/2 tsp. dried basil
3/4 tsp. dried tarragon

1/4 c. red wine vinegar
2 T. plus 2 tsp. canola oil
Salt and pepper to taste

Place tomatoes and onions in shallow bowl, overlapping slightly.

In small bowl, combine remaining ingredients. Pour over vegetables. Chill several hours to blend flavors. Note: tastes better a day later. (Fat: less than 10% calories from fat)

— Tomato 'N Rice Salad —
(8 servings)

1 T. low-sodium soy sauce
1 T. red wine vinegar or rice vinegar
3 c. long-grain brown rice (cooked and cooled)
3 medium tomatoes (seeded and diced)

1/2 red onion (diced)
1 medium green bell pepper (chopped)
2 T. fresh basil (chopped)

Sprinkle soy sauce and vinegar over rice. Mix lightly with fork. Add tomatoes, green pepper, red onion, and basil. Toss lightly. Chill until serving time. (Fat: less than 20% calories from fat)

— Medley Congealed Salad —
(8 servings)

1 package (0.6-ounce) sugar-free, lime
   gelatin
2 c. boiling water
1-3/4 c. cold water
1/4 c. vinegar
1 c. celery (chopped)

1 c. carrot (shredded)
2 T. sweet red pepper (chopped)
2 T. green onions (chopped)
Nonstick cooking spray
Lettuce leaves (optional)

Dissolve gelatin in boiling water in a medium bowl, stirring well. Stir in cold water and vinegar. Chill until mixture is the consistency of unbeaten egg white.

Fold in vegetables and pour gelatin mixture into eight 2/3-cup molds, coated with cooking spray.

Chill until firm. Unmold onto lettuce leaves, if desired. (Fat: less than 10% calories from fat)

— Cauliflower Salad —
(10 - 1/2 cup servings)

1 medium cauliflower (broken into flowerets)
1/2 c. celery (sliced)
1/2 c. commercial low-calorie Italian dressing

2 small cloves garlic (minced)
1/4 tsp. salt
1/4 tsp. pepper
1/4 tsp. red pepper

Combine by tossing gently. Chill 30 minutes to 1 hour before serving. (Fat: less than 10% calories from fat)

— Green Bean Salad —
(4 - 1/2 cup servings)

2 cans (10-ounce) cut green beans (undrained)
1/2 c. dill pickles (chopped)
1 clove garlic (minced)

1/2 tsp. dried whole basil
1 small red onion (sliced)
1 c. commercial low-calorie Italian dressing

Heat beans in medium saucepan for 5 minutes. Drain.

Combine beans and remaining ingredients in a medium bowl. Toss slightly. Cover and refrigerate at least 8 hours. Serve salad using slotted spoon. (Fat: less than 10% calories from fat)

— Vegetable and Rice Salad —
(10 servings)

1-1/4 c. water
1-1/2 c. instant brown rice
2/3 c. prepared, fat-free Italian dressing
1 c. fresh sliced mushrooms

1 c. green peas (fresh or frozen)
1 c. red and green pepper strips
1/4 c. chopped parsley

Bring water to boil. Stir in rice. Reduce heat, cover and simmer 5 minutes. Remove from heat and let stand 5 minutes.

Mix rice and 1/3 cup dressing. Add remaining ingredients. Toss gently. Cool to room temperature. Just before serving, toss with remaining 1/3 cup dressing. (Fat: less than 25% calories from fat)

— Asparagus Salad —
(4 servings)

1 pound fresh asparagus
1/8 c. canola or olive oil
1 T. tarragon vinegar
1 T. fresh lemon juice

1 T. fresh scallions (chopped)
1/2 T. Dijon-style mustard
1 clove garlic (crushed)
1/4 to 1/2 tsp. dried leaf tarragon (crushed)

Wash asparagus and break off tough bottom ends. Lay asparagus flat on a steamer rack over about 1 inch of water. Cook for 4 to 7 minutes or until they reach peak green color. (If color dulls, you have overcooked.) Drain. Place asparagus in shallow dish. In small bowl, mix 1/4 cup water with remaining ingredients. Pour over asparagus. Cover and chill overnight. Drain before serving. (Fat: less than 20% calories from fat)

— Low-Fat Potato Salad —

8 c. potatoes (cooked and cubed)
1 c. onion (chopped)
1 c. celery (chopped)
1-1/2 tsp. salt
1/4 tsp. dry mustard

1 c. fat-free mayonnaise
1 T. vinegar
1 envelope artificial sweetener (optional)
1/2 c. low-fat coleslaw dressing
Sweet pickle juice

While potatoes are warm, combine them with onions, celery, and salt with enough sweet pickle juice to marinate it. Stir or toss this mixture in a large flat pan or dish with fork. Let set about 1/2 hour.

Mix fat-free mayonnaise, low-fat coleslaw dressing vinegar, sweetener, vinegar, and dry mustard. Add this to potato mixture. Chill in refrigerator several hours or overnight in a covered container.

Note: Macaroni salad can be made the same way. Cook 2 cups of raw macaroni. Combine celery and onions with macaroni to marinate. Then add chopped cucumbers and large pieces of chopped tomatoes when ready to serve. (Fat: less than 20% calories from fat)

— Mrs. Darl Hetrick, New Bethlehem, PA

— Potato 'N Carrot Salad —
(12 servings)

6 medium potatoes (boiled and cubed)
3 eggs (hard boiled and diced)
1/2 small onion (grated)
2 carrots (diced)
1 bell pepper (diced)
2 stalks celery (sliced thin)
1 c. plain low-fat yogurt

1/4 c. low-fat mayonnaise
1/4 tsp. garlic powder
Fresh-ground black pepper to taste
1 tsp. tarragon
1 T. Dijon mustard
1 tsp. salt

Combine all ingredients. Chill and serve. (Fat: less than 30% calories from fat)

— Red Potato Salad —
(14 servings)

6 medium, red potatoes (unpeeled)
1/4 c. green onions (chopped)
1 jar (2-ounce) diced pimento (drained)
1/3 c. nonfat mayonnaise
2 T. prepared mustard
1 T. sugar

1 T. white wine vinegar
1/2 tsp. salt
1/2 tsp. celery seeds
1/4 tsp. pepper
1/8 tsp. garlic powder

Place potatoes in pan. Cover with water and bring to boil. Cover. Reduce heat and simmer potatoes 25 minutes or so. Drain and let cool. Peel potatoes and cut into 1/2-inch cubes. Combine potatoes, onion, and pimento in large bowl.

Combine mayonnaise and remaining ingredients in small bowl. Stir well. Add this mixture to potato mixture. Toss gently. Cover and chill. (Fat: less than 30% calories from fat)

— Tangy Potato Salad —
(4 servings)

12 ounces cooked potatoes (unpeeled, cut
   into 1-inch chunks)
1 T. red wine vinegar
2 tsp. coarse, grainy mustard
1 generous T. nonfat mayonnaise

2 tsp. dried chives
2 tsp. dried parsley
1/8 tsp. pepper
Salt to taste

Place potatoes in large bowl.

In small bowl, combine remaining ingredients. Mix well. Add to potatoes. Toss until well blended. Chill before serving. (Fat: 25% calories from fat)

— Sweet 'N Sour Bean Salad —
(6 servings)

1 c. cooked kidney beans
1 c. cooked garbanzo beans
1/2 c. carrots (diced)
1 small red onion (thinly sliced)
1/4 tsp. salt

1/8 tsp. pepper
1/2 tsp. dry mustard
3 T. vinegar
1 T. honey

Combine all ingredients in large bowl. Toss gently. Chill before serving. (Fat: less than 20% calories from fat)

— Easy Bean Salad —

1 can (16-ounce) each of:
   kidney beans
   wax beans
   cut green beans
   garbanzo beans (chick peas)

1/2 c. canola oil
1/2 c. fresh lemon juice
1/3 c. sugar
1 medium onion (chopped)
1 stalk celery (chopped)

Drain beans well. Blend oil, lemon juice, and sugar in blender. Toss beans with onion and celery. Add oil mixture and toss again. Marinate overnight. For best results store in flat, covered container so beans are covered in oil mixture. (Fat: approx. 30% calories from fat)

— Colorful Vegetable Salad —

2 cans tiny, gourmet-type peas
2 cans niblet corn
2 cans sliced water chestnuts
1 c. celery (chopped)
1 medium jar pimentos

1 medium onion (chopped)
1 medium green pepper (chopped)
1/2 c. white vinegar
1/4 c. canola oil
3/4 c. sugar

Mix sugar, oil and vinegar together until sugar is dissolved. Drain peas, corn, and pimentos well. Mix with other vegetables in sugar mixture. Let set overnight. (Fat: 25% calories from fat)

— Broccoli Salad —

2 pounds fresh broccoli florets
1/2 pound fresh mushrooms (sliced)

2 c. bean sprouts

Dressing:
1/3 c. oil
1/3 c. vinegar

2 tsp. catsup
1/2 tsp. salt

Steam broccoli for 2 minutes. Mix with mushrooms and sprouts. Pour dressing over salad. Refrigerate until cold. (Fat: 30% calories from fat)

— Tart 'N Tangy White Bean Salad —
(makes 14 cups)

1 pound small dry white beans
2 stalks celery
2 tsp. salt
1 red onion (diced)
2 ripe tomatoes (diced)
2 stalks celery (diced)

Your favorite low-fat vinaigrette
1/2 c. fresh parsley (chopped)
Black pepper to taste
1 bunch fresh spinach (washed and trimmed)
1 lemon (sliced in rounds)

Wash beans and put into stock pot. Add 2 quarts water. Cover and bring to boil. Remove from heat and let soak 1 hour. Drain. Return beans to stock pot with 2 quarts fresh water. Bring to boil. Add 2 stalks celery and salt. Reduce heat to medium. Cook 35-40 minutes or until beans are tender. Drain. Discard celery stalks.

Rinse beans with cold water and chill. Just before serving, toss beans with onion, tomatoes, diced celery and just enough vinaigrette to moisten. Sprinkle with parsley and season generously with black pepper.

Line a shallow salad bowl with spinach greens. Spoon beans into center. Ring beans with lemon rounds. (Fat: Trace)

— Molded Health Salad —
(12 servings)

2 T. unflavored gelatin
1/4 c. cold water
1 c. boiling water
2 T. lemon juice
1/4 c. sugar
1 tsp. salt

1/4 c. vinegar
1 medium onion (chopped)
1/4 green pepper (chopped)
1 c. nonfat mayonnaise
3 c. vegetables (chopped) — use cabbage,
    carrots, celery

Soak gelatin in cold water. Add boiling water and other ingredients in order. Pour into individual molds or one big mold. (Fat: 25% calories from fat)

— Gini Tharrington, Raleigh, NC

— Eight-Vegetable Salad —
(4 servings)

6 green onions (chopped)
3 stalks celery (chopped)
1 carrot (shredded)
1 onion (thinly sliced)
6 radishes (thinly sliced)

1 c. cucumbers (sliced)
1/2 c. raw cauliflower florets
1/2 c. low-fat vinaigrette dressing
1 head romaine or bibb lettuce
1 large tomato (sliced)

In a glass bowl, marinate all vegetables, except lettuce and tomato, in vinaigrette for 1/2 hour. When ready to serve, tear lettuce into pieces and put into salad bowl. Add marinated vegetables and tomatoes. Toss lightly and serve immediately. (Fat: 20% calories from fat)

— Georgia Vegetable Salad —
(6 servings)

1 can (1 pound) whole, vertical packed
   green beans
1 c. thinly sliced fresh cauliflower
1 c. fresh orange sections

2 T. sliced radishes
1/4 tsp. seasoned salt
Dash of seasoned pepper
Low-calorie salad dressing (see below)

Drain beans. Arrange in bundles (wheel spoke fashion) on serving plate. Place cauliflower and orange sections between beans with cauliflower nearest rim of plate. Place sliced radishes in center. Sprinkle seasoned salt and seasoned pepper over all. Chill well. Serve with dressing that follows:

Dressing:
2 T. instant minced onion
2 tsp. cornstarch
1/2 tsp. paprika
1/2 tsp. Worcestershire sauce

1 T. canola oil
2 T. sugar
1/2 tsp. salt
1/3 c. vinegar
Dash of Tabasco sauce

Combine dry ingredients in saucepan. Stir in 1 cup water, vinegar, Worcestershire sauce, and Tabasco sauce. Cook and stir until mixture comes to a boil and is thickened. Remove from heat. Stir in oil. Chill until ready to use. (Fat: approximately 25% calories from fat)

— Mushroom Lover's Salad —
(16 servings)

1/4 c. canned (no-salt) chicken broth
   (undiluted)
2 T. minced fresh parsley
3 T. fresh lemon juice
1 tsp. olive oil

1 tsp. salt
1 clove garlic (minced)
1/4 tsp. freshly ground pepper
1-1/2 pounds fresh mushrooms (quartered)

Combine first 8 ingredients in a large bowl. Add mushrooms. Toss gently. Cover. Marinate in refrigerator 2 hours, tossing occasionally. (Fat: 20% calories from fat)

— Chinese Wonder Salad —
(makes 3 pints)

1 can (16-ounce) French-style green beans
1 flat can water chestnuts (thinly sliced)
3 medium onions (thinly sliced)
3/4 c. cider vinegar
Pepper to taste
1 can (16-ounce) small green peas (drained)

1 can (16-ounce) fancy Chinese vegetables
(without meat and drained)
1-1/2 c. celery (thinly sliced)
3/4 c. sugar
1 tsp. salt

Drain and discard liquid from all canned vegetables. Mix all ingredients in a large bowl. Cover and refrigerate several hours or overnight before serving. This will keep well for several weeks in the refrigerator. (Fat: less than 20% calories from fat)

— Gini Tharrington, Raleigh, NC

— Zucchini Rice Salad —
(8 servings)

4 c. rice (cooked)
2 small apples (unpeeled, diced)
1/4 c. raisins
1 c. zucchini (unpeeled, diced)

2 T. plus 2 tsp. canola oil
2 T. fresh lemon juice
1/2 tsp. ground cinnamon
2 tsp. sugar (or equivalent in sweetener)

In a large bowl, combine rice, apples, raisins, and zucchini. Toss to blend.
In a small bowl, combine remaining ingredients. Pour over rice mixture. Mix well. Chill overnight to blend flavors. (Fat: less than 10% calories from fat)

Fruit Salads

— Gingered Fruit Salad —
(6 servings)

1/4 c. unsweetened orange juice
1 T. honey
1 tsp. grated orange rind
1/4 tsp. ground ginger

1 c. fresh plums (sliced)
1 c. apple (chopped)
1 c. pear (chopped)
Lettuce leaves

Combine first 4 ingredients in a jar. Cover and shake well. Chill dressing mixture.
Place plums, apple, and pear in a large bowl. Add dressing. Toss gently. Spoon onto individual lettuce-lined salad plates. (Fat: 0.4 grams per serving)

— Apple-Celery Medley —
(4 servings)

1/4 c. low-fat cottage cheese
1/2 c. plain, low-fat yogurt
Juice of 1 lemon
1 red apple

3 stalks (inner ones) celery (chopped)
Heart of romaine lettuce
Pepper to taste

Blend yogurt, cottage cheese and lemon juice in salad bowl. Quarter apple, remove core, and thinly slice into bowl. Add chopped celery and lettuce leaves torn into bite-size pieces. Season as desired with pepper. Toss gently. (Fat: 1 gram per serving)

— Apple Delight —
(4 one-cup servings)

2 large red delicious apples
   (cored, unpeeled, cut into chunks)
2/3 c. crushed pineapple (drained) or
Fresh pineapple (minced) — juice reserved
1/3 c. celery (diced)
2 T. raisins

Dressing:
3 T. plain, low-fat yogurt
2 tsp. nonfat mayonnaise
1 T. pineapple juice
1/8 tsp. cinnamon

In medium bowl, combine salad ingredients.
In small bowl, combine dressing ingredients. Blend. Add to fruit mixture. (Fat: 20% calories from fat)

— Pineapple Lover's Salad —
(6 servings)

Curly leaf lettuce leaves
1 medium-size fresh pineapple

2 medium kiwi fruit (peeled)
Poppy Seed Dressing (see below)

Place lettuce leaves on a serving platter. Set aside.
Peel and trim eyes from pineapple, removing core. Cut pineapple into 6 slices. Arrange over lettuce leaves. Cut kiwi into 6 slices. Arrange over pineapple slices. Pour 2 tablespoons Poppy Seed Dressing over each serving.

Dressing:
3/4 c. unsweetened orange juice
2 tsp. cornstarch

1 T. honey
1-1/2 tsp. poppy seeds
1/4 tsp. grated orange rind

Combine orange juice and cornstarch in a 2-cup glass measure. Stir well. Microwave at high for 2-1/2 minutes or until thickened. Stir once. Add honey, poppy seeds, and orange rind. Stir well. Cover and chill. (Fat: 1.1 grams per serving)

— Sparkling Fruit —
(8 servings)

4 medium-size fresh pears (cored and diced)
2 T. fresh lemon juice
2 c. fresh strawberries (halved)
2 c. fresh peaches (peeled and diced)

3/4 pound fresh plums (pitted and thinly sliced)
2 c. sparkling apple cider (chilled)

Place diced pears in large bowl. Sprinkle with lemon juice. Toss gently. Add strawberries, plums, and peaches. Toss gently.

Place 1 cup fruit mixture in individual dessert cups. Pour 1/4 cup sparkling apple cider over each serving. Serve immediately. (Fat: 0.8 grams per serving)

— Apple Gelatin Salad —
(4 servings)

2 c. low-calorie cranapple juice
1 envelope low-calorie strawberry gelatin
1/4 tsp. salt

1 c. apple (chopped)
1/2 c. celery (chopped)

Bring 1 cup juice to a boil. Stir in gelatin until dissolved. Add remaining juice and salt. Chill until partially set. Gently stir in apples and celery. Pour into individual molds. Chill until set. (Fat: less than 20% calories from fat)

— Fruit Delight —
(6 servings)

1 pineapple (cut in cubes) (reserve shell)
3 oranges (peeled and sectioned)

2-1/2 c. strawberries or raspberries
1 c. your choice low-fat fruit salad dressing

Toss fruit together with dressing. Return salad to pineapple shell and garnish with a few berries. (Fat: less than 20% calories from fat)

— Low-Fat Fruit Salad —

1 can chunk pineapple (in it's own juice)
1 can fruit cocktail in lite syrup
1 package sugar-free banana pudding mix
1 can mandarin oranges

1 medium banana
1 medium apple
Nuts and raisins to taste (optional)

Drain juice from pineapple, fruit cocktail, and oranges into medium size bowl. Add pudding mix and mix with electric mixer until smooth and slightly thickened. Slice the banana and dice the apple. Add all fruit to pudding. Fold in nuts and raisins if desired. (Fat: approx. 25% calories from fat)

— Carol Hamilton, Ashville, OH

— Fruit-Veggie Salad —
(4 servings)

1-1/2 c. cabbage (finely shredded)
1 can (10-1/4 ounce) unsweetened mandarin
    oranges (drained)
1 medium-size Red Delicious apple (cored
    and cubed)
1/2 c. vanilla low-fat yogurt
1 T. brown sugar

Place first 3 ingredients in a medium bowl. Toss gently.

Combine yogurt and brown sugar in small bowl. Stir well. Add yogurt mixture to cabbage mixture. Toss gently. Cover and chill one hour. (Fat: 0.5 grams per serving)

— Six-Fruit Salad —
(6 servings)

2 apples (cubed)
2 bananas (sliced)
2 peaches or nectarines (sliced)
1 cantaloupe (cubed)

1/2 pound green, seedless grapes
1 small can mandarin oranges OR
    1 c. fresh orange slices

Dressing:
8 ounces fat-free sour cream

4 T. honey
1/3 c. sugar (optional)

Mix all three dressing ingredients together. Pour over fruit mixture. Toss gently just before serving. (Fat: less than 20% calories from fat)

— Rice 'N Fruit Salad —
(4 servings)

1 c. plain, low-fat or fat-free yogurt
3 T. sugar (or sweetener equivalent to 9 tsp.
    sugar)
1/4 tsp. coconut extract
1 tsp. vanilla extract
1 c. cooked brown rice

1/2 c. canned, crushed pineapple (unsweetened
    and drained)
2 T. juice from pineapple
1 medium, ripe banana (sliced)
1 small orange (peeled and sectioned)

In large bowl, combine yogurt, sugar, and extracts. Mix well. Add remaining ingredients. Toss to blend. Chill. Toss again before serving. (Fat: less than 20% calories from fat)

— Seasonal Fruit Salad —
(4 servings)

1/2 c. fresh strawberries (cut in halves)
1/2 c. melon balls
1/2 c. canned pineapple chunks (unsweetened)
1/2 c. grapes (cut in halves)

1/2 c. orange juice (unsweetened)
1 tsp. coconut extract
2 tsp. honey

Combine all ingredients in bowl. Mix well.
Chill several hours to blend flavors, stirring occasionally. (Fat: None)

— Momma's Ambrosia —

2 cans crushed pineapple (unsweetened)
4 c. peeled, sectioned, and cut up oranges
  (including juice)
4 c. apples (peeled and diced)

4 c. bananas (peeled and diced)
1/2 c. sugar (or to taste with substitutes)
Diet Sprite or Ginger Ale

Combine fruit in order given. Add sweetener and Sprite or Ginger Ale to cover. Stir good. Chill well. (Fat: less than 20% calories from fat)

— Harriet Cottingham, Charleston Heights, SC

— Fruit Mixture —
(7 servings)

1 c. water-packed pineapple chunks or tidbits
1 c. fresh orange slices
1 c. apple (unpeeled and diced)

1 c. canned, unsweetened cherries (drained)
1 c. plain, unsweetened, low-fat yogurt

Combine fruit with yogurt. Chill well before serving. (Fat: less than 20% calories from fat)

— Easy Waldorf Salad —
(5 servings)

3 medium apples (unpeeled and diced)
1/2 c. celery (sliced)
1/4 c. raisins

1/2 c. nonfat mayonnaise
1 T. lemon juice

Combine apple, celery, and raisins in medium bowl.
Combine nonfat mayonnaise and lemon juice. Stir to blend. Add to fruit mixture. Toss lightly.
Cover and refrigerate until chilled. (Fat: less than 30% calories from fat)

— Lime-Cottage Cheese Mold —
(10 servings)

1 package (0.6-ounce) sugar-free, lime
  gelatin
2 c. boiling water
2 c. cold water
2 T. nonfat mayonnaise

1 c. nonfat cottage cheese
1 can (8-1/4-ounce) crushed, water-packed
  pineapple (drained)
Nonstick cooking spray
Lettuce leaves

Dissolve gelatin in boiling water in medium bowl. Stir well. Stir in cold water. Chill until mixture is consistency of unbeaten egg white.
Fold in mayonnaise, cottage cheese, and pineapple. Pour gelatin mixture into a 6-cup mold coated with cooking spray.
Chill until firm. Unmold salad onto lettuce leaves. (Fat: less than 20% calories from fat)

— Gelatin Fruit Salad —
(10 servings)

1 package (0.3-ounce) sugar-free strawberry gelatin
3/4 c. boiling water
1 package (10-ounce) frozen, unsweetened strawberries (partially thawed)

1 can (8-1/4-ounce) crushed, water-packed pineapple (undrained)
1 medium banana (mashed)
Nonstick cooking spray
1 c. plain, unsweetened low-fat yogurt

Dissolve gelatin in boiling water in large mixing bowl. Stir well. Chill until mixture is slightly thickened.

Fold in strawberries, pineapple, and banana. Pour half of mixture into a 13x9x2-inch baking dish coated in nonstick cooking spray. Chill until firm. Store remaining gelatin mixture at room temperature.

Spread yogurt evenly over congealed layer. Pour remaining gelatin mixture over yogurt. Chill until firm. Cut into squares to serve. (Fat: less than 10% calories from fat)

Salads With Meat

— Leftover Turkey Salad —
(4 servings)

2 c. turkey (cooked, diced)
1-1/2 c. fresh bean sprouts
1 apple (unpeeled, diced)

1 stalk celery (diced)
1/4 c. raisins
3 T. walnuts (chopped)

Dressing:
3 T. plain, low-fat yogurt
2 T. nonfat mayonnaise

2 T. orange juice
1 tsp. grated orange rind

In medium bowl, combine all salad ingredients.

In small bowl, combine all dressing ingredients. Pour dressing over turkey mixture and toss. (Fat: 30% calories from fat)

— Tuna Salad —
(6 servings)

1 can (12-1/2-ounce) water-packed tuna (drained)
2 T. fresh lemon juice
1 T. capers
1/4 tsp. salt
1/4 tsp. (or less) black pepper
3/4 pound fresh baby green beans

1 pound small red potatoes (unpeeled)
3/4 pound cherry tomatoes (halved)
1/2 medium purple onion (thinly sliced)
Vinaigrette (recipe follows)
1 large head curly leaf lettuce (torn)
2 T. fresh parsley (chopped)

(Continued)

Combine tuna, lemon juice, capers, salt and pepper. Toss gently. Set aside.

Wash beans. Trim ends and remove strings. Cook beans in small amount of boiling water for 5 minutes or until crispy-tender. Drain. Plunge beans into ice water to cool. Drain. Set aside.

Cook potatoes in boiling water for 15 minutes or until tender. Drain. Plunge potatoes into ice water to cool. Drain. Let cool. Cut into quarters.

Place beans, potatoes, tomatoes, and onion in separate bowls. Add 2 tablespoons vinaigrette to each bowl. Toss gently. Cover and chill.

Arrange lettuce leaves on large serving platter. Mound tuna mixture in center of platter. Arrange chilled vegetables around tuna. Drizzle remaining vinaigrette over salad. Sprinkle with parsley.

Vinaigrette:

1/2 tsp. chicken-flavored bouillon granules	1 T. lemon juice
1/2 c. boiling water	2 cloves garlic (minced)
2 T. red wine vinegar	1 T. canola oil

Dissolve bouillon granules in boiling water. Set aside to cool. Combine bouillon and remaining ingredients. Blend with wire whisk. (Fat: less than 25% calories from fat)

— Chicken Salad With Vinaigrette —

(4 servings)

Marinated cucumbers and onions:

1 c. rice wine vinegar	1/8 tsp. red pepper flakes
1 tsp. honey	1 cucumber (thinly sliced, diagonally)
	1 red onion (thinly sliced)

In large bowl, combine vinegar, honey, and pepper flakes. Add cucumber and onion. Toss. Marinate 2 hours.

Vinaigrette:

8 cloves garlic (unpeeled)	1/2 c. red wine vinegar
2 large ripe tomatoes (peeled, seeded, chopped)	1 T. fresh basil (minced)
	1 tsp. dried basil

Place garlic in a custard cup. Cover with foil and bake at 450 degrees for 20 minutes or until tender and lightly browned. Let cool slightly. Remove cloves from peels. Place garlic in blender. Add tomatoes, vinegar, fresh basil, and dried basil. Process until smooth. Set aside.

Marinated chicken breasts:

1 T. lemon juice	1 tsp. olive oil
1 clove garlic (minced)	4 boneless, skinless chicken breast halves

In a small cup, combine lemon juice, minced garlic, and olive oil. Rub over all sides of chicken. Place the breasts on a baking sheet. Bake at 450 degrees for 8 to 10 minutes or until done. Remove from the oven and slice chicken on bias.

Place lettuce or greens in large bowl. Process vinaigrette for a few seconds to recombine ingredients. Pour over greens and toss well. Divide among 4 dinner plates.

Drain cucumber and onion. Arrange next to greens. Place chicken over greens. (Fat: 13% calories from fat)

— Easy Chicken Salad —
(8 servings)

2-1/2 c. canned or leftover cooked chicken (diced)
1 c. celery (chopped)
1 c. white grapes (sliced)
2 T. parsley
1 c. nonfat mayonnaise
Salt to taste
1/2 c. toasted, slivered almonds

Mix all ingredients. Serve on bed of lettuce, in a whole tomato or on top of sliced fresh pineapple. (Fat: approx. 30% calories from fat)

— Tuna Salad —

1/2 c. nonfat mayonnaise
Dash pepper
1 can tuna in water (drained)
1 c. cooked peas
1/2 c. (or less) minced onion
2 T. wine vinegar
4 ounces salad macaroni (cooked)
1 c. celery (sliced)
Dillweed and parsley to taste
Paprika

Mix well. Top with paprika. Chill before serving. (Fat: less than 30% calories from fat)
— *Fran Knoblock, Burson, CA*

— Quick Tuna Salad —

Rinse and drain 1 can of tuna. Put in food processor and chop 8 to 10 seconds. Add: 1 tsp. dill pickle juice (or more) and 6 dill pickle slices. Add mustard and nonfat mayonnaise to taste. Mix in processor for 20 seconds. (Fat: 30% calories from fat) — *Mary Alice Stevens, Springhill, LA*

— Chinese Chicken Salad —
(4 servings)

4 chicken breasts (skinless)
1 can (11-ounce) mandarin oranges
4 c. romaine lettuce, torn
4 c. iceberg lettuce, torn
1 bunch cilantro (chopped)
1 red bell pepper (chopped)
1/4 c. avocado (diced)
1/3 c. cashews
1/2 c. chow mein noodles

Dressing:
1/3 c. seasoned rice vinegar
1-1/2 garlic cloves (minced)
1 tsp. ginger (freshly grated)
1 tsp. soy sauce
1 tsp. sesame oil

Glaze:
3 T. honey
2 T. soy sauce
1-1/2 tsp. sesame oil

Slice chicken into bite-size pieces and poach in water. Combine glaze ingredients and drizzle over chicken. Mix chicken and glaze thoroughly. Cool in refrigerator.

Drain mandarin oranges. Combine with remaining salad ingredients and set aside. Mix salad dressing ingredients and stir well. Add glazed chicken to salad. Serve salad dressing on the side. (Fat: 26% calories from fat)

— Seafood Salad —
(4 servings)

1 c. salad shrimp (cooked)
1 c. flaked crab or mock crab
1/2 c. celery (chopped)
1/4 c. pimento (chopped)
2 T. onion (minced)
1 c. green peas

1/2 c. reduced-calorie Thousand Island
   dressing
1 tsp. lemon juice
1/4 tsp. pepper
1/4 tsp. marjoram
1/4 c. plain, nonfat yogurt

Combine shrimp, crab, celery, pimento, onion, and peas in a serving bowl. In shaker container, mix remaining ingredients and pour dressing over salad. Toss and serve. (Fat: 26% calories from fat)

— Fiesta Turkey Salad —
(8 servings)

1 c. quick rice
1 c. water
1 tomato (sliced)

1 green pepper (chopped)
2 T. green chiles
2 c. turkey (cooked)

Dressing:
1/2 c. nonfat yogurt
1 T. canola oil
1-1/2 tsp. chile powder

1/2 tsp. cumin
1/2 tsp. sugar
1/4 tsp. garlic powder
1/4 tsp. salt (optional)

Combine rice and water in 1-quart microwave dish. Cover tightly and microwave on high for 3 minutes. When rice is cooked, rinse quickly with cold water and transfer to colander to drain. In salad bowl, combine vegetables, turkey, and rice. In shaker container, blend ingredients for dressing and pour over salad just before serving. (Fat: 20% calories from fat)

— Turkey 'N Fruit Salad —
(8 servings)

1/4 c. nonfat mayonnaise
2 T. honey
1/4 tsp. ginger
1/2 c. celery (diced)
2 c. turkey (cooked and chopped)

1 can (11-ounce) mandarin oranges (drained)
1 c. apple (chopped)
1 c. grape halves
1 can (8-ounce) pineapple chunks (drained)

In a serving bowl, combine mayonnaise, honey, and ginger. Mix well. Add remaining ingredients and mix lightly. (Fat: less than 19% calories from fat)

Pasta Salads

—Scallop Pasta Salad —
(6 servings)

1 pound scallops
1/2 c. celery (thinly sliced)
1 can (8-ounce) sliced water chestnuts
4 green onions (cut in strings)

1 package (8-ounce) buckwheat noodles
 (cooked and drained)
1 head red leaf lettuce (shredded)
1/4 c. reduced-sodium soy sauce
2 T. rice vinegar

In nonstick skillet, saute scallops 2 to 3 minutes or until cooked. Chill scallops, celery, water chestnuts, onions, noodles, and lettuce. Just before serving, arrange lettuce over chilled salad plates. Top with noodles. Add scallops, celery, water chestnuts, and green onions.

Combine soy sauce and vinegar. Drizzle over salads. (Fat: 8% calories from fat)

— Pasta Salad —
(4 servings)

2 c. elbow macaroni (cooked)
1/2 c. celery (thinly sliced)
1/4 c. green pepper (finely chopped)
1/4 c. carrots (finely chopped)
1 T. pimento (chopped)
1/4 c. nonfat mayonnaise

1 T. minced onion flakes
1/8 tsp. dry mustard
1/2 tsp. dillweed
1 tsp. sugar (or equivalent amount of
 sweetener)
Salt and pepper to taste

In large bowl, combine macaroni, celery, green pepper, carrots, and pimento.
Combine remaining ingredients. Mix well. Add to macaroni. Toss to blend. Chill. (Fat: less than 30% calories form fat)

— Vegetable Pasta —
(6 servings)

6 ounces spaghetti (uncooked)
Nonstick cooking spray
1 c. broccoli flowerets
1 c. carrots (thinly sliced)
1 c. zucchini (sliced)
1/4 c. onion (sliced)
1/2 c. cucumber (sliced)

1/2 c. fresh mushrooms (sliced)
1 small tomato (cut into 8 wedges)
2 T. wine vinegar
1/4 c. plus 2 T. grated Parmesan
cheese
1 T. fresh parsley (minced)
1/2 tsp. sweet red pepper flakes

Cook pasta according to package directions, omitting salt. Drain. Set aside.

Coat large nonstick skillet with cooking spray. Place over medium heat until hot. Add broccoli and next 3 ingredients. Saute 4 minutes. Add cucumber and mushrooms. Saute 4 minutes. Add pasta, tomato, and wine vinegar. Toss gently. Cook until thoroughly heated. Sprinkle with cheese, parsley, and pepper flakes. Toss gently. Serve immediately. (Fat: less than 25% calories from fat)

— Macaroni Salad —

3/4 c. fat-free mayonnaise
2 T. vinegar
1 T. prepared mustard
1 tsp. sugar
1 tsp. salt

1/8 tsp. pepper
1 c. celery (sliced)
1 c. green and sweet red pepper (chopped)
1/4 c. onion (chopped)
8 ounces elbow macaroni (cooked, drained)

To cook macaroni, bring 3 quarts of water to rapid boil. Add macaroni and stir to separate and return to boil. Boil uncovered, stirring occasionally 8 to 12 minutes until tender. Drain thoroughly.

In large bowl, stir together mayonnaise, vinegar, mustard, sugar, salt, and pepper until smooth. Add macaroni, celery, green pepper, and onion. Toss to coat well. Cover. Chill. (Fat: less than 20% calories from fat)

— Pasta Tomato Salad —
(makes 2 quarts or 8 cups)

1 pound package rotini (cooked until tender)
2 c. fresh basil
2 c. diced ripe tomatoes
1/4 pound part-skim mozzarella cheese
   (cubed)

Oil-free Italian dressing (see Dressings
   section)
Black pepper (optional and to taste)

In a salad bowl, combine rotini, basil, tomatoes, and cheese. Pour dressing into cruet and pass it with salads. Offer black pepper. Serve hot or cold. (Fat: 12% calories from fat per 1/2-cup serving)

— Shrimp Pasta Salad —
(8 servings)

Although I rarely use any cheese except nonfat cheeses, I still like to treat myself to a little feta cheese occasionally. When used in moderation, feta cheese makes a great addition to certain salads.

1/2 pound shrimp (cooked, deveined)
2/3 c. feta cheese (crumbled)
2 large fresh tomatoes (chopped)
1 large cucumber (peeled and chopped)
1/2 c. no-fat prepared Italian dressing

2 T. fresh lemon juice
1/2 tsp. oregano
1/2 tsp. fresh ground black pepper
3 c. pasta (cooked and cooled)

Mix shrimp, feta cheese, tomatoes, cucumber, dressing, lemon juice, and seasonings. Toss with pasta. Chill. (Fat: less than 30% calories from fat)

— Colorful Pasta Salad —
(6 servings)

8 ounces tri-colored pasta (green, red, white)
2 c. assorted raw vegetables (chopped) — i.e. green or red peppers, summer squash, onions, tomatoes, cauliflower, broccoli, carrots
1 c. fat-free, prepared Italian dressing

Cook and drain pasta according to package directions.
Add chopped vegetables and dressing. Toss well. Chill before serving. (Fat: less than 20% calories from fat)

— Quick Spaghetti Salad —
(4 servings)

3 ounces whole-wheat spaghetti
1 zucchini (thinly sliced)
1/4 c. celery (chopped)
4 ounces mushrooms (thinly sliced)
1/3 c. no-salt tomato juice

1-1/2 tsp. dry garlic and herb salad dressing mix
1 tsp. canola oil
1 tsp. lemon juice

Cook spaghetti according to package directions. Rinse with cold water. Drain well. Place zucchini, celery, and mushrooms in a 2-quart salad bowl.

In a shaker container, combine tomato juice and dressing mix, oil, and lemon juice. Transfer drained spaghetti to bowl. Pour dressing over spaghetti and vegetables just before serving. (Fat: 13% calories from fat)

INTRODUCTION TO SAUCES

Know Your Oils —

Mechanics say that one of the most important ways to take care of your car is to change the oil on a regular basis. In recent years doctors have been saying that, in order to take proper care of our body's engine, the heart, many of us need to change the kind of oil we are using.

We basically eat three kinds of oil (or fat): saturated, polyunsaturated, and monounsaturated. Several years ago, scientists found that replacing saturated fats with polyunsaturated ones would help bring down cholesterol levels. So people began cooking with vegetable oil instead of lard and soft margarine instead of butter. As a result, cholesterol levels did come down.

However, today doctors are saying we need to change oil again. They now recommend monounsaturated oil. Tests conducted in Mediterranean countries showed that where highly-monounsaturated olive oil is eaten, people have a lower incidence of heart disease. Like polyunsaturated oil, monounsaturated oil was found to reduce total cholesterol but with one big difference — without reducing the HDL or good cholesterol. This is one of its advantages over polyunsaturated oil.

There is more good news. Testing with over 5,000 men and women revealed that monounsaturated oils also help reduce high blood pressure and help control diabetes by balancing glucose levels.

There is no need to stop using polyunsaturated oils; but it would be wise to add monounsaturated oils to your diet while reducing use of polyunsaturated ones.

Read labels. Find the oil highest in monounsaturated fat. For example, olive oil is 77% monounsaturated, 9% polyunsaturated, and 14% saturated. Canola oil is 74% monounsaturated, 14% polyunsaturated, and 12% saturated. Margarine is 46% monounsaturated, 33% polyunsaturated, and 21% saturated.

Breaking Old Habits —

> Having therefore these promises, dearly beloved let us cleanse ourselves
> from all filthiness of the flesh and spirit, perfecting holiness in the fear of God
> (2 Cor. 7:1).

Old habits, whether they be diet, life style, or sin-habits, do not always disappear when we come to Christ. But, as we look to our Heavenly Father, He will gradually and lovingly show us those habits in us that do not please Him.

I remember shortly after I was saved, God showed me how I carried a gluttonous attitude toward fried chicken. In a restaurant, one day, I carefully ordered fried chicken breast. I wanted white meat — absolutely no dark meat for me. Unfortunately, the waitress was new at her job and accidentally brought me a HUGE chicken thigh. I remember my disappointment and despair as I looked at that thigh and lamented, "That is not what I ordered!"

At that moment God convicted me of the sin of lusting after fried white chicken breast. Yes, I had been lusting after food.

Have you ever had that problem? Don't backslide into your old eating habits just because you are feeling tempted and weak. Instead reach for God's Word and read Psalm 34:1, "I will bless the Lord at all times: His praise shall continually be in my mouth." In other words, put praise for God in your mouth and not those bad-for-you foods you used to love. Remember, there is power in God's Word to fight whatever temptation or discouragement you might face.

Habits that you once thought impossible to break can be removed forever from your life as you learn to apply God's Word to your particular situation. Give your bad habits to the Lord.

> Blessed is she that believed; for there shall be a performance of those things
> which were told her from the Lord (Luke 1:45).

A Viewer Writes —
Dear Beverly,

The Holy Spirit has really been working with me concerning the care of my body since I have been working with you. I enjoy your comments so much. Here is a poem God gave me since I have been exercising with you:

God gave me a body with certain traits,
But God didn't make me overweight.
God gave me food to give me strength,
But I must eat a very short length.
God gave me a mind with which to think,
But my will determines what kind of thing.
God gave me eyes to see His beauty,
But what I look at is my duty.
God gave me ears with which to hear,
But I must choose what they are near.
God gave me a tongue with which to speak,
But the words I choose my heart must seek.
God gave me hands with which to work,
But I must decide that I'll not shirk.
God gave me feet with which to move,
But where they take me my life will prove.
God gave me a will that is my own,
But how to make it His, Jesus has shown.
God gave me His Son to show me His love,
But I must believe He came in the flesh, from above.
God gave me His Spirit to teach me in every way,
But I must ask for His guidance every day.
God gave me things on which the angels desire to look,
But I must find out what they are by reading His book.
God gave me this poem to help me reform,
But I must obey so His Spirit can perform.

May God continue to bless you. I get you on Channel 16, WRDG, Burlington, NC. I support them because of you. I told them your . . . program ministered to our spirit, soul, and body . . .

Sylvia Hough, Greensboro, NC

Thank you, Sylvia.

SAUCES

— Handy Barbecue Sauce —

Melt and blend over low heat: 1 stick low-fat margarine and 2 T. peanut butter.

Add:

2 T. chili powder	1 T. lite salt
1 T. celery seed	1 T. black pepper
	1 c. white vinegar

Stir and bring to boiling point. Do not boil. Put aside to cool and then add 3 tablespoons lemon juice. Refrigerate until ready to use (up to 2 weeks) and freeze what's left. Good on any kind of meat, chicken, or fish. (Fat: 30% calories from fat)
— *Janet Hardy, Mauldin, SC*

— Barbecue Sauce Delight —
(makes 1-1/4 cups)

1/4 c. cider vinegar
1/2 c. water
2 generous T. brown sugar
1 T. prepared mustard
1/4 tsp. salt (optional)
1/4 tsp. (or less) black pepper

Juice of 1 lemon (about 1/4 cup)
1 to 1-1/2 T. dried onion flakes
1 T. low-fat margarine (optional)
1 T. Worcestershire sauce
1/2 c. ketsup

In medium saucepan, combine all ingredients except ketsup. Bring to boil and simmer over medium-low heat for 20 minutes. Sauce will be of medium thickness. Stir in ketsup. Remove from heat.

Serving Suggestion: Coat skinless, defatted, baked chicken breasts with sauce. Place under oven broiler and watch closely until sauce bubbles. Do this to both sides of chicken. (Fat: less than 20% calories from fat)
— *Gale R. Cox, Taylors, SC*

— Texas Barbecue Sauce —
(makes 1 cup)

1 can (8-ounce) tomato sauce
1 T. vinegar
1 tsp. Worcestershire sauce
1 tsp. dry mustard

2 tsp. chopped, fresh parsley
1/4 tsp. salt
1/8 tsp. pepper
1/4 tsp. garlic powder

Combine all ingredients. Serve over chicken, pork chops, or beef. (Fat: None)
— *Ann Buel, Fairfax VA*

— All-Purpose Tomato Sauce —

3 T. canola or safflower oil
2 T. chopped onion
2 T. chopped green pepper
1/4 c. sliced mushrooms
2 c. stewed or fresh tomatoes

1/2 tsp. salt
Dash black pepper
Few drops Tobasco sauce (optional)
1/2 tsp. basil (optional)

Cook onion, green pepper, and sliced mushrooms in oil over low heat for about 5 minutes. Add tomatoes and seasonings and simmer until sauce is desired thickness (about 30 minutes).

Serving Suggestions: Serve as Seafood Creole by adding cooked fish, shrimp, lobster, or crabmeat to sauce and heating thoroughly. Serve over rice. (Fat: 30% calories from fat)

— Thick and Tasty Spaghetti Sauce —
(8 servings)

Nonstick cooking spray
1 T. olive oil
3-4 medium onions (sliced)
4 cloves garlic (minced)
1 green pepper (chopped)
10 ounces mushrooms (sliced)
Water as needed

1 pound ground turkey
1 can (28-ounce) tomato sauce
1 can (6-ounce) tomato paste
1 can (10-ounce) tomato puree
1 tsp. salt
1/2 tsp. pepper
1 tsp. basil

Spray bottom of a deep saucepan with cooking spray. Add olive oil, onion, garlic, green peppers, and mushrooms. Saute, covered, over medium heat until vegetables are tender, adding a tablespoon of water or more if necessary to prevent sticking.

Meanwhile, in a skillet, cook ground turkey until browned. Drain liquid. Add to cooked vegetables. Stir in tomato sauce, tomato paste, tomato puree, and seasonings.

Simmer, covered, for 1 to 2 hours. Serve over pasta of choice. (Fat: less than 30% calories from fat)

— Basic Cream Sauce —
(makes about 1-1/2 cups)

1 c. low-fat cottage cheese
1/4 c. skim milk
2 T. grated Parmesan

2 tsp. dried dillweed
Generous dash nutmeg (optional)
Black pepper to taste

Combine all ingredients in blender until smooth.

Serving Suggestions: Toss with hot pasta. Or combine sauce with 1 to 2 cups of diced cooked chicken or turkey. Heat gently and serve over pasta. (Fat: 30% calories from fat)

— Mock Sour Cream —

2 T. skim milk
1 T. lemon juice

1 c. low-fat cottage cheese
1/4 tsp. salt

Place all ingredients in a blender and mix on medium high speed until smooth and creamy. Use as a sour cream substitute.

This sauce may be added to hot dishes at the last moment. Or serve it cold, adding herbs, as a salad dressing or sauce for other main dishes. (Fat: 25% calories from fat)

— Mrs. Hazel McConnell, Alma, MI

— Quick Fruit Sauce —

1/2 c. frozen blueberries

1 envelope Equal sweetener

Wash berries and microwave for 1-1/2 to 2 minutes until juices flow. Sprinkle with sweetener. Serve over yogurt or ice milk. (Fat: less than 10% calories from fat)

— Harriet Cottingham, Charleston Hgts., SC

— Mock Sour Cream with Buttermilk —
(makes 1-1/2 cups)

1 c. low-fat cottage cheese
1/2 c. buttermilk

1 tsp. fresh lemon juice (strained)
Pinch of salt

Put all ingredients in a blender and blend until smooth. This recipe may be used in any recipe calling for sour cream. (Fat: less than 20% calories from fat) — *Gini Tharrington, Raleigh, NC*

— Low-Cal Ketchup —

1 can (46-ounce) tomato juice
1/4 c. wine vinegar
3 T. onion flakes
1/2 tsp. salt

1 tsp. lemon juice
1-1/8 tsp. garlic powder
Artificial sweetener to equal 4 tsp. sugar
2 T. Worcestershire sauce

Combine ingredients in saucepan. Cook over low heat for 3 to 5 hours, stirring occasionally. Cool. Store in refrigerator. (Fat: less than 20% calories from fat) — *Ann Buel, Fairfax, VA*

DRESSINGS

— Old Fashioned Buttermilk Dressing —
(makes 1-1/4 cups)

1 c. buttermilk
1/4 c. grated cucumber
2 T. minced scallions
1 T. Dijon mustard

2 tsp. minced fresh parsley
2 tsp. lemon juice
1/4 tsp. dried dillweed
1/4 tsp. (or less) black pepper

Combine all ingredients in a screw-top jar, shake well and chill. (Fat: less than 20% calories from fat)

— Poppy Seed Dressing —
(for fruit salads)
(makes 1-1/4 cups)

1 c. plain, low-fat yogurt
2 T. orange juice
2 T. honey
1 T. fresh lemon juice

1 tsp. poppy seeds
Salt to taste (optional)
Black pepper to taste (optional)

Combine all ingredients in a small jar, shake well. (Fat: less than 20% calories from fat)

— Oil-Free Vinegar Dressing —
(makes 1 cup)

1/4 c. cider vinegar
3/4 c. cold water

3/4 tsp. salt
1/4 tsp. (or less) black pepper

Combine ingredients in covered jar. Shake well. (Fat: trace)

— Vinegar 'N Herb Dressing —
(makes about 1/2 cup)

1/2 c. white vinegar
3 or 4 sage leaves (crushed)
1/4 tsp. tarragon
1 tsp. dried parsley flakes (crushed)

1/2 clove garlic (crushed)
1/4 tsp. dried dillweed
1/2 tsp. salt (optional)
Black pepper to taste

Combine all ingredients in jar. Shake well. (Fat: less than 20% calories from fat)

— Savory Vinaigrette —
(makes 1-1/4 cups)

2/3 c. plain, low-fat yogurt
1/3 c. apple cider vinegar
2 T. olive oil
1 T. Dijon mustard

1 T. fresh lemon juice
1 very large clove garlic (crushed)
1 T. low-sodium soy sauce (optional)
1/4 tsp. dried dillweed

Combine all ingredients in bowl or jar with tight-fitting lid. Shake well. (Fat: 30% calories from fat)

— Cole Slaw Dressing —
(makes 2 cups)

3 T. honey
1 c. low-fat yogurt (plain)
2 eggs (beaten)

1/2 c. tarragon vinegar
1 tsp. celery (finely chopped)

In top of double boiler, blend all ingredients and cook until mixture becomes smooth and custardy. (Fat: 30% calories from fat)

— Fruit Salad Dressing —
(makes 1-1/2 cups)

1/2 c. apricot juice or any other unsweetened
   fruit juice
4 T. honey

2 egg yolks (beaten)
1 c. plain, low-fat yogurt
Cinnamon to taste

In top of double boiler, mix juice and honey. Add egg yolks gradually and beat well. Stir constantly over simmering water until mixture thickens slightly. Remove from heat and cool. When cooled, fold in yogurt and spice. (Fat: 30% calories from fat)

— No-Fat Lemon Vinaigrette —
(makes 1/3 cup)

1/3 c. fresh lemon juice
1/2 tsp. salt

1/4 tsp. (or less) black pepper

Combine ingredients in covered jar. Shake well.

— Fresh Vegetable Dip —
(Makes 1-1/2 cups)

1 c. low-fat cottage cheese
1/2 c. (4 ounces) plain, low-fat yogurt
1/2 tsp. dillweed

1 garlic clove (minced)
2 green onions (chopped)
1 T. fresh parsley (chopped)

Place cottage cheese in food processor or blender. Blend until smooth. Add next 5 ingredients and process well. Place mixture in bowl. Cover and chill until ready to serve. (Fat: approx. 25% calories from fat)

— Martha Elson, Anchorage, AK

GRAVIES

— Fat-Free Brown Gravy —

1 tablespoon browned flour for every 1/2 cup broth

To make browned flour: place flour in shallow baking pan. Spread evenly to a depth of about 1/2 to 3/4-inch. Bake in a low oven at 250 degrees, stirring occasionally until lightly browned. Store unused flour in a covered jar in refrigerator for future use.

To make gravy: put 1 tablespoon browned flour in a jar with 1/2 cup cold broth of choice (fat-free beef, turkey, chicken, or vegetable). Cover and shake well. For additional gravy, use the same ration of flour to broth. Slowly add gravy mixture to hot liquids in pan. Stir until thickened.

— Chicken Gravy —
(makes 2-3/4 cups)

6 T. flour
2-1/2 cups fat-free chicken broth
1/2 tsp. poultry seasoning

1/2 tsp. salt (optional)
Black pepper to taste

In a medium saucepan, whisk flour, stock, and poultry seasoning together until smooth. Adjust heat to moderate and cook, stirring constantly, until gravy thickens. This is a fat-free recipe as long as you use fat-free broth. (Fat: 25% calories from fat)

— Easy Microwave Gravy —
(makes 1 cup)

1 T. reduced-calorie margarine
1 T. all-purpose flour
1/2 c. evaporated skimmed milk
1/4 c. canned, salt-free chicken broth (undiluted)

1/4 tsp. salt
1/4 tsp. ground white pepper
2 T. fresh chives (chopped)

Place margarine in a 4-cup glass measuring cup. Microwave, uncovered, on high for 30 seconds or until melted. Add flour and stir until smooth. Gradually add milk and broth. Stir until smooth. Microwave on high for 3 to 5 minutes or until thickened, stirring once. Stir in salt, pepper, and chives. Serve immediately. (Fat: approx. 30% calories from fat)

5

Grains, Beans, & Pasta

INTRODUCTION

The Food Problem —

I will never forget the testimony of a minister. Let's call him Pastor Bob. He loves to tell people that God did not deliver him from a weight problem but from a food problem.

Pastor Bob had suffered from obesity to the point of declining health. He tried and failed over and over to lose weight. No diet helped for long. If he lost weight, as soon as he finished the diet, he would put that weight back on plus some more. He began to feel totally helpless and hopeless. Finally, in desperation, he made the decision to fast and pray, shut away from everyone, until he heard from God.

And hear he did! God met Bob in his closet of prayer and told him exactly where his weight problem lay. God showed him what to do about his weight and revealed the source of his problem.

The Lord revealed to Pastor Bob's heart and mind that his problem basically stemmed from the fact that he was always trying to lose weight without really changing his daily eating habits. God helped him see himself as being like an alcoholic who wants to be able to drink constantly without suffering the effects of alcohol. He saw himself as a man who wanted to eat nine times a day but still weigh 165 pounds.

"The bottom line," Bob stated, "was I was a glutton who wanted to continue in gluttony and escape the consequences of it. God would not be partner to that."

In His Word, my friend, God places gluttony in the same category as drunkenness. It is a sin. This precious man of God came to realize that in the past he had actually been asking God to let him get away with sin without suffering sin's consequences.

The first thing this minister did was change the prayer he had been praying. He repented of the sin of gluttony.

"That was tough," he admits. "For the first time, I finally understood how tough it is for a person who drinks to face the fact of his alcoholism. So instead of asking God for deliverance from my weight problem, as I had in the past, I began asking Him to deliver me from my food problem."

One can give up alcohol totally, but a person cannot totally give up food. So what is a food-aholic to do? As Bob continued seeking, God revealed that He was going to deliver him, not from all food, but from certain kinds of food. Unhealthy foods — those full of sugar and fat. I believe Proverbs 23:3 warns us against such food, calling it "deceitful meat."

Bob continues: "I knew God wanted me on a permanently healthy diet. My problem, however, was I didn't like healthy foods. I had never eaten vegetables, for example. So I had to ask God to change my appetite."

Good Food Decisions —

The change did not occur overnight. Pastor Bob had to make a firm commitment, as anyone does, to put gluttony behind him and stand on the Word of God in faith. Instead of jumping on every fad diet, he began letting God teach him about the foods he needed. With God's help, he began making good food decisions. Instead of constantly eating cakes, pies, and fried foods, he began to feed on the Word of God and on healthy physical foods. The more he was committed to this new life style, the more he experienced victory.

This is the story of one man who found 2 Corinthians 12:9 to be real and true in his life — God's strength was made perfect in his weakness. Today food is no longer an area of struggle for Pastor Bob. He now controls that which once had him bound. His last word of testimony was, "Praise God, I'm free!"

If you or someone you know has such a food problem, there is freedom from food abuse. Go to the Lord and ask for deliverance from the food problem, not the weight problem. Once the food problem is corrected, the weight problem will gradually correct itself. And don't forget to add exercise to your healthy diet.

You may be asking, "Would God do that for me?" Yes, my friend, He surely will.

> And he said unto me, my grace is sufficient for thee: for my strength is made perfect in weakness. Most gladly therefore will I rather glory in my infirmities, that the power of Christ may rest upon me.
> Therefore, I take pleasure in infirmities, in reproaches, in necessities, in persecutions, in distresses for Christ's sake: for when I am weak, then am I strong (2 Cor. 12:9-10).

Something New —

The Food and Drug Administration and the Health and Human Services Department have recently released a new set of suggested weights based on height. Their table makes allowances for weight gain as you age. The lower weights generally apply to women. The higher ones to men. (Weights are without shoes and clothes.)

Height	19 to 34 years	35 years or more
5'0"	97-128	108-138
5'1"	101-132	111-143
5'2"	104-137	115-148
5'3"	107-141	119-152
5'4"	111-146	122-157
5'5"	114-150	126-162
5'6"	118-155	130-167
5'7"	121-160	134-172
5'8"	125-164	138-178
5'9"	129-169	142-183
5'10"	132-174	146-188
5'11"	136-179	151-194
6'0"	140-184	155-199
6'1"	144-189	159-205
6'2"	148-195	164-210
6'3"	153-200	168-216
6'4"	156-205	173-222

Tips on Legumes —

— Legumes are the fruit or seeds of pod-bearing plants. Their common names are beans or peas.

— Some common types of beans are kidney, pinto, navy, black, lima, garbanzo, and soy.

— Other types include: split peas, lentils, and black-eyed peas.

— A popular legume is peanuts. However, peanuts are higher in fat and in cost than most other legumes.

— Legumes are complex carbohydrates and are a good source of dietary fiber.

— Legumes provide iron, B vitamins, zinc, calcium, potassium, magnesium, and phosphorus.

— Beans and peas are low in fat. What little fat they do contain is mostly unsaturated.

— Legumes have no cholesterol.

— Since most beans cost very little, they make a good inexpensive meal.

— One cup of most dried beans will weigh about 6 ounces and will make about 3 cups of cooked beans.

— It is best to soak most legumes in water overnight, except for split peas and lentils, both of which need no soaking. Soaking overnight will reduce cooking time. Use 2 to 3 times their volume of water. Discarding soaking water will help eliminate digestive problems that beans usually cause.

— To cook legumes, use 3 to 4 cups of water for each cup of beans. Bring water and beans to boil in pot, reduce heat, cover. Simmer until tender.

— When cooking beans or peas, prepare extra for freezer. Freeze in small containers or bags for use in various other recipes.

— Canned beans can be used in recipes calling for cooked beans. However, in most cases, they contain unnecessary sugar and salt.

Cooking Times for Legumes —

Legume:	Cooking Time:
Black Beans	1-1/2 to 2 hours
Black-eyed Peas	30 to 45 minutes
Garbanzo Beans	2 to 3 hours
Great Northern Beans	1 to 1-1/2 hours
Kidney Beans	1-1/2 to 2 hours
Lentils	30 to 45 minutes
Lima Beans	1 to 1-1/2 hours
Navy Beans	1-1/2 to 2 hours
Pinto Beans	1-1/2 to 2 hours
Pink Beans	1 to 1-1/2 hours
Soybeans	2 to 3 hours
Split Peas	30 to 45 minutes

The above cooking times apply to soaked beans, except for split peas and lentils. Cooking times will vary with size, quality, and freshness of beans as well as mineral content of water being used.

Rice Dishes

— Rainbow Rice Dish —
(4 servings)

1/3 c. green onions (chopped)
1/2 c. zucchini (sliced)
1 c. frozen corn (thawed)
1 c. tomatoes (chopped)
1-1/2 c. cooked white rice (1/2 cup uncooked)
2 T. fresh parsley (chopped)

1/4 tsp. lite salt
1/4 tsp. pepper
1/4 tsp. dried whole oregano
2 garlic cloves (peeled and minced)
Nonstick cooking spray

Coat electric skillet or wok with spray. Heat to 350 degrees. Add zucchini and onions. Cook 3 to 5 minutes until crisp/tender. Add remaining ingredients. Cover. Reduce heat and simmer 10 to 15 minutes. (Fat: approx. 20% calories from fat)

— *Martha Elson, Anchorage, AK*

— Versatile Rice Stuffing —
(20 to 24 servings)

3 c. low-fat chicken broth
1-1/2 c. regular long grain rice
2 T. diet margarine
2 medium onions (chopped)
1 large carrot (shredded)
4 stalks celery (thinly sliced)
1 clove garlic (minced or mashed)
1/4 c. parsley (minced)

1/4 pound mushrooms (sliced)
1 tsp. poultry seasoning
1-1/2 tsp. grated lemon peel
1/4 tsp. pepper
1/4 tsp. thyme
1/2 tsp. salt (optional)
1/3 c. low-fat chicken broth
1/2 c. almonds (sliced)

Boil chicken broth. Add rice. Stir. Reduce heat to low. Cover and let stand for 20 minutes or until liquid is absorbed. Melt margarine in large skillet. Add onions and saute 5 minutes. Add carrot, celery, garlic, parsley, and mushrooms.

Stir in poultry seasoning, lemon peel, pepper, thyme, and salt. Saute 5 more minutes or until liquid from vegetables evaporates.

Combine vegetables with rice. Add broth and nuts. Toss lightly with fork. Bake in covered casserole for about 30 minutes at 350 degrees. (Fat: approx. 30% calories from fat)

— Rice Casserole —
(6 servings)

1 c. converted white rice
6 paper-thin slices of lemon
Non-stick cooking spray
2 scallions (minced)
1/2 c. green bell pepper (minced)

2 c. parsley (minced)
Salt (optional)
Ground black pepper to taste
2 c. skim milk
2 whole eggs

In a medium saucepan, combine rice with lemon slices and 2-1/2 cups of cold water. Bring to boil over high heat. Immediately reduce heat to low and cover. Cook until rice has absorbed all liquid (18-25 minutes). After cooking, turn rice out into large bowl. Discard lemon slices.

Preheat oven to 350 degrees. Lightly coat casserole dish with cooking spray. In a small skillet, combine scallions, bell pepper, and 1 tablespoon of water. Cover and cook over low heat until vegetables are softened (about 5 minutes). Drain off excess moisture and scrape vegetables into bowl of rice. Add parsley, salt, and pepper. Toss ingredients well. Spoon into casserole. Beat milk and eggs until slightly foamy. Pour this slowly and evenly over casserole. Bake for 45 minutes to 1 hour or until knife inserted into center comes out clean. Serve warm. (Fat: 30% calories from fat)

— Healthy Casserole —

1 c. brown rice
1 package frozen broccoli
1 c. carrots (sliced)

1 small squash, yellow or zucchini (sliced)
Low-fat cheese of choice

Cook rice 45 minutes. Cook vegetables separately and drain. Place cooked rice in casserole dish. Layer vegetables and rice. Top with low-fat cheese. Bake until cheese melts in a 350-degree oven. (Fat: 30% calories from fat)

— *Phyllis Witwer, Camp Springs, MA*

— Rice Side Dish —
(5 servings)

1 c. uncooked wild rice
4 c. de-fatted chicken broth
7 large fresh mushrooms (thinly sliced)

2 T. fresh parsley (chopped)
1/2 ripe tomato (diced)

Pour rice into a 6-quart saucepan. Cover with hot water. Soak 1/2 hour. Drain. Add broth and heat to boiling (do not boil). Reduce heat. Cover and simmer 45 minutes. Stir in mushrooms. Remove from heat. Let stand 15 minutes. Stir in parsley and tomatoes. (Fat: 6% calories from fat)

— South of the Border Rice —
(6 servings)

1-2/3 c. water
1/2 tsp. dry mustard
1/2 tsp. beef-flavored bouillon granules
1-1/2 c. uncooked instant rice

1/4 c. green pepper (chopped)
1 can (4-ounce) chopped green chiles
  (undrained)

Combine water, dry mustard, and bouillon granules in a 2-quart casserole. Stir in rice and chopped green peppers. Cover with heavy-duty plastic wrap and microwave on high for 8 to 10 minutes or until liquid is absorbed. Let stand 3 minutes. Stir in chopped green chiles. Fluff with fork before serving. (Fat: approx. 20% calories from fat)

— Spanish Rice —
(8 to 10 servings)

1-1/2 c. uncooked long grain rice
1 to 1-1/2 c. green peas (frozen)
1 can (16-ounce) sliced tomatoes (drain,
  reserve juice)
1/2 c. tomato paste or fruit sweetened catsup
1 medium onion (finely chopped)
1 small bell pepper (chopped)
1/4 c. celery (finely chopped)

1/2 can (10-1/2-ounce) beef broth
1 T. brown sugar
1 to 2 tsp. Worcestershire sauce
1/2 tsp. chili powder
1/8 tsp. black pepper
Dash of garlic powder
Paprika
Low-fat cheddar cheese (optional)

After draining tomatoes and reserving juice, add enough hot water to tomato juice to equal 1 cup. Combine all ingredients, except paprika, in a large skillet or saute pan. Bring to boil. Reduce heat and simmer, covered, for 15 to 20 minutes. Spoon mixture into a 10-inch pie plate or a 13x9x2-inch baking dish, lightly sprayed with cooking spray. Sprinkle with paprika. Bake, covered, at 350 degrees for 25 to 30 minutes. May lightly sprinkle with shredded cheddar cheese if desired. (Fat: less than 20% calories from fat)

— Karen Cooper, Flat Rock, NC

— Microwave Rice Dish —
(6 servings)

1-2/3 c. water
1/4 c. onion (grated)
1 tsp. low-calorie margarine
1/4 tsp. salt
1/4 tsp. pepper

1-1/2 c. uncooked instant rice
1 medium tomato (peeled, seeded, and chopped)
2 T. fresh parsley (chopped)
2 T. unsalted sunflower kernels (toasted)

Combine first 5 ingredients in a 2-quart casserole. Stir in rice and tomato. Cover with heavy-duty plastic wrap and microwave on high for 8 to 10 minutes or until liquid is absorbed. Let stand 2 minutes. Fluff rice with a fork. Sprinkle parsley and sunflower kernels over rice. (Fat: approx. 25% calories from fat)

— Standard Rice Pilaf —
(6 servings)

1 c. brown rice (uncooked)
2 stalks celery (chopped)
1 medium onion (chopped)
2 T. reduced-calorie margarine

1 can (4-ounce) small mushrooms (whole)
1 can (10-3/4-ounce) beef consomme
1/4 tsp. fresh-ground black pepper
1-1/4 c. water

Combine all ingredients in a 1-1/2-quart casserole dish. Cook, covered, at 350 degrees for 1 hour. (Fat: less than 30% calories from fat)

— Zucchini-Rice Supper —
(8 servings)

1-1/2 pounds lean ground beef
1/2 c. green pepper (diced)
1/2 c. celery (chopped)
1/2 c. onion (chopped)
1/2 tsp. garlic powder
1/4 tsp. salt (optional)
1/4 tsp. black pepper
2 c. zucchini (diced)

2 T. dried parsley
1 c. quick rice (uncooked)
1/4 tsp. oregano
6 ounces of no-salt tomato paste
3 c. water
1 c. bread crumbs
1/4 c. Parmesan cheese
1 tsp. reduced-calorie margarine

Preheat oven to 450 degrees. Brown ground beef in large skillet. Drain. Add green peppers, celery, onions, and garlic powder. Cook until vegetables are tender. Stir in salt, pepper, zucchini, parsley, rice, oregano, tomato paste, and water. Bring to boil. Simmer 20 minutes, covered. Pour mixture into 3-quart baking dish. Sprinkle with bread crumbs and Parmesan cheese and dot with margarine. Bake for 15 minutes or microwave on high for 8 to 10 minutes until cheese and margarine melt and crumbs brown. Freezes well. (Fat: 23% calories from fat)

— Nutty Rice and Vegetables —
(4 servings)

1/2 c. brown rice (uncooked)
1-1/2 c. water
1 tsp. chicken bullion granules
8 ounces fresh mushrooms (sliced)
3 carrots (matchstick-size cuts)

1/4 c. fresh parsley (chopped)
1/3 c. green onions (chopped)
1/4 tsp. black pepper
3 T. pecans (chopped)

Mix water and bouillon in a large saucepan and bring water to a boil. Add rice and let it come to a boil. Reduce heat and simmer 40 minutes or until done. Add next 5 ingredients. Mix. Cover and let simmer another 10 minutes. Sprinkle with pecans just before serving. (Fat: 30% calories from fat)

— Martha Elson, Anchorage, AK

Bean Dishes

— Bean Pie —
(4 servings)

1 medium zucchini (grated) — 2 cups
1 medium onion (grated) — 1/2 cup
1/2 c. low-fat Cheddar cheese (grated)
3 c. kidney beans (cooked)

2 T. hot picante sauce
2 cloves garlic (pressed)
1/2 tsp. canola oil
4 corn or flour tortillas

Grate zucchini and onion together and set aside. Grate cheese and set aside. Put beans in blender with picante sauce and garlic. Blend until almost smooth.

Put thin layer of blended bean mixture in bottom of an 8-inch iron skillet brushed with oil. Place 2 tortillas on top, breaking them as needed to cover bean mixture.

Layer half of the remaining beans with half of the zucchini and onions. Then add half the grated cheese. Cover with the last 2 tortillas and layer again until you end with cheese on top.

Bake at 350 degrees for about 35 minutes or until cheese on top begins to brown. (Fat: approx. 30% calories from fat)

— Bean Casserole —
(8 servings)

4 strips lean bacon
1 c. onion (chopped)
1 green pepper (diced)
2 T. reduced-calorie margarine
2 cans (15-ounce) pinto or kidney beans (drained)
4 tsp. chili powder

1 tsp. garlic powder
1 tsp. dried jalapeno pepper (optional)
1 can (14-ounce) chopped tomatoes or 2 cups fresh chopped tomatoes
1/2 c. part-skim American cheese (shredded)
1/2 c. part-skim Monterey Jack cheese (shredded)

Broil bacon until crisp. Crumble and set aside. Saute onion and pepper in margarine. Combine sauteed vegetables, beans, seasonings, and tomatoes in a 3-quart baking dish. Stir well. Bake for 35 minutes at 350 degrees. Sprinkle with cheeses and crumbled bacon and bake for 5 more minutes. Serve. Freezes well. (Fat: 28% calories from fat)

— Black Bean Stir-Fry —
(8 servings)

1 tsp. canola oil
1 pound lean pork tenderloin (cut in strips)
2 T. chili powder
1 small onion (chopped)
1/4 tsp. garlic powder

1 can (16-ounce) black beans (drained)
1 pint cherry tomatoes (halved)
1 c. frozen corn (thawed)
1 T. lemon juice
1/4 tsp. salt (optional)

Heat oil in large skillet over medium heat. Stir-fry pork with chili powder until pork is browned and cooked thoroughly (3 to 5 minutes). Set pork aside. Add onion and garlic powder to pan and stir-fry for 1 minute. Add remaining ingredients and stir-fry for 3 more minutes. Stir in pork, heat through and serve. (May be frozen and reheated in microwave.) (Fat: 18% calories from fat)

— Bean Dip —
(12 servings)

2 c. cooked, pureed black beans or pinto beans

1 c. spicy salsa

Combine ingredients until well blended. Serve with corn chips and whole-wheat flour tortillas. (Using vegetarian refried beans and ready-made salsa will make this a quick fix.) (Fat: 4% calories from fat)

— Arizona Pinto Beans —

2 small cans of pinto beans
1 small bell pepper (chopped)
1 small onion, Vidalia if possible, (chopped)

Ham-flavored seasoning to taste
Jalapeno peppers to taste (finely chopped)
Black pepper to taste

Combine all ingredients and bring to a boil. Simmer on low until tender and flavors are blended. (Fat: approx. 30% calories from fat)

— *Margie Hopkins, Vidalia, GA*

— Basic Kidney Beans —
(makes 2-3/4 quarts)

1 pound dry red kidney or pinto beans
2 stalks celery
1 large yellow onion (quartered)

2 cloves garlic (peeled)
1 tsp. salt

Thoroughly wash beans. Drain. In a small stock pot, combine beans with 2 quarts water. Cover and bring to a boil. Remove from heat. Set aside 1 hour. Drain.

Return beans to stock pot with 2 quarts fresh water, celery, onion, and garlic. Cook 20 minutes. Add salt. Cook 15 minutes or until beans are tender. Drain. Discard celery, onion, and garlic.

Serve as a vegetable side dish or as a base for chili, refried beans or red bean dip. (Fat: 4% calories from fat)

— Spicy Pinto Beans Tortillas —
(6 servings)

1-1/2 c. dried pinto beans
4 c. water
1 can (4-ounce) chopped green chiles (undrained)
1/3 c. green onions (chopped)
1/2 tsp. salt
1/2 tsp. dried Italian seasoning

6 (6-inch) corn tortillas
3 c. shredded lettuce
1 small tomato (chopped)
1 c. (4 ounces) part-skim Monterey Jack cheese (shredded)
1/4 c. plus 2 T. plain, nonfat yogurt

Sort and wash pinto beans and place in large Dutch oven. Add water to cover and let beans soak overnight.

Drain beans. Return to Dutch oven and add 4 cups water. Add green chiles and next 3 ingredients. Stir well. Bring to boil. Cover. Reduce heat and simmer 1-1/2 hours. Pour 1 cup of bean mixture into blender or food processor and blend until smooth. Return this mixture to Dutch oven. Cover and simmer 30 minutes. Uncover and simmer an additional 15 to 20 minutes or until mixture thickens. Stir frequently.

Wrap tortillas in aluminum foil. Bake at 350 degrees for 10 minutes or until thoroughly heated. Unwrap and spread 1/2 cup bean mixture over each tortilla. To serve, place 1/2 cup shredded lettuce on each tortilla. Sprinkle chopped tomato and cheese evenly over them. Top each with 1 tablespoon nonfat yogurt. Serve immediately. (Fat: approx. 30% calories from fat)

— Ryland's Chili —

1/2 pound very lean ground beef (double ground)
1/2 c. onion (chopped)
1 clove garlic (minced)
3 cans (8-ounce) tomato sauce

1 can (26-ounce) Hanover light red kidney beans
1/4 tsp. black pepper
2 tsp. chili powder
1-1/2 tsp. cumin

Brown ground beef in heavy saucepan. Drain. Add onion and garlic. Cook until tender. Add remaining ingredients and simmer 30 minutes, stirring occasionally. (Fat: less than 30% calories from fat)

— Ryland Chesser, Anderson, SC

— Chili Con Carne —

1 can (28-ounce) plum tomatoes (diced)
2 T. cider vinegar
1 T. pure ground chili powder (mild)
1/8 tsp. ground cumin
1/8 tsp. cayenne pepper
1/8 tsp. black pepper
1/8 tsp. oregano

1/2 tsp. paprika
1/2 tsp. salt
1 pound extra-lean ground round (browned and drained)
2 cans (15-ounce) red kidney beans with liquid

In a saucepan, combine tomatoes, vinegar, and seasonings. Heat to boiling but do not boil. Add ground beef. Simmer, uncovered, for 45 minutes. Add kidney beans. Heat and serve. (Fat: 26% calories from fat)

— Black Beans and Corn —
(4 servings)

1 T. plus 1 tsp. canola oil
1 c. onions (chopped)
1 c. carrots (diced)
1 c. celery (chopped)
2 cloves garlic (minced)
1/4 tsp. dried thyme

1/4 tsp. oregano
1 c. water
1 packet instant chicken-flavored broth mix
1 tsp. Worcestershire sauce
1 package (10-ounce) frozen corn (thawed)
12 ounces cooked black beans

Heat oil in a large nonstick skillet over medium heat. Add onions, carrots, celery, and garlic. Cook until vegetables are tender, adding small amounts of water as necessary to prevent drying. Reduce heat to low.

Add remaining ingredients, cover and cook until heated thoroughly. Stir occasionally. (Fat: less than 25% calories from fat)

— Zesty Lima Beans —
(8 servings)

1 tsp. plus 1 T. olive oil
1/2 c. onion (finely chopped)
1 medium clove garlic (peeled and minced)
1 medium carrot (peeled and minced)
1 medium rib celery (minced)
1 can (16-ounce) tomatoes

1/8 tsp. hot red chili flakes
Black pepper to taste
1 pkg. (16-ounce) frozen lima beans (defrosted)
1/4 c. parsley (minced)
1/3 c. bread crumbs
2 T. Parmesan cheese (finely grated)

Heat 1 teaspoon olive oil in a nonstick skillet over medium heat. Add onion, garlic, carrot, and celery. Saute until vegetables begin to soften. Break up tomatoes and add to the pan with the juice. Add chili flakes and pepper. Simmer until thickened (approx. 10 minutes). Stir in lima beans and cook 5 minutes. Test for tenderness. Stir in parsley and transfer to a baking dish. Combine bread crumbs and Parmesan. Sprinkle over top and drizzle with 1 tablespoon of oil. Bake in preheated 350-degree oven for 15 minutes. Turn oven to broil and toast the crumb topping. Let cool. (Fat: 20% calories from fat)

— Lentil Stew with Rice —
(4 servings)

2 T. (generous) reduced-calorie margarine
1 c. onions (chopped)
1 c. celery (chopped)
2 cans (1-pound) tomatoes (undrained, chopped)
2 c. water

6 ounces lentils (uncooked)
4 ounces brown rice (uncooked)
1/2 tsp. dried thyme
1/4 tsp. garlic powder
Salt and pepper to taste

Melt margarine in large nonstick skillet over medium heat. Add onions and celery and cook until tender (approx. 10 minutes). Add water if necessary to prevent drying. Reduce heat to low.

Add remaining ingredients. Cover and cook 40 minutes, stirring occasionally. Add small amounts of water while cooking if more liquid is desired. (Fat: 20% calories from fat)

— Hoppin' John —
(4 servings)

6 ounces dry black-eyed peas
1 T. plus 1 tsp. canola oil
1 c. chopped onions
2 cloves garlic (minced)
1-1/2 c. water

1/2 tsp. dried thyme
1 bay leaf
Salt and pepper to taste
2 c. cooked brown rice

Place peas in large bowl. Add 3 to 4 cups water and soak overnight.

Heat oil in large saucepan over medium heat. Add onions and garlic. Saute until tender (approx. 10 minutes). Add small amounts of water, if necessary, to prevent drying. Reduce heat to low.

Rinse and drain peas. Add to saucepan.

Add 1-1/2 cups water and remaining ingredients, except rice. Cover and simmer 30 minutes, until peas are tender. Add rice. Cook 10 minutes, stirring occasionally. Remove from heat and discard bay leaf before serving. (Fat: 25% calories from fat)

— Lentil Loaf —

12 ounces cooked lentils
2-1/4 ounces wheat germ
1/2 c. onions (finely chopped)
2 eggs (beaten)
1/2 c. tomato sauce
1/4 tsp. dried basil

1/4 tsp. dried thyme
Salt and pepper to taste
2 ounces low-fat Cheddar cheese (shredded)
   or Alpine Lace nonfat Cheddar
2 ounces part-skim mozzarella cheese (shredded)
   or Alpine Lace nonfat mozzarella

Preheat oven to 350 degrees.

Place lentils in large bowl and mash lightly, using a fork or potato masher.

Add remaining ingredients. Mix well.

Place mixture in a 4x8-inch loaf pan that has been sprayed with a nonstick cooking spray. Bake 30 minutes until firm. (Fat: less than 30% calories from fat)

— Barbecue Beans —
(4 servings)

2 T. (generous) reduced-calorie
  margarine
1/2 c. onions (chopped)
1/2 c. green pepper (chopped)
1 clove garlic (minced)
1 can (8-ounce) tomato sauce

1 tsp. Worcestershire sauce
1 T. molasses
1/2 tsp. dry mustard
1 T. sweet pickle relish
2 T. water
8 ounces kidney or pinto beans (cooked)

Melt margarine in large nonstick skillet over medium heat. Add onions, green pepper, and garlic. Saute until tender (approx. 10 minutes).

Stir in remaining ingredients, adding beans last.

Reduce heat to low. Cover and cook 10 minutes, stirring occasionally. Serving suggestion: serve over rice or noodles. (Fat: 25% calories from fat)

— Dressed-Up Lima Beans —
(4 servings)

1 package (10-ounce) frozen baby lima beans
1/2 c. frozen whole kernel corn
Nonstick cooking spray
1 T. onion (diced)
2 tsp. green pepper (diced)
1/4 c. no-salt tomato sauce

3 T. vinegar
1 T. brown sugar
1 T. pimento (diced)
1 T. Worcestershire sauce
2 tsp. prepared mustard
1/2 tsp. chili powder

Combine lima beans and corn in medium saucepan. Cook according to package directions, omitting salt. Drain and set aside.

Coat medium nonstick skillet with cooking spray. Place over medium heat until hot. Add onion and green pepper. Saute until tender. Stir in tomato sauce and next 6 ingredients. Reduce heat and simmer 5 minutes. Stir in lima beans and corn. Bring to boil. Cover. Reduce heat and simmer 5 minutes. (Fat: 0.6 grams per serving)

— Peppers Stuffed with Beans —
(6 servings)

6 medium green peppers
12 ounces cooked chick peas (garbanzo beans)
1/4 c. onions (finely minced)
1/2 c. celery (finely minced)
1/2 c. carrots (finely shredded)
1/8 tsp. garlic powder

1/4 tsp. ground cumin
1/4 tsp. dried oregano
1/2 c. tomato sauce
Salt and pepper to taste
3 T. dry bread crumbs
2 T. reduced-calorie margarine

Preheat oven to 350 degrees. Slice off top of each pepper. Finely chop the slice and remove seeds from peppers.

Place peppers in a pot of boiling water. Boil 5 minutes. Remove peppers from water and drain, upside down, on paper towels.

Mash beans, using fork or potato masher. Add chopped peppers, onions, celery, carrots, spices, and tomato sauce. Mix well.

Fill green peppers with bean mixture. Sprinkle evenly with bread crumbs. Dot with margarine. Place peppers in shallow baking pan that has been sprayed with nonstick cooking spray. Bake, uncovered, for 30 minutes. (Fat: less than 30% calories from fat)

Pasta Dishes

— Zucchini Lasagna Bake —
(4 servings)

1 onion (chopped)
1 green pepper (chopped)
4 ounces mushrooms (sliced)
1/2 tsp. canola oil
4 small zucchini (peeled and thinly sliced lengthwise)
1 pound lean ground beef (browned and drained)
8 ounces no-salt tomato sauce

1/4 tsp. garlic powder
1/4 tsp. fennel
1/4 tsp. pepper
1 tsp. basil
1/2 tsp. oregano
2/3 c. nonfat cottage cheese
2 ounces skim mozzarella cheese (shredded)
1/3 c. Parmesan cheese

Preheat oven to 375 degrees. Saute onion, pepper, and mushrooms in oil in a Dutch oven or microwave 4 minutes in a 2-quart casserole dish. Steam zucchini for 6 minutes on stove top or microwave with 1 tablespoon water for 8 minutes in covered container.

Stir meat, tomato sauce, and seasonings into sauteed vegetables. Combine cottage and mozzarella cheeses in separate bowl. Spray 8-inch square baking dish with nonstick cooking spray. Layer zucchini, cheeses, and meat sauce twice. Sprinkle Parmesan cheese over top layer. Bake for 45 minutes or microwave 20 minutes. (Fat: 30% calories from fat)

— Pasta 'N Broccoli Sauce —
(4 servings)

3 small bunches broccoli
4 garlic cloves (peeled)
1/4 tsp. salt (optional)
1/4 tsp. pepper

3 T. plus 1 tsp. fresh Parmesan (grated)
1 c. skim milk
8 ounces thin spaghetti

Bring 2 large pots of water to a boil over high heat. Cut the florets off the top of each head of broccoli. Pull off and discard leaves on stems, then peel stems to remove outer layer. Cut stems into 1/4-inch slices. Cook florets and stems with garlic in one pot of boiling water for about 15 minutes or until broccoli is very tender but still bright green. Drain well and transfer to a blender or food processor. Add salt and pepper along with 2 tablespoons of Parmesan and the milk. Blend until smooth. Scrape into a medium saucepan and warm over low heat.

Cook spaghetti in other pot of boiling water to desired degree of doneness. Drain and divide between 4 plates. Pour some of sauce over each portion of spaghetti and top with remaining Parmesan (1 teaspoon per portion). (Fat: less than 25% calories from fat)

— Cheesy Macaroni —
(4 servings)

1/2 c. sharp low-fat Cheddar cheese (grated)
  (or use Alpine Lace Cheddar — no fat)
1-1/2 T. cornstarch
1-1/2 c. skim milk
1/2 c. grated Parmesan cheese
1/4 c. no-fat cottage cheese
1/2 c. onion (finely chopped)
1 tsp. dry mustard

1/2 teaspoon seasoned salt substitute
1/8 teaspoon pepper
2 dashes hot sauce (optional)
8 ounces macaroni (cooked and drained)
Nonstick cooking spray
2 T. seasoned bread crumbs
1/4 tsp. paprika

Mix cornstarch and milk in a saucepan. Bring to a low boil. Reduce heat, stirring constantly with a wire whisk, until slightly thickened. Remove from heat.

To this mixture, add Cheddar and Parmesan cheeses with cottage cheese, onion, mustard, salt substitute, pepper, hot sauce, and cooked macaroni. Mix well.

Coat an 8-inch square baking dish with cooking spray. Pour mixture into pan and top with bread crumbs and paprika. Bake at 350 degrees for 30 minutes. (Fat: 30% calories from fat)

— Martha Elson, Anchorage, Alaska

— Vegetable Medley Lasagna —
(6 servings)

6 ounces lasagna noodles (6-7, halved)
1 can (1-lb.) plum tomatoes
1 T. canola oil
1 medium onion (chopped)
2 cloves garlic (minced or pressed)
1/4 lb. (1/2 c.) zucchini (chopped)
1/4 lb. (1/2 c.) broccoli (chopped)

1/4 tsp. oregano
1/4 tsp. dried basil
1/4 tsp. garlic powder
1/4 tsp. black pepper
1/4 tsp. dried red pepper (crushed)
1-1/2 c. low-fat cottage cheese
2 T. Parmesan cheese

Prepare lasagna noodles according to package directions, but do not add salt to cooking water. Drain noodles and place in a single layer on a large tray.

Drain and chop tomatoes. Reserve liquid. Heat oil in a large skillet. Saute onion and garlic until golden brown. Add zucchini, broccoli, tomatoes, tomato liquid, and seasonings. Simmer, covered, for 10 minutes, stirring occasionally.

In a round, 2-quart baking dish, layer sauce, noodles, and cottage cheese, beginning and ending with sauce layer. Sprinkle with parmesan cheese. Bake 25 minutes at 350 degrees. (Fat: less than 30% calories from fat)

— Ravioli With Lite Sauce —
(4 servings)

16 ounces cheese ravioli
1 c. nonfat cottage cheese
1/4 c. evaporated skim milk
1 tsp. dried rosemary
1/4 tsp. salt

1/4 tsp. pepper
2 tsp. fresh lemon juice
3 T. fresh chives (chopped)
4 T. grated Parmesan cheese

(Continued)

Cook ravioli according to package directions. Meanwhile, in a blender or food processor, puree next 5 ingredients until smooth. Set aside.

Drizzle lemon juice over drained ravioli. Add sauce. Toss lightly. Serve with chives and Parmesan cheese. (Fat: 24% calories from fat)

— Macaroni and Cheese —
(4 servings)

2 c. macaroni noodles (cooked and drained)
2 T. reduced-calorie margarine
1 T. whole-wheat flour
1/2 tsp. dry mustard (optional)
1/2 tsp. salt

Dash of pepper
1-1/4 c. skim milk
1/4 c. chopped onion (optional)
1-1/2 c. nonfat Alpine Lace Cheddar cheese

Preheat oven to 350 degrees.

Melt margarine in saucepan. Blend in flour, mustard, salt and pepper. Add milk. Stir. Cook until thick and bubbly. Remove from heat. Add onion and cheese and stir well.

Mix cheese sauce with noodles. Place in 1-quart casserole dish and cover. Bake 35-40 minutes. (Fat: less than 30% calories from fat)

— Hot Macaroni Tuna —
(6 servings)

1 c. elbow macaroni
1/4 c. prepared Italian dressing
1 tsp. celery seed
3/4 tsp. dry mustard
1/8 tsp. pepper

1/2 tsp. salt
1 can (7-ounce) tuna (drained and rinsed)
1/2 c. celery (chopped)
1/2 c. green pepper (chopped)
3 T. fat-free mayonnaise

Bring 1 quart of water to full boil. Add macaroni and cook until tender (about 8 minutes). Drain and rinse. Combine salad dressing and seasonings in a skillet and heat to boiling. Add macaroni, tuna, celery, and green pepper and toss. Continue to heat until heated through. Remove from burner and stir in mayonnaise. (Fat: less than 30% calories from fat)

— Chicken-Noodle Bake —
(8 servings)

1 package (8-ounce) medium egg noodles
  (uncooked)
1/4 c. fresh parsley (chopped)
Nonstick cooking spray
1/2 c. onion (chopped)
2 cloves garlic (minced)
1 can (28-ounce) no-salt whole tomatoes
  (undrained)
1 can (8-ounce) no-salt tomato sauce
1/4 tsp. ground oregano

1/4 tsp. pepper
1/3 c. fine, dry bread crumbs
3 T. Parmesan cheese (grated)
1 egg (beaten)
1 T. water
6 chicken breast halves (4-ounces each) —
  skinned, boned, and cut into 1-inch pieces
1 T. canola oil
1/2 c. (2 ounces) part-skim mozzarella cheese
  (shredded)   *(Continued)*

Cook noodles according to package directions, omitting fat and salt. Drain. Stir in parsley and set aside.

Coat large nonstick skillet with cooking spray. Place over medium-high heat until hot. Add chopped onion and garlic. Saute until tender. Set aside.

Drain tomatoes. Reserve 1/2 cup liquid. Coarsely chop tomatoes. Add tomatoes, 1/2 cup tomato liquid, tomato sauce, oregano, and pepper to reserved onion mixture. Set aside.

Combine bread crumbs and Parmesan cheese in small bowl. Combine egg and water in small bowl. Dip chicken in egg mixture. Then dredge in bread crumb mixture.

Coat large nonstick skillet with cooking spray. Add oil. Place over medium-high heat until hot. Add chicken and cook 3 to 5 minutes or until lightly browned.

Coat a 13x9x2-inch baking dish with cooking spray. Spoon noodles into dish. Arrange chicken over noodles. Pour reserved tomato mixture over chicken. Sprinkle with mozzarella cheese. Bake, uncovered, at 350 degrees for 25 minutes. (Fat: 30% calories from fat)

NOTE: All pasta recipes calling for Ricotta cheese can be made lighter by using nonfat cottage cheese instead of Ricotta.

— Garden Lasagna —
(8 servings)

Nonstick cooking spray
1 c. onion (chopped)
2/3 c. green pepper (chopped)
2 cloves garlic (minced)
2 c. zucchini (coarsely chopped)
1-1/2 c. tomato (peeled and chopped)
1-1/2 c. fresh mushrooms (sliced)
1/2 c. carrot (shredded)
1/2 c. celery (chopped)
1-1/4 c. no-salt tomato sauce
1 can (6-ounce) no-salt tomato paste

1 T. plus 1-1/2 tsp. red wine vinegar
1 tsp. dried whole basil
1/2 tsp. dried Italian seasoning
1/2 tsp. salt
1/2 tsp. pepper
1 bay leaf
6 lasagna noodles (uncooked)
1-1/2 c. nonfat cottage cheese
1 c. (4 ounces) part-skim mozzarella cheese
  (shredded and divided)
1 T. Parmesan cheese (grated)

Coat a large Dutch oven with cooking spray. Place over medium-high heat until hot. Add onion, green pepper, and garlic and saute until tender. Add zucchini and next 12 ingredients. Cover and bring to boil. Reduce heat and simmer 20 to 30 minutes, stirring occasionally. Remove and discard bay leaf. Set aside.

Cook noodles according to package directions, omitting salt and fat. Drain noodles. Set aside.

Combine cottage cheese and 1/2 cup mozarella cheese in a small bowl. Stir well.

Coat an 11x7x1-1/2-inch baking dish with cooking spray. Spoon 2 cups reserved vegetable mixture into dish. Layer 1/3 each of lasagna noodles, cheese mixture, and vegetable mixture. Repeat layers twice. Cover and bake at 350 degrees for 25 minutes. Uncover and sprinkle with remaining 1/2 cup mozzarella cheese and Parmesan cheese. Bake an additional 10 minutes. Let lasagna stand 10 minutes before serving. (Fat: approx. 30% calories from fat)

— Pasta, Cheese, 'N Tomatoes —
(6 servings)

2 c. low-fat Cheddar cheese (cubed)
1 c. skim evaporated milk
1 T. Dijon mustard
2-1/2 c. elbow macaroni (cooked until tender)

1/2 tsp. dried basil
1 can (16-ounce) plum tomatoes with liquid (diced)
1 T. bread crumbs

In medium saucepan, combine cheese, milk, and mustard. Cook over low heat, stirring constantly, until cheese melts. Add pasta and mix well. Add basil to tomatoes.

In an ovenproof baking dish, layer 1/3 of the macaroni and cheese. Top with 1/3 of the tomato mixture. Repeat layers, ending with macaroni and cheese but reserving a generous dollop of the tomatoes to put in center of the top layer. Sprinkle with bread crumbs. Bake, covered, at 350 degrees for 30 minutes or until mixture is hot and bubbly. (Fat: 22% calories from fat)

— Traditional Macaroni 'N Cheese —
(6 servings)

2 c. low-fat Cheddar cheese (grated) — or substitute Alpine Lace no-fat Cheddar cheese
2 c. macaroni (cooked)
3/4 c. evaporated skim milk

2 T. onion (finely chopped)
2 T. fresh parsley (chopped)
1 tsp. salt
1/4 tsp. white pepper
Paprika for topping

Coat a shallow 3-quart casserole dish with nonstick cooking spray. Reserve half of cheese for topping. Combine remaining ingredients in dish. Top with reserved cheese and sprinkle with paprika. Broil in oven until light brown (about five minutes). (Fat: 26% calories from fat)

— Easy Pasta Mix —
(makes 8 cups)

1 medium onion (chopped)
1-2 cloves garlic (minced)
Nonstick cooking spray
3 c. beef or chicken stock or broth or 3 c. water with 3 bouillon cubes
1 can (8-ounce) sliced mushrooms with liquid

1 box (12-ounce) of pasta (try a garden trio)
1 can (19-ounce) garbanzo beans
1/2 c. parsley (optional)
1-2 c. cooked vegetables of choice
Salt and pepper to taste

Saute onion and garlic in a medium-large pot sprayed with nonstck cooking spray. Add a tablespoon or two of water or of the broth if onion and garlic begin to stick.

Add the stock or the water and bouillon cubes and bring to a boil. Add mushrooms with liquid and pasta. Cover and simmer for 20 to 25 minutes or until pasta is tender.

Add the garbanzo beans, parsley, and cooked vegetables. Season with salt and pepper. Toss and serve hot or chilled. (Fat: less than 20% calories from fat)

— Quick Marinara Sauce 'N Pasta —

1 can (2-lb.) plum tomatoes (diced)
2 T. tomato paste
1/4 tsp. oregano
1/2 tsp. dried basil
1/2 tsp. black pepper

1 T. olive oil
1/4 tsp. cider vinegar
1 package (1-lb.) spaghetti, rigatoni, rotini, or penne pasta (cooked until tender)

In medium saucepan, combine tomatoes, tomato paste, oregano, basil, and black pepper. Simmer 20 minutes (do not allow to boil). Stir in olive oil and vinegar. Simmer 10 minutes. Serve over pasta.

For variety: Add one 8-ounce can drained mushroom stems and pieces and one 15-ounce can drained artichoke hearts. (Fat: 10% calories from fat)

— Vegetable Lasagna —
(8 servings)

3 c. chunky-style bottled spaghetti sauce of choice
2 medium zucchini (shredded)
1 medium carrot (shredded)
6 lasagna noodles (uncooked)

1 c. nonfat cottage cheese
1/4 c. grated Parmesan cheese
1/2 tsp. dried oregano
2 c. Alpine Lace fat-free mozzarella cheese (shredded)

Mix spaghetti sauce, raw shredded zucchini with juices, and shredded carrot.

Spread 1 cup mixture in an ungreased oblong baking dish, 11x7x1-1/2 inches. Top with 3 uncooked noodles. Mix cottage cheese with Parmesan and oregano. Spread over noodles in dish. Spread with 1 cup sauce mixture.

Top with remaining uncooked noodles, sauce mixture, and the mozzarella cheese. Bake uncovered in a preheated oven (350 degrees) until hot and bubbly (about 45 minutes). Let stand 15 minutes before cutting. (Fat: less than 20% calories from fat)

— Beverly's Lasagna —
(12 servings)

1/2 pound lasagna noodles
1 medium onion (chopped)
2 cloves garlic (minced)
1 T. olive oil
Water as needed
1 pound nonfat cottage cheese
1/4 c. grated Parmesan
2 egg whites (beaten)

1/4 tsp. fresh-ground black pepper
2-3 T. fresh parsley (chopped)
Nonstick cooking spray
6 c. tomato or meatless spaghetti sauce of choice
6 ounces Alpine Lace fat-free mozzarella cheese (grated)

Cook lasagna noodles according to package directions. While noodles are cooking, saute onion and garlic in olive oil, adding a tablespoon or two of water as needed to keep from sticking. Combine the cottage cheese, Parmesan, egg whites, black pepper, parsley, and sauteed onion and garlic. Mix well.

(Continued)

Spray a 9x13x2-inch casserole dish with nonstick cooking spray. Spread 1/4 of tomato or spaghetti sauce over bottom and then arrange a layer of noodles. Top with 1/3 of cheese mixture. Sprinkle with 1/3 of mozzarella and then top with tomato sauce. Repeat layers twice more, ending with sauce.

Cover pan with aluminum foil, crimping edges tightly. Bake at 350 degrees for 40 minutes. Remove foil and bake 10 to 15 minutes more. (Fat: less than 30% calories from fat)

Note: Always use cheeses that are as low in fat as you can find them.

— Beverly Chesser, Anderson, SC

— Pasta 'N Lentils —
(8 servings)

Nonstick cooking spray
1 tsp. olive oil
1 c. onion (diced)
1 c. carrot (diced)
2/3 c. celery (diced)
3 c. canned no-salt chicken broth (undiluted)
1 c. dried lentils

1 bay leaf
1/4 tsp. salt
1/4 tsp. pepper
10 ounces fresh Parmesan cheese (grated)
2 T. fresh parsley (minced)
1 T. fresh basil (chopped)

Coat a large nonstick skillet with cooking spray. Add oil. Place over medium heat until hot. Add onion, carrot, and celery. Cook until vegetables are tender but still crisp. Stir in chicken broth, lentils, and bay leaf. Bring mixture to a boil. Cover and reduce heat. Simmer 25 minutes or until lentils are tender. Remove an discard bay leaf. Stir in salt and pepper.

Cook pasta according to package directions omitting salt and fat. Combine pasta, lentil mixture, and remaining ingredients. Toss well. (Fat: approx. 30% calories from fat)

— Lasagna With Meat —
(12 servings)

1 pound lean ground chuck
1 can (16-oz.) stewed tomatoes (undrained)
1/2 c. water
1 clove garlic (minced)
2 tsp. dried whole Italian herb seasoning
1 package (8-oz.) whole-wheat lasagna
   noodles

1 package (10-oz.) frozen chopped spinach
1 c. nonfat cottage cheese
2 T. grated Parmesan cheese
1 T. dried parsley flakes
1/2 tsp. oregano
Nonstick cooking spray
1 c. (4-oz.) fat-free cheese of choice (shredded)

Cook ground chuck in a medium skillet over medium heat until browned. Drain and pat dry with paper towels. Wipe skillet with paper towel.

Return meat to skillet and stir in tomatoes, water, garlic, and Italian herb seasoning. Cover and bring to boil. Reduce heat and simmer 20 minutes.

Cook noodles according to package directions, omitting salt and fat. Drain well and set aside.

Cook spinach according to package directions, omitting salt and fat. Drain well and squeeze excess moisture from spinach. Combine spinach and next 4 ingredients, stirring until well combined. Set mixture aside.

(Continued)

Place half of cooked noodles in a 12x8x2-inch baking dish coated with cooking spray. Top with half each of cottage cheese mixture and other cheese. Spread half of meat mixture over top.

Repeat layers with remaining cooked noodles, cottage cheese mixture, shredded cheese, and meat mixture. Bake at 350 degrees for 30 minutes. Let stand 10 minutes before serving. (Fat: less than 30% calories from fat)

— Macaroni 'N Chili —

1 large onion (chopped)

1 pound extra-lean ground beef

2 cans tomato sauce

1 can tomato soup

1 can red kidney beans

2 soup cans of water

1 T. chili powder

1 tsp. allspice

1 c. elbow macaroni

Brown onion in small amount of olive oil (1

tablespoon). Add ground beef and brown. Drain off excess fat. Add tomato sauce, soup, kidney beans, water, chili powder, and allspice. Bring to boil, reduce heat, simmer 30 minutes. Add macaroni. Cook, stirring often, until macaroni is tender. Let stand few minutes before serving. (Fat: less than 30% calories from fat)

— Harriet Cottingham, Charleston Heights, SC

— Baked Macaroni 'N Cheese —

2 T. reduced-calorie margarine

1/8 c. flour

1 tsp. salt

1/2 tsp. dry mustard

1/4 tsp. pepper

2-1/2 c. skim milk

2 c. Free 'N Lean Alpine Lace Cheddar Cheese (shredded)

8 ounces elbow macaroni (cooked 6 minutes and drained)

Bread crumbs (to sprinkle on top)

In a 2-quart saucepan, melt margarine over low heat. Stir in flour, salt, mustard, and pepper until smooth and add a little milk. Gradually add remainder of milk and stir constantly. Add about 1/2 of the Cheddar cheese and continue stirring until mixture comes to a boil. Turn macaroni into a 2-quart casserole that has been sprayed with a nonfat spray. Pour cheese mixture over macaroni. Place the remaining cheese on top and sprinkle with bread crumbs. Bake in 375-degree oven for 20 to 25 minutes or until topping is lightly browned. (Fat: less than 20% calories from fat)

— Beverly Chesser, Anderson, SC

6

Meats, Fish, & Poultry

Introduction

Following is a letter from a precious young lady who listens to my radio program on WLFJ in Greenville, South Carolina:

Dear Beverly,

I am a full-time student at college and work 30 hours during the school week and full time during the summer. Three years ago, I lost 40 pounds. I rarely exercise . . . and have little energy. I know the Lord is showing me a need to take care of my whole person.

This morning, after listening to *Your Health Coach* program, I left for a class I'm taking and upon requesting prayer for strength (we pray before class) my professor said the Lord had shown him Luke 2:52 and confronted him with caring for his physical as well as spiritual being.

I'm seeking some sources for both diet and exercise that can help me please God in my outer man as well as inner man. I appreciate your help . . .

Beverly's reply:

Thank you so much for your letter. I am so glad you are able to listen to my program on WLFJ.

You certainly do have an exhausting schedule and if there is anyone who needs to eat right and exercise to keep up that pace, it has to be you. You tell me that you exercise rarely. That certainly explains your low energy level. I don't know what your meals are like, but you certainly need to be following a low-fat diet. I believe my book, *Your Health Coach,* would be a good source of material for you. Also, I do hope you can continue listening to my daily programs as they contain a lot of information.

I have enclosed a low-fat bulletin which just gives you an idea of low-fat foods. There is so much more in my book.

I would like to suggest that you immediately make some time for exercise.

Try to work in a brisk 30-minute walk every day. It will help give you so much more energy.

I like the Bible verse your professor gave you. I immediately looked it up.

"And Jesus increased in wisdom and stature and in favor with God and man" (Luke 2:52).

He matured four ways: in wisdom (mentally); in stature (physically); in favor with God (spiritually); and in favor with man (socially). We, too, need to increase in all these ways.

God bless you, my sweet friend. I am praying for God's guidance in your life and strength for you.

Proper Maintenance —

Perhaps you can identify with this young lady — going to college full time and working 30 hours per week. Just going to school full time is the same as holding a full-time job by the time you study and get all your assignments done.

Our bodies are wonderfully made by God Almighty. However, they do require proper maintenance. How about you? Are you feeding your body properly? Are you getting enough sleep? We cannot indefinitely ignore our health without experiencing serious problems in our whole person. Fatigue, loss of energy — such problems are just warning signs of serious health risks to our bodies. God expects us to take care of our bodies — His holy temples.

God wants you in health today.

Beloved, I wish above all things that thou mayest prosper and be in health, even as thy soul prospereth (3 John 1:2).

Our Heavenly Father wants us to be healthy mentally, physically, and spiritually. Eating good, nutritious food and exercising regularly helps our physical bodies and our minds; while studying God's Word, meditating on it, and praying helps us spiritually and mentally.

Watching the Salt —

Have you been told to get your blood pressure down? What key words should we watch for when we need to avoid salt or sodium? Watch out for sodium as in sodium chloride or salt, sodium bicarbonate as in baking soda, and sodium citrate as in preservatives. These chemicals have long been black listed from a heart-healthy diet. The reason? Sodium is known to contribute to high blood pressure which often results in heart attack, stroke or kidney disease.

If you love salt and regularly include it in your diet, you are a candidate for high blood pressure. In a recent study of 10,000 people in 32 countries, it was confirmed that the higher the salt intake, the higher the blood pressure.

Many people with high blood pressure are salt-sensitive people. The best ways to control blood pressure problems are to cut back on salt intake and make life style changes in diet and exercise.

How much sodium should a person with high blood pressure consume? Such a person should reduce sodium intake to under 1,800 milligrams per day, that is less than 1 teaspoon per day. In addition, such a person should exercise regularly, but moderately, and keep weight within healthy limits.

Where does most of the sodium in our diets come from? It comes from the salt shaker on our tables. Overindulgence in salt will result in fluid retention and stress on the kidneys. Evidence also points to the possibility that a high-salt diet can damage blood vessels even when a person has no problems with high blood pressure.

However, the body cannot do without salt completely. Our bodies require a certain amount of salt in order for nerves and muscles to function properly and to keep blood volume and pressure normal. But we are talking about a tiny amount that is needed — less than a quarter of a teaspoon. This can easily be provided by a healthy diet.

The National Academy of Sciences advises normal, healthy people to limit their sodium intake to 2,400 milligrams or about 1-1/2 teaspoons per day. To do this, we need to eat a diet high in fresh fruits and vegetables, grains, fish, and low-fat dairy products.

Salt Hides in Condiments —
The following chart shows salt content in some of the most popular condiments:

Condiment	Sodium Per Teaspoon
Table salt	1,955 mg.
Lite salt	1,570 mg.
Low-sodium soy sauce	220 mg.
Dijon mustard	150 mg.
Green olive (minced)	74 mg.
Anchovy (minced)	74 mg.
Brown mustard	68 mg.
Sweet pickle (minced)	64 mg.
Parmesan cheese (grated)	39 mg.
Black olive (minced)	39 mg.
Butter flavor granules	28 mg.

The Number One Enemy —
Many overweight people claim they use no salt at all. Many of them focus so much on totally excluding sodium that their foods taste bland. So what do they do? They will be heavy on the fats such as butter, oil, and margarine in order to give taste to their food. This is counterproductive to say the least.

Always, the Number One Enemy in weight control is FAT. Lowering the fat in your diet is so important in controlling cholesterol and weight. Many high-fat foods are also high in salt and should not be eaten at all — salami, hot dogs, potato chips, and high-fat cheeses. Just cutting these foods completely from your diet will do your heart and weight a lot of good.

Foods of a low-fat diet are just naturally low in salt — unprocessed grains, fruits, vegetables, skim milk products, fresh lean meats, poultry, and fish. Eating a diet high in these foods also provides calcium and potassium, both of which are needed to control high blood pressure.

Removing the Fat From Chicken —

Is it myth or fact that we need to remove the skin from chicken before cooking it?

Now, all you cooks know that for a long time we were told to remove the skin from chicken before cooking if we wanted to reduce fat intake. But recent studies at the University of Minnesota revealed that it doesn't matter whether you remove the skin before or after cooking — just so you remove it.

You see, about one-half of the fat in poultry comes from the skin, BUT the fat is not transferred from the skin to the meat during cooking. If you skin poultry before cooking, you will have a much drier, tougher piece of meat — and not one bit leaner than if you wait until after it cooks. When you do remove the fat after cooking, however, be sure to remove ALL visible fat from the meat before you eat it.

What about other types of meat? Removing the fat from various cuts of beef before broiling or roasting eliminates only slightly more fat and calories than if you wait until after cooking to remove it. But no matter how you do it, the important thing it to throw the fat away before you eat the meat.

Tips for Red Meats —

— Always choose lean cuts such as flank steak, round steak, pork tenderloin, or center loin.

— In general, the higher the grade of meat the more fat it contains.

— No matter what cut you use of red meat, the fat in it will mostly be saturated and will be turned into cholesterol by your body.

— Trim all visible fat from all meats.

— Instead of gravy, try basting meats with broth, lemon juice, or cooking wine.

— Tomato products are also a great alternative to gravies.

— In most marinades, 3/4 of the oil can be removed and replaced with fruit juice, wine, broth, or water.

— When possible, brown ground meat or stew meat under the broiler so much of the fat can drip away.

— Cook meat and roasts on a rack by broiling, roasting, baking, or grilling.

— We all eat too much meat. Reduce the size of the meat portion you eat and add more grains and vegetables to your diet.

— Replace bacon with imitation bacon bits.

— Sausage and many lunch meats are extremely high in fat and salt. Try turkey sausages and lunch meats or other low-fat varieties.

Meats

— Pork Chops 'N Apples —
(4 servings)

4 lean, center-cut, 4-ounce pork chops (trimmed)
1 medium onion (chopped)
Nonstick cooking spray
1-1/4 c. water

1 tsp. chicken-flavored bouillon granules
1/4 tsp. pepper
3 medium cooking apples (peeled and sliced)
1/2 tsp. ground cinnamon

Brown pork chops and onion in a large skillet coated with cooking spray.

Combine water, bouillon granules, and pepper, stirring to dissolve. Add to skillet. Cover and bring to boil. Reduce heat and simmer 20 minutes. Skim off fat.

Add apple slices and cinnamon to mixture in skillet. Cover and simmer an additional 15 minutes. Transfer to a serving platter and serve hot. (Fat: less than 30% calories from fat)

— Veal Chops —
(4 servings)

4 small veal chops (cut from rump if possible)
2 T. fresh lemon juice
1/4 tsp. black pepper

1 T. fresh parsley (chopped)
1/2 fresh lemon (cut in wedges)

Arrange veal chops in a shallow dish. Sprinkle with lemon juice, black pepper, and parsley. Marinate 2 hours.

In a nonstick skillet over high heat, cook veal chops 2 to 3 minutes on each side. Remove veal to a platter. Squeeze a lemon wedge over each chop.(Fat: 29% calories from fat)

— Veal Parmigiana —
(6 servings)

1 egg substitute (beaten)
1/2 tsp. salt
1/4 tsp. pepper
1/4 c. soft breadcrumbs
1 T. Parmesan cheese (grated)
Nonstick cooking spray

1 pound thin veal cutlets (cut into 6 serving-size pieces)
1 can (8-ounce) tomato sauce
2 slices (1-ounce) part-skim mozzarella cheese (or Alpine Lace nonfat mozzarella cheese)

Combine egg, salt, and pepper. Beat with wire whisk until blended. Combine breadcrumbs and Parmesan cheese, stirring well. Dip veal into egg mixture and dredge in breadcrumb mixture.

Saute veal in large skillet coated with nonstick cooking spray until golden brown.

Transfer veal to shallow baking dish. Pour tomato sauce over veal and top with cheese slices. Bake at 350 degrees for 15 to 20 minutes. Serve immediately. (Fat: 30% calories from fat)

— Barbecued Sirloin —
(8 servings)

2 pounds sirloin or round, well trimmed
1/2 tsp. salt
1/4 tsp. pepper
1 tsp. canola oil
1/3 c. water
1 can (8-ounce) tomato sauce

1/2 c. onion (chopped)
1/2 tsp. garlic powder
2 tsp. lemon juice
2 tsp. vinegar
2 tsp. brown sugar
1 tsp. dry mustard

Place sirloin in a shallow pan. Combine remaining ingredients and pour over meat. Cover and marinate for at least 30 minutes in the refrigerator. Broil or grill sirloin for 12 minutes on each side, placing meat 4 inches from heating element. Brush with marinade during last 5 minutes of cooking. (Fat: 28% calories from fat)

— Lean Beef Stew —
(8 servings)

1 T. olive oil
3/4 pound lean beef (fat trimmed)
1 onion (chopped)
3 cloves garlic (minced)
1 can (14-1/2-ounces) reduced-salt chicken broth
1 can (16-ounce) whole peeled tomatoes
12 ounces low-fat beef broth

2 c. water
1/2 tsp. crushed red pepper
1/4 small cabbage (about 1/4 pound)
1/2 pound carrots
2 stalks celery
1 pound potato (peeled)
Black pepper to taste
1/2 T. soy sauce

Cut beef into bite-size cubes. In a heavy stew pot, heat olive oil. Add beef. When beef is browned, add onion, garlic, and a small amount of chicken broth. Simmer until onions and garlic are limp. Add tomatoes, beef broth, water, remaining chicken broth, red pepper, cabbage, and carrots. Bring to a boil and let simmer. Meanwhile chop celery and potatoes and add to mixture. Cook until potatoes and carrots are tender (about 45 minutes). Add soy sauce and pepper to taste. (Fat: 25% calories from fat)

— Green Pepper and Goulosh —
(4 servings)

1 pound lean, boneless chuck roast (trimmed and cut into 1-1/2 inch cubes)
Nonstick cooking spray
2 medium onions (chopped)

1 c. water
1 T. paprika
1 tsp. beef-flavored bouillon granules
1 small green pepper (chopped)

Brown roast over medium heat in a small Dutch oven coated with nonstick cooking spray.

Add onion and continue to cook over medium heat 2 to 3 minutes or until onion is tender. Add water, paprika, bouillon granules, and green pepper. Stir well.

Cover and cook over low heat 2 hours or until meat is very tender.

Serving suggestion: May be served hot over cooked noodles or rice cooked without salt or fat. (Fat: 30% calories from fat)

— Lean Meat Loaf —
(4 servings)

1/4 c. egg substitute
1/2 c. low-calorie catsup or 4-ounce can
   tomato sauce
1/4 c. onion (finely chopped)
2 T. green pepper (chopped)
1/2 tsp. salt substitute

Dash thyme (crushed)
Dash marjoram (crushed)
1/2 c. crushed cracker crumbs, dried bread
   crumbs, or leftover cooked rice
3/4 pound extra-lean ground beef

Combine all ingredients except ground beef and mix well. Add ground beef and mix well. Shape mixture into a loaf in 12x7-1/2x2-inch baking dish. Bake at 350 degrees for about 1-1/4 hours. (Fat: 30% calories from fat)

— Martha Elson, Anchorage, AK

— Teriyaki Beef Stir-Fry —

(4 servings)
3 T. teriyaki sauce
4 tsp. canola oil (divided)
2 tsp. cornstarch

1 pound top round of beef (cut in thin strips)
2 red, green, or yellow bell peppers (cut
   into 3/4-inch cubes)

6 green onions (cut into 2-inch slices)
Combine teriyaki sauce, 2 teaspoons oil, and cornstarch in a medium to large bowl.
Add beef strips and marinate in refrigerator for at least 45 minutes.
In a wok or skillet, stir-fry bell peppers and onions in 2 teaspoons oil for about 3 minutes. Remove from pan.
Stir-fry beef (half at a time) for 3 minutes.
Return vegetables to pan and cook until hot. Serve with rice and steamed broccoli. (Fat: 11 grams per serving)

— Steak in a Casserole —

(4 servings)
4 beef top or bottom round steaks (4 ounces
   each)
1 can (1-pound) tomatoes (chopped,
   undrained)
1 packet instant beef-flavored broth mix

1 T. minced onion flakes
1/2 tsp. dried oregano
1/8 tsp. garlic powder
1 T. wine vinegar
1 tsp. sugar (or equivalent in sweetener)

Salt and pepper to taste
Broil steaks on a rack until lightly browned on each side. Transfer to casserole.
Preheat oven to 350 degrees.
In medium bowl, combine remaining ingredients. Pour over steak.
Bake, uncovered, for 1 hour, until steaks are tender. (Fat: 30% calories from fat)

— Swiss Steak —
(6 servings)

1-1/2 pounds lean round steak (trimmed and cut into 6 serving-size pieces)
1 T. reduced-calorie margarine (melted)
1 can (16-ounce) stewed tomatoes (undrained)
1 small onion (sliced)
1 stalk celery (sliced)
1 medium carrot (scraped and thinly sliced)
1 tsp. Worcestershire sauce
1 T. all-purpose flour
1/2 tsp. salt
1/4 c. water

Place each piece of steak between two sheets of heavy-duty plastic wrap and flatten to 1/4-inch thickness using a meat mallet or rolling pin.

Brown meat on both sides in melted margarine in a large skillet. Drain off excess fat. Add stewed tomatoes, sliced onion, celery, carrot, and Worcestershire sauce to skillet. Cover and cook over low heat 1 hour and 15 minutes or until meat is tender. Transfer meat to a serving platter and keep warm.

Skim excess fat from tomato mixture. Combine flour and salt. Add water and stir until well blended. Stir into tomato mixture. Cook over medium heat, stirring frequently for 2 minutes or until thickened and bubbly.

Remove sauce mixture from heat and pour over meat. Serve immediately. (Fat: less than 30% calories from fat)

— Green Pepper Steak —
(6 servings)

1-1/2 pounds lean round steak (fat trimmed)
1 T. olive oil
5 T. low-sodium soy sauce
1 c. diced green peppers
1 c. chopped onions
3 c. water
Flour or cornstarch for thickening

Cut tenderized steak into bite-size cubes. Pour soy sauce over and stir to get to all sides of meat. Brown at high heat, stirring; then add onions and peppers and stir 2 minutes. Add 3 cups water and cover and simmer until tender. Thicken with flour or corn starch and serve over white cooked rice. (Fat: 30% calories from fat)
— *Harriet Cottingham, Charleston Heights, SC*

— Beef, Stir-Fried and Tasty —
(12 servings)

1 pound lean, boneless top round steak (trimmed)
2/3 c. water
1/4 c. onion (chopped)
3 T. reduced-salt soy sauce
1 tsp. beef-flavored bouillon granules
1 tsp. Worcestershire sauce
1 clove garlic (minced)
1/2 tsp. salt
1/8 tsp. pepper
2 medium carrots (scraped and diagonally sliced)
2 c. cauliflower flowerets
Nonstick cooking spray
1 c. fresh mushrooms (sliced)
1 package (16-ounce) frozen snow pea pods (partially thawed)
1/4 c. water
1 T. cornstarch

(Continued)

Partially freeze steak. Then slice diagonally across grain into 1/4-inch strips. Set aside.

Combine 2/3 cup water, onion, soy sauce, bouillon granules, Worcestershire sauce, garlic, salt, and pepper in a large bowl. Mix well. Add steak, stirring to coat. Cover and refrigerate 1 hour, stirring once. Drain steak, reserving marinade. Set steak aside.

Cook carrots and cauliflower in boiling water to cover, for 3 minutes. Drain and set aside.

Coat a wok or large skillet with cooking spray. Heat at medium high for 2 minutes. Add steak and stir-fry 3 minutes. Add mushrooms. Stir-fry 1 minute. Add pea pods, carrots, and cauliflower. Stir-fry 2 minutes or until vegetables are tender but still crisp. (Fat: 25% calories from fat)

— Teriyaki Beef Stir-Fry —
(4 servings)

3/4 pound flank steak (fat trimmed)
1/4 c. reduced-salt soy sauce
1/4 c. water
2 T. honey
1/2 tsp. ground ginger
4 cloves garlic (minced)
Nonstick cooking spray

1 tsp. canola oil
1 onion (chopped)
2 c. broccoli (chopped)
1 c. fresh mushrooms (chopped)
1 green pepper (chopped)
1 tomato (chopped)

Cut beef into strips. Combine next 5 ingredients in an 8-inch square pan. Add steak to marinade. Turn to coat. Cover and marinate in refrigerator 30 minutes to 1 hour.

Coat a wok or electric skillet with nonstick cooking spray. Add oil and turn to medium high (325 degrees). Add steak, onion, pepper, and broccoli. Cook for 3 to 5 minutes. Add mushrooms and tomato. Cook additional 3 minutes or until done. (Fat: 30% calories from fat)

— Martha Elson, Anchorage, AK

— Beef Stroganoff —
(4 servings)

3/4 pound sirloin
1 clove garlic
1-1/2 c. fresh mushrooms (chopped)
2 T. flour
1 c. evaporated skim milk

1 package Lipton's Instant Onion Mushroom Soup mix
8 ounces plain nonfat yogurt
2 c. hot, cooked noodles

Slice beef into bite-size pieces. Fry pieces with garlic in a nonstick skillet or a pan coated with nonstick cooking spray. Just before beef is done, add mushrooms.

While meat cooks, prepare sauce. Add flour to evaporated skim milk and stir until flour dissolves. In a medium saucepan combine milk mixture with Instant Onion Mushroom Soup mix over medium heat, stirring constantly until boiling. Add yogurt and stir until simmering.

Combine sauce with beef mixture and serve over hot noodles. Garnish with chopped parsley, if desired. (Fat: 20% calories from fat)

— Pot Roast with Vegetables —
(6 servings)

1 pound lean, boneless chuck roast (trimmed)	1/4 tsp. salt
Nonstick cooking spray	1/8 tsp. pepper
2 medium onions (peeled and sliced)	4 large carrots (scraped and sliced)
2 stalks celery (sliced)	2 medium red boiling potatoes (peeled
1/4 c. water	and coarsely chopped)

Brown boneless chuck roast evenly on all sides over medium heat in a small Dutch oven coated with nonstick cooking spray. Add sliced onion, celery, water, salt, and pepper.

Cover Dutch oven and bake at 350 degrees for 1 hour and 15 minutes. Add sliced carrots and coarsely chopped potatoes. Continue to bake, covered, for 1 hour or until meat and vegetables are tender.

Transfer roast and vegetables to a serving platter. Cut roast into 2-ounce slices. Serve hot. (Fat: less than 30% calories from fat)

— Roast Leg of Lamb —
(10 servings)

1 — 3- to 4-pound leg of lamb	Salt and pepper to taste
3 cloves garlic (slivered)	

Preheat oven to 325 degrees.

Make small slits in all meat surfaces with the tip of a sharp knife. Insert slivers of garlic in each slit.

Place meat on a rack in a shallow roasting pan. Sprinkle with salt and pepper.

Roast, uncovered, 30 to 35 minutes per pound or until a meat thermometer registers 175 degrees. (Fat: 30% calories from fat)

Fish and Seafood

— Shrimp Creole —
(4 servings)

1 medium to large onion (chopped)	Pepper to taste
1/2 c. celery (chopped)	Pinch of parsley
1 medium green pepper (chopped)	Pinch of basil
1-2 T. canola oil	1/2 tsp. garlic salt
1 can (10-oz. or so) tomato sauce	7 dashes of Tabasco sauce (or to taste)
1 can (10-oz. or so) stewed tomatoes	1 pound shrimp (peeled and deveined)
Salt to taste	Cooked long-grain rice

Saute onion, celery, and green pepper in oil until onion is clear looking. Add tomato sauce and stewed tomatoes. Stir. Add seasonings. Mix well. Lower heat, cover and simmer 1 to 2 hours. Right before serving, drop in peeled and deveined shrimp. Set off heat. Cover. Ready to serve in 5 minutes. Serve over rice. (Fat: approx. 30% calories from fat)

— Gale R. Cox, Taylors, SC

— Louisiana Fish Stew —
(8 servings)

1 pound white fish (thawed) — haddock, cod,
   or trout
2 scallions (chopped)
4 ounces fresh mushrooms (sliced)
1 small zucchini (sliced)
1 green pepper (chopped)
1 can (12-ounce) chopped tomatoes

1 c. quick rice
1/2 tsp. garlic powder
1/2 tsp. cumin
Cayenne pepper to taste
8 ounces no-salt tomato sauce
1 tsp. basil
1 tsp. Worcestershire sauce

Steam fish with 1 tablespoon water in the microwave for 3 minutes. Cool and cut into small cubes. Saute scallions, mushrooms, zucchini, and pepper in the bottom of a Dutch oven that has been sprayed with nonstick cooking spray. Add fish and all remaining ingredients and simmer for 30 minutes, or microwave uncovered in a 3-quart casserole dish for 15 minutes. (Fat: 5% calories from fat)

— Broiled Ginger Fish —
(4 servings)

1 c. flour
1 tsp. salt
1/2 tsp. freshly ground pepper
4 six-ounce fish filets (monkfish, haddock, etc.)

2 tsp. reduced-calorie margarine
4 tsp. diced ginger root
Lemon slices to cover filets

Set oven to broil and spray broiler pan with nonstick cooking spray.

Combine flour, salt, and pepper on a large plate. Dip filets in flour, covering both sides. Dot filets with tiny bits of margarine, sprinkle them with ginger and cover with lemon slices. Broil for 5 to 15 minutes or until fish flakes easily. (Fat: less than 30% calories from fat)

— Beverly Hyde, Talladega, AL

— Light Fish Fry —
(4 servings)

1 pound catfish or haddock filet
2 T. Dijon mustard
1 T. nonfat yogurt
1 T. chives (chopped)

1 T. fresh parsley (chopped)
Pinch of ground red pepper
1 c. fresh bread crumbs

Rinse fish and pat it dry. Cut into 8 equal pieces.

In a cup, combine mustard, yogurt, chives, parsley, and pepper. Rub this mixture onto all sides of fish filets. Refrigerate about 30 minutes.

Thoroughly coat fish pieces with bread crumbs.

Coat a baking sheet with nonstick cooking spray. Add fish. Bake at 375 degrees for 10 to 12 minutes or until fish flakes easily when tested with fork. (Fat: 15% calories from fat)

— Crab Boil Shrimp and Corn —
(Can prepare to serve as many as you like)

Bag of frozen shrimp (peeled and deveined)
Corn on cob

1 package crab boil mix
Water

Bring water and crab boil mix to a boil. Add corn on cob and cook until tender (about 10 to 15 minutes). Add shrimp and cook until tender and pink (about 2 or 3 minutes). Remove from heat and serve. (Fat: approx. 20% calories from fat)   — *Cheryln Sanders, Taylors, SC*

— Seafood Stir-Fry —
(4 servings)

6 ounces rice-stick noodles
2 tsp. canola oil
6 ounces sea scallops
6 ounces shrimp (peeled and deveined)
2 stalks celery (thinly sliced on the diagonal)
1 large carrot (cut into thin strips)
1 red pepper (cut into thin strips)
1 yellow pepper (cut into thin strips)

6 fresh mushrooms (sliced)
4 scallions (cut on the diagonal)
1 tsp. garlic (minced)
Juice of 1 lime
Red pepper flakes to taste
2-1/2 T. low-salt soy sauce
1-1/2 T. water

Cook noodles in a large pot of boiling water until tender (about 8 minutes). Drain and place in a bowl. Set aside.

While noodles are cooking, place a wok or large frying pan over medium-high heat until hot (about 2 minutes). Add oil, scallops, and shrimp. Stir-fry for 1 minute.

Add celery, carrot, red pepper, yellow pepper, and mushrooms. Stir-fry for 2 minutes. Stir in scallions and garlic. Mix well. Add lime juice and pepper flakes. Stir-fry for 30 seconds.

Stir in soy sauce, water, and noodles. Toss well to coat. (Fat: 10% calories from fat)

— Poached Stuffed Salmon Roll —
(6 servings)

6 ounces fresh shrimp (peeled and deveined)
1/2 c. spinach leaves
2 tsp. cider vinegar

1/8 tsp. white pepper
1-1/4 pound skinless, boneless salmon filet

Puree shrimp and spinach in food processor or blender. Stir in vinegar and pepper. Set aside. Cut salmon filet in half horizontally. Spread spinach mixture evenly between the two layers of salmon. Starting with long edge of salmon, roll up jelly-roll fashion.

Tightly wrap salmon with plastic wrap, tying both ends closed with string. Poach salmon roll in simmering water (180 degrees) about 30 minutes or until internal temperature reaches 120 degrees. Remove from water and keep warm. Before serving, gently remove plastic. Slice salmon into six equal portions. (Fat: 25% calories from fat)

— Crispy Baked Fish Filets —
(4 servings)

This recipe produces a crisp coating almost like deep-fried fish.

1 pound fish filets
1/4 tsp. salt
Dash pepper

2 T. canola oil
1/3 c. cornflake crumbs

Preheat oven to 500 degrees. Wash and dry filets and cut into serving pieces. Season, dip in oil, and coat with cornflake crumbs. Arrange in single layer in a lightly oiled shallow baking dish. Bake 10 minutes without turning or basting. (Fat: less than 30% calories from fat)

— Mrs. Hazel McConnell, Alma, MI

— Oven-Fried Catfish —
(4 servings)

2 T. skim milk
2 egg whites
1/2 c. yellow cornmeal
1/4 tsp. paprika
1/4 tsp. salt

1/4 tsp. onion or garlic powder
1 pound catfish filets (or other white fish)
Nonstick cooking spray
1/2 tsp. olive oil

In a shallow bowl, beat milk and eggs together. In another shallow bowl, combine cornmeal and dry ingredients.

Dip each fish filet in the egg mixture and then coat thoroughly in the cornmeal.

Spray a shallow baking dish with nonstick cooking spray and then add olive oil, turning the dish to coat. Place fish in single layer in the baking dish.

Bake in a 500-degree oven for about 12 minutes or until fish flakes easily with a fork. (Fat: less than 30% calories from fat)

— Baked Red Snapper —
(4 servings)
(May substitute with similar fish)

1 pound red snapper filets (cut into 3-inch cubes)
2 tsp. powdered rosemary

1/2 tsp. black pepper
2 fresh lemons (peeled and finely diced)
1/4 c. fresh parsley (chopped)

Sprinkle fish generously with powdered rosemary and black pepper. Arrange in a nonstick baking pan. Bake at 325 degrees for 15 to 20 minutes, or until fish flakes easily when tested with a fork. Remove to serving plate. Cover with lemons and sprinkle with parsley. (Fat: 11% calories from fat)

— Filet of Sole —
(4 servings)

1 medium white onion (chopped)
2/3 pound fresh mushrooms (sliced)

1 c. part-skim mozzarella cheese (grated)
1 pound filet of sole

In a covered vegetable steamer basket over boiling water, steam onions 3 minutes. Add mushrooms and steam 2 minutes. In a shallow baking dish, layer half the onions, then half the mushrooms, then half the cheese. Arrange the sole over the cheese. Top sole with remaining onions, mushrooms, then cheese. Bake at 400 degrees for 20 to 25 minutes, or until cheese is melted and fish flakes easily when tested with fork. (Fat: 25% calories from fat)

— Fish Filets 'N Mustard Sauce —
(2 servings)

8 ounces flounder or sole filets
2 tsp. nonfat mayonnaise

3 T. plus 1 tsp. Dijon-style mustard
1/16 tsp. cayenne pepper

Preheat broiler to high. In a small bowl, stir together the mayonnaise, mustard, and cayenne pepper until blended. Cover a broiler tray with foil and arrange the filets on top in a single layer. Spread with sauce, dividing evenly. Broil until brown and bubbly. (Fat: 3 grams per serving)

— Skillet Fish —
(4 servings)

1 pound flounder or sole filet
2 T. canola oil
1 medium onion (chopped)
1/2 green pepper (chopped)
2 T. fresh parsley (chopped)

2 medium tomatoes (coarsely chopped)
1/2 tsp. dried basil
1/4 tsp. dried oregano
1/2 c. water, tomato juice, or broth
Dash of pepper

Heat oil in large skillet. Add onion, green pepper, and parsley. Cook until vegetables soften (about 3 to 4 minutes). Add tomatoes, seasonings, and liquid. Cook until tomatoes are soft. Add raw fish filets. Cover and cook over moderate heat until fish flakes easily (about 10 minutes). (Fat: 30% calories from fat)

— Poached Fish 'N Vegetables —
(2 servings)

1 medium tomato (seeded and diced)
1 small green pepper (diced)
1 small scallion (sliced diagonally into
    1/4-inch pieces)
4 fresh mushrooms (diced)
2 T. dry white wine

8 ounces flounder filets (or other firm-fleshed
    white fish)
1/4 tsp. thyme
Freshly ground pepper
Lemon wedges

(Continued)

Preheat oven to 350 degrees. Put tomato, green pepper, scallion, mushrooms, and white wine in a small skillet. Cover and cook over low heat until softened (about 5 minutes). Tear off two, 14-inch pieces of aluminum foil. Center half the filets on each sheet. Top with half the vegetables, dividing evenly. Sprinkle each with 1/8 teaspoon thyme and freshly ground pepper. Fold in the corners and seal the edges to form 2 pouches. Place on a baking sheet. Bake until the fish is cooked through (7 to 10 minutes). Place each pouch on a plate and open at table. Serve with lemon wedges. (Fat: 1 gram per serving)

— Barbecued Catfish —
(6 servings)

1/3 c. reduced-calorie catsup	1/2 tsp. dried whole marjoram
1 T. lemon juice	1/4 tsp. garlic powder
1 tsp. brown sugar	1/4 tsp. ground red pepper
2 tsp. canola oil	6 (4-ounce) catfish filets
1 tsp. low-sodium Worcestershire sauce	Nonstick cooking spray

Combine first 8 ingredients in a small bowl. Arrange filets in a 13x9x2-inch baking dish coated with nonstick cooking spray. Pour catsup mixture over filets. Cover and marinate in refrigerator 30 minutes, turning once.

Remove filets from marinade, reserving marinade. Bring marinade to boil in a small saucepan. Boil 2 minutes. Place filets on rack of broiler pan that has been coated with cooking spray. Broil 6 inches from heat 14 to 15 minutes or until fish flakes easily when tested with a fork, basting occasionally with marinade. Transfer to serving platter. (Fat: 30% calories from fat)

— Flounder With Rice —

4 (6-ounce) flounder filets or orange roughy filets	4 garlic cloves (chopped)
2 large tomatoes (chopped)	2 c. brown long-grain rice (cooked)
1 large onion (chopped)	Salt and pepper to taste

Heat onions and garlic over medium heat for 2 minutes in a large, nonstick pan with lid. Add salt, pepper, and tomatoes. Cover and cook for 7 minutes. Mix in rice and heat thoroughly. Lay filets on top of this mixture and cover. Cook until fish flakes (about 5 minutes). Carefully remove fish to platter and spoon rice mixture over fish. Serve with a steamed vegetable. (Fat: 30% calories from fat)

— Debitha Harrelson, Elba, AL

— Pasta Tuna Bake —
(6 servings)

1 c. medium shell macaroni (uncooked)
Nonstick cooking spray
2 T. reduced-calorie margarine (divided)
1/2 c. onion (minced)
1/2 c. green pepper (minced)
2 T. all-purpose flour
1-1/2 c. skim milk

2 cans (6-1/2-ounce) spring water-packed
  white tuna (drained)
1/4 c. reduced-calorie chili sauce
1/4 tsp. salt
1/4 tsp. dried whole basil
1/8 tsp. ground red pepper

Cook macaroni according to package directions, omitting fat and salt. Drain and set aside.

Coat a large nonstick skillet with cooking spray. Add 1 teaspoon margarine and place over medium heat until hot. Add onion and green pepper. Saute until tender. Remove from skillet and set aside.

Melt remaining margarine in skillet. Add flour, and cook over medium heat, stirring constantly for 1 minute. Gradually add milk. Cook over medium heat, stirring constantly until mixture thickens and bubbles. Remove mixture from heat. Stir in pasta, onion mixture, tuna, and remaining ingredients.

Place tuna mixture in a 2-quart baking dish coated with cooking spray. Bake, uncovered, at 350 degrees for 30 minutes. If desired, garnish with lemon slices. (Fat: 30% calories from fat)

— Crab 'N Vegetables —
(8 servings)

6 medium tomatoes (skinned and chopped)
1 c. evaporated skim milk
2 T. reduced-calorie margarine
2 T. lemon juice
1/8 tsp. nutmeg
1/4 tsp. salt

1/2 tsp. pepper
2 c. (16-ounce) imitation crab
1/4 pound mushrooms
1/2 c. frozen peas
1/2 c. spiral vegetable pasta
1/4 c. Parmesan cheese

Cook tomatoes for 5 minutes. Add milk and margarine. Cook for 10 minutes. Add next four ingredients. Stir in crab and remove from heat. Meanwhile, steam mushrooms and peas. Cook pasta for 8 minutes in boiling water. Drain. Mix crab sauce with pasta and vegetables in large serving bowl. Sprinkle with cheese and serve. (Fat: 16% calories from fat)

— Seafood 'N Vegetables —
(4 servings)

1 T. canola oil
4 small red potatoes (sliced)
1/2 red onion (sliced)
1/2 tsp. white pepper
1/2 tsp. thyme
1/4 tsp. garlic powder
1/4 tsp. salt

4 lemon slices
1 pound perch or haddock
1 zucchini (thinly sliced)
1 green pepper (chopped)
1 tomato (chopped)
1/4 c. white wine

(Continued)

Preheat oven to 375 degrees. In skillet, heat oil and add red potatoes, sliced onion, white pepper, thyme, garlic powder, and salt. Cover and cook 15 minutes, stirring occasionally. Place lemon slices in a 9x9-inch baking dish. Place fish over lemon and top with zucchini, green pepper, and tomato. Pour on wine. Top with potato mixture.

Cover and bake for 25 minutes in a conventional oven or microwave in a covered dish at 70% power for 11 to 12 minutes until vegetables are tender. (Fat: 14% calories from fat)

— Shrimp Casserole —
(4 servings)

1/2 c. celery (chopped)	2 tsp. Worcestershire sauce
1 c. onion (chopped)	Red pepper sauce to taste
2 T. reduced-calorie margarine	1/2 c. soda cracker crumbs (crushed)
1/4 tsp. celery seed	1 egg (beaten) or 1/4 cup liquid egg substitute
1 can (16-ounce) chopped tomatoes	1 pound shrimp (peeled and deveined)
1/4 c. catsup	1 tsp. dried parsley
2 tsp. horseradish	

Preheat oven to 375 degrees. Saute celery and onion in margarine in 2-quart Dutch oven. Stir in remaining ingredients and transfer to a shallow 2-quart casserole dish sprayed with nonstick cooking spray. Bake for 25 minutes or microwave 12 to 15 minutes. (Fat: 28% calories from fat)

Poultry

— Chicken with Garlic 'N Broccoli —

1 large chicken breast (boneless, skinless, sliced thin)	5 large cloves garlic
	1 T. olive oil
2 c. broccoli in small pieces	Salt and pepper

In a large frying pan, cook garlic and broccoli in olive oil over medium-low heat, covered, for approximately 10 minutes. Add chicken, salt, and pepper. Cook over medium heat for 5 to 6 minutes, stirring often. Do not overcook. Serve with wild rice. (Fat: 25% calories from fat)

— DeBitha Harrelson, Elba, AL

— Microwave Chicken Cacciatore —
(6 servings)

2-1/2 to 3 pound chicken (skinned and cut up)	1/2 tsp. dried oregano (crushed in hand)
	1/2 tsp. basil (crushed)
1-2 medium onions (thinly sliced)	1/2 tsp. celery seed (optional)
2 cloves garlic (minced)	1 bay leaf
1 can (1-pound) tomatoes	1/4 c. dry white wine
1/2 tsp. pepper	3 c. spaghetti (cooked)

Assemble all ingredients, except pasta. Cook at medium-high in microwave for 25 minutes, stirring twice. After cooking, remove chicken and cut meat off bones. Return meat to the sauce, reheat and serve over cooked spaghetti or noodles. (Fat: 30% calories from fat)

— Parmesan Breaded Chicken —
(4 servings)

1/4 c. seasoned bread crumbs
1/4 c. Parmesan cheese (grated)
1/2 tsp. oregano
1/4 tsp. rosemary
1/4 tsp. basil

1/4 tsp. pepper
4 chicken breasts (skinless)
1/2 c. low-fat buttermilk
Nonstick cooking spray

Combine first 6 ingredients in a shallow bowl. Dip chicken in buttermilk and roll in bread crumb/herb mixture.

Coat a baking dish with cooking spray. Place chicken (bone side down) on pan. Bake, covered, at 350 degrees for 25 minutes. Remove cover and bake another 20 minutes or until done. (Fat: 30% calories from fat)
— *Martha Elson, Anchorage, AK*

— Chicken Meatballs in Tomato Sauce —
(4 servings)

Meatballs:
1 pound extra-lean ground chicken
1/4 c. onions (finely diced)
1/4 c. dry bread crumbs
1 egg white

2 tsp. low-sodium soy sauce
1/4 tsp. dried oregano
1/4 tsp. dried basil
1 clove garlic (minced)

Sauce:
6 large ripe tomatoes
1/2 c. red wine vinegar
1-1/2 c. defatted chicken stock
2 yellow peppers (sliced in thin strips)
2 green peppers (sliced in thin strips)

1 red onion (sliced in thin strips)
2 ounces fresh basil (chopped)
3 cloves garlic (finely chopped)
1/2 tsp. dried oregano
8 ounces pasta

To make meatballs: In a large bowl, mix together chicken, onions, bread crumbs, egg white, soy sauce, oregano, basil, and garlic. Form mixture into 12 meatballs. Place on nonstick baking sheet. Bake at 350 degrees for 25 minutes.

To make sauce: On a grill or under a broiler, char the tomatoes until they are blackened on all sides. Remove peelings and coarsely chop tomatoes. (Should have about 4 cups including juice). Place this in Dutch oven. Add vinegar, stock, yellow peppers, green peppers, onion, basil, garlic, and oregano. Simmer over medium heat for 30 minutes.

While sauce is cooking, cook pasta in a large pot of boiling water until tender. Drain and place in large serving bowl. Top with sauce and meatballs. (Fat: 25% calories from fat)

— Ida's Baked Chicken —

Desired amount of skinless thighs and
 drumsticks
Tomatoes (chopped)
Onions (diced)
Celery (diced)

Fresh Mushrooms (sliced)
Garlic to taste
Bread cubes
Pepper to taste

(Continued)

Place desired amounts of all ingredients in baking dish. Cover with plastic wrap and make a small slit in it. Bake in microwave for 15 minutes or until meat is done. (Fat: 25% calories from fat)
— *Ida Blankenship, Peoria, IL*

— Ann's Fried Chicken —
(4 servings)

4 chicken breasts (skinless and boneless)   1/2 tsp. pepper
1 tsp. seasoned salt

Sprinkle salt and pepper on both sides of chicken. Place in nonstick frying pan and cover. Cook on medium heat 10 to 15 minutes. Turn chicken and continue cooking on medium heat for about 10 more minutes. Remove lid and allow moisture to evaporate and chicken to brown. (Fat: 25% calories from fat)
— *Ann Buel, Fairfax, VA*

— Turkey Breast —
(4 servings)

1 fresh turkey breast (about 2 to 3 pounds)   Garlic powder
Powdered rosemary   Black pepper

Remove and discard 3/4 of the skin from turkey breast. Leave on remaining skin for moisture. Rub breast on both sides with generous amounts of rosemary, garlic powder and black pepper. Roast at 325 degrees for 60 to -90 minutes. Discard remaining skin after cooking is complete. (Fat: 19% calories from fat)

— Turkey Sausage —
(8 servings)

1 pound lean ground turkey
1/2 c. breadcrumbs
2 cloves garlic (minced)
2 T. fresh parsley (finely chopped)
1 tsp. thyme
1 tsp. sage

1/2 tsp. marjoram
1/2 tsp. salt
Freshly ground black pepper to taste
1/2 to 1 tsp. crushed, hot red pepper
Nonstick cooking spray

Combine all ingredients and form into 8 small patties.

Fry in a nonstick skillet sprayed with cooking spray until brown and crisp on both sides (about 20 minutes). Add a little water during cooking if patties begin to stick.

Serving Suggestions: This can be made into a loaf by adding onion and mushrooms. You may also substitute canned salmon for the turkey — add 2 egg whites to 2 cans (7-1/2-ounces) of salmon. (Fat: less than 30% calories from fat)

— Indonesian Peanut Chicken —
(4 servings)

4 chicken breast halves (skinless and
   boneless)
2 tsp. olive oil
1/4 tsp. seasoned salt substitute
4-1/2 tsp. lemon juice (reserve 3-1/2 tsp.)
3/4 tsp. cumin (reserve 1/4 tsp.)
1/2 tsp. ground ginger

1 c. low-fat buttermilk
3 T. peanut butter
3 T. reduced-sodium soy sauce
1 clove garlic (minced)
1 tsp. dry mustard
1 tsp. tumeric
1/4 tsp. crushed red pepper (optional)

Cut chicken into bite-size pieces. Stir-fry chicken with 2 teaspoons oil, 1 teaspoon lemon juice, 1/2 teaspoon cumin, and 1/4 teaspoon seasoned salt substitute until cooked through.

In saucepan, combine 3-1/2 teaspoons lemon juice, 1/4 teaspoon cumin, and remaining ingredients. Bring to a boil over medium heat, stirring continuously with wire whisk. Reduce heat to simmer for 3-5 minutes.

Pour sauce over chicken and serve over brown rice. (Fat: 30% calories from fat)

— *Martha Elson, Anchorage, AK*

— Pepper Meal —
(8 servings)

4 large green peppers
Water
Dash salt
Nonstick cooking spray
1 pound ground turkey
1/2 c. onion (finely chopped)
1 can (16-ounce) tomatoes (chopped,
   undrained)

1/2 c. long-grain rice
1/2 c. water
1/4 tsp. salt
1/4 tsp. pepper
1-1/2 T. Worcestershire sauce
1/2 tsp. dried oregano (crushed)
3/4 c. part-skim mozzarella (grated)

Halve peppers lengthwise, removing membranes, seeds, and stems. Cook peppers in boiling water for 3 minutes. Drain and sprinkle insides of peppers with small amount of salt.

Spray a skillet with nonstick cooking spray. Cook turkey and onion until onion is tender. Drain well.

Stir in tomatoes (undrained), uncooked rice, 1/2 cup water, salt, pepper, Worcestershire sauce, and oregano. Bring to boil. Reduce heat to simmer.

Cover and simmer for 20 minutes or until rice is tender. Stir in half of the cheese and fill pepper halves with the rice-meat-cheese mixture.

Place stuffed pepper in an ovenproof baking dish and bake for 15 to 20 minutes at 375 degrees. Remove from oven and immediately sprinkle with remaining cheese. (Fat: less than 30% calories from fat)

— Chicken Dijon —
(8 servings)

1/2 carton (8-ounce) plain, unsweetened
 low-fat yogurt
1/4 c. Dijon mustard

8 (3-ounce) chicken breast halves (skinless)
1/2 c. soft breadcrumbs
Nonstick cooking spray

Combine yogurt and mustard, stirring until well blended. Brush breast halves evenly with yogurt mixture and dip in breadcrumbs.

Arrange chicken in a 12x8x2-inch baking dish coated with cooking spray. Cover and bake at 400 degrees for 30 minutes.

Increase temperature to 450 degrees. Bake, uncovered, for 15 minutes or until chicken is done and coating is browned. (Fat: less than 30% calories from fat)

— Chicken 'N Potatoes Meal —
(4 servings)

Stuffed Chicken Breasts:
4 chicken breast halves (boneless, skinless)
1 jar (8-oz.) roasted red peppers (drained and
 cut in thin strips)
1/2 c. spinach (cooked and chopped)

2 T. coarse mustard
1 potato
2 tsp. olive oil
1 T. lemon juice
1/8 tsp. ground black pepper

Stewed Potatoes:
2 c. defatted chicken stock
8 small red potatoes (halved)
2 tomatoes (peeled, seeded, and cut in 1-inch
 cubes)

2 medium onions (cut into 1/2-inch wedges)
2 green peppers (cut in 1/2-inch strips)
2 tsp. garlic
1/2 tsp. dried oregano
1/2 tsp. dried rosemary

To make stuffed chicken breasts, cut a pocket lengthwise in each chicken breast. Fill with the peppers and spinach. Close the pockets and secure with toothpicks. Place the breasts on a baking sheet. Spread with mustard.

Shred the potato into a bowl drizzle with oil and lemon juice. Sprinkle with black pepper. Toss well. Divide mixture into 4 portions and cover each breast with a portion.

Bake at 350 degrees for 35 to 40 minutes or until chicken is cooked through.

To make stewed potatoes, while chicken is baking, combine the stock, potatoes, onions, tomatoes, peppers, garlic, oregano, and rosemary in a Dutch oven or very large frying pan. Partially cover and simmer over medium heat until potatoes are tender (about 25 minutes). Remove potatoes with a slotted spoon. Increase heat to medium-high and cook until remaining ingredients are reduced by one-third (or about 10 minutes). Return potatoes to pan and warm through. Serve with chicken. (Fat: 17% calories calories from fat)

— Cauliflower Chicken Casserole —
(6 servings)

1 package (10-ounce) cauliflower (frozen, chopped)
1/2 c. onion (coarsely chopped)
1/2 c. water
1 c. skim milk
1 T. cornstarch
1 tsp. chicken-flavored bouillon granules

1/2 tsp. salt
1/4 c. (1 ounce) low-fat process American cheese (shredded)
1 c. chicken (chopped, cooked)
1 jar (4-ounce) pimento (diced, drained)
Nonstick cooking spray

Combine cauliflower, onion, and water in a medium saucepan. Cover and bring to a boil. Reduce heat and simmer 5 minutes or until vegetables are crisp but tender. Drain well. Set aside.

Add milk, cornstarch, bouillon granules, and salt to saucepan, beating well with a wire whisk to blend. Bring to a boil. Reduce heat and simmer, stirring constantly, until thickened and bubbly. Add cheese. Stir with wire whisk until cheese melts. Remove from heat.

Add cauliflower-onion mixture, chicken, and pimento to cheese sauce. Spoon mixture into a 1-1/2-quart casserole dish coated with cooking spray. Bake at 325 degrees for 20 minutes or until thoroughly heated. (Fat: less than 20% calories from fat)

— DeBitha's Southern Fried Chicken —
— With Creamed Potatoes —

Chicken:

Skin and remove all fragments of fat from chicken breast. Sprinkle with garlic salt and black pepper. Rub chicken with nonfat yogurt and shake in bag with corn flake crumbs. Place chicken breasts on baking sheet with meat side up. Cover with foil and bake approximately 1-1/2 hours at 350 degrees. Remove foil during last 30 minutes of cooking time.

Creamed Potatoes:

Peel and chop potatoes in desired amount. Cook until tender in small amount of water. Drain excess water. Add approximately 1 tablespoon of Molly McButter and beat with mixer until creamy. Add skim milk (about 3/4 cup) while beating. (May top with one of our no-fat gravies — see Sauces section.) (Fat: 20% calories from fat)   — DeBitha Harrelson, Elba, AL

— Vegetable Chicken Parmesan —
(8 servings)

8 chicken breast halves (skinned, boned)
1 package (10-ounce) broccoli (frozen, chopped)
Nonstick cooking spray
1/4 can (10-3/4-ounce) cream of chicken soup (undiluted)

1/4 can (10-3/4-ounce) cream of potato soup (undiluted)
1/2 c. skim milk
1-1/2 tsp. lemon juice
2 T. Parmesan cheese (grated)

(Continued)

Combine chicken and water to cover in a large saucepan. Cover and bring to a boil. Reduce heat and simmer 20 minutes or until chicken is done. Drain well. Chop chicken and set aside.

Cook broccoli according to package directions, omitting salt and fat. Drain well. Arrange broccoli in a 2-quart baking dish coated with cooking spray and top with chicken.

Combine soups, milk, and lemon juice, stirring to blend. Pour over chicken and broccoli. Sprinkle cheese over top. Bake at 350 degrees for 25 minutes or until thoroughly heated. (Fat: less than 30% calories from fat)

— Oven-Baked Mustardy Chicken —
(8 servings)

8 chicken breast halves (skinned)
1/2 tsp. salt
1/8 tsp. pepper
2 T. prepared mustard

1 egg
1/4 c. plus 2 T. Parmesan cheese (grated)
1/4 c. soft bread crumbs
Nonstick cooking spray

Sprinkle chicken breast halves with salt and pepper

Combine mustard and egg, beating with a wire whisk until well blended. Combine cheese and bread crumbs. Stir well.

Dip chicken in egg mixture and then dredge in bread-crumb mixture. Let stand at room temperature on wax paper 10 minutes to set coating.

Transfer chicken to rack of a roasting pan coated with cooking spray. Bake at 400 degrees for 40 minutes or until chicken is done and coating is lightly browned. (Fat: less than 30% calories from fat)

— Chicken Florentine —
(2 servings)

2 chicken breast halves (skinned)
1/4 c. onion (chopped)
Nonstick cooking spray
1 package (10-ounce) frozen spinach
  (chopped, thawed)
2 T. (1/2 ounce) low-fat shredded Swiss cheese

1/8 tsp. ground nutmeg
1/2 c. fresh mushrooms (sliced)
1/2 c. skim milk
1/2 c. boiling water
1 T. reduced-calorie margarine (melted)
1/2 tsp. chicken-flavored bouillon granules

Place chicken between 2 sheets of heavy-duty plastic wrap and flatten to 1/4-inch thickness, using a meat mallet or rolling pin. Set aside.

Saute onion in a large skillet coated with cooking spray. Remove from heat and stir in spinach, cheese, and nutmeg.

Divide mixture in half and shape into mounds. Transfer mounds to a 10x6x2-inch baking dish coated with cooking spray. Top each portion with a chicken breast half. Bake at 350 degrees for 25 minutes or until chicken is done.

Place mushrooms in skillet. Stir in milk and remaining ingredients and bring to a boil. Boil 6 minutes, stirring frequently until liquid is reduced and thickened. Spoon sauce evenly over each portion and serve hot. (Fat: less than 25% calories from fat)

— Chicken Pot Pie —
(makes 2 pies)

4 chicken breasts (boneless)
2 cans reduced-calorie cream of chicken soup (undiluted)

2 small cans of "veg-all" vegetables (drained)
4 pie crusts (see our recipes for low-fat crusts)
1/2 tsp. curry powder

Boil chicken and curry powder in water until done and cut into small pieces. Mix vegetables, chicken, and soup together. Divide mixture and pour into pie crusts and top each with another pie crust. (Fat: 30% calories from fat)

— *Cheryln Sanders, Taylors, SC*

— Chicken Cordon Bleu —
(4 servings)

4 chicken breast halves (skinned and boned)
2 slices cooked, lean ham (cut in half)
2 slices low-fat Swiss cheese (cut in half)
1 egg (beaten)
2 T. all-purpose flour

Nonstick cooking spray
1/3 c. onion (chopped)
1/4 can (10-1/2-ounce) reduced-calorie cream of chicken soup (undiluted)

Place chicken between 2 sheets of heavy-duty plastic wrap and flatten to 1/4-inch thickness, using a meat mallet or rolling pin.

Place one-half slice each of ham and cheese in center of each chicken breast half. Roll up lengthwise and secure with wooden picks.

Dip each chicken roll in egg and dredge in flour. Place chicken rolls, seam side down, in a shallow casserole dish coated with cooking spray and bake at 350 degrees for 20 minutes.

Combine onion and soup, stirring until well combined. Pour over chicken and continue to bake at 350 degrees for 15 minutes or until chicken is done. (Fat: less than 30% calories from fat)

— Chicken Bake —
(4 servings)

8 small new potatoes (cut in half)
4 carrots (cut in 2-inch chunks)
4 chicken breasts (skinned)
1/8 tsp. garlic powder
1 tsp. curry powder
1/2 tsp. ground mustard

1 tsp. tarragon
1/2 tsp. dried red pepper (crushed)
2 T. lemon juice
1/2 c. cooking wine
4 stalks celery (sliced thin)
4 onions (sliced thin)

Combine potatoes and carrots in a casserole dish. Place chicken breasts on top.

Combine spices, lemon juice, and wine and pour over chicken. Top with celery and onions. Cover and bake at 350 degrees for 1 hour. (Fat: less than 30% calories from fat)

— Chicken 'N Spinach Pasta Casserole —
(8 servings)

10 ounces uncooked pasta of choice
1 package (10-ounce) frozen, chopped
   spinach (thawed and drained)
Nonstick cooking spray
2 tsp. canola oil
1 large onion (chopped)
4 garlic cloves (minced)
1 pound chicken breasts (bone, skinned, and
cut into 1-inch pieces)
1 can (28-ounce) whole tomatoes (undrained,
   coarsely chopped)
3 T. tomato paste
1-1/4 tsp. dried basil
1/2 tsp. dried oregano
1/4 tsp. hot, red pepper (crushed)
1/2 c. Parmesan cheese (grated)

Cook pasta according to package directions. Drain. Place spinach on paper towels and squeeze until barely moist.

Coat large nonstick skillet with cooking spray. Add oil and place over medium heat until hot. Add onion and garlic and saute until tender.

Add chicken and cook until it loses its pink color, stirring constantly.

Stir in tomatoes, tomato paste, basil, oregano, and crushed peppers. Bring to a boil and reduce heat. Simmer 5 minutes, uncovered, stirring occasionally.

Combine pasta, spinach, chicken mixture, and 1/4 cup cheese in a bowl. Spoon into a 13x9x2-inch baking dish coated with cooking spray. Sprinkle remaining 1/4 cup of cheese over top. Bake at 350 degrees for 20 minutes. (Fat: less than 30% calories from fat)

— Traditional Chicken Cacciatore —
(5 servings)

1 T. reduced-calorie margarine
1/2 pound chicken breast halves (boned and
   skinned)
1/2 c. onion (chopped)
1/2 c. celery (chopped)
1 clove garlic (minced)
1 can (26-ounce) whole tomatoes (undrained
   and chopped)
1 c. fresh mushrooms (sliced)
1/2 c. fresh parsley (chopped)
1/4 c. green pepper (chopped)
1 tsp. dried whole basil
1/2 tsp. dried whole oregano
1/4 tsp. salt
1/4 tsp. pepper
1/8 tsp. red pepper

Melt margarine over low heat in a large skillet. Add chicken and cook until lightly browned. Chop chicken and set aside.

Add onion, celery, and garlic to margarine in skillet. Saute until vegetables are tender.

Return chicken to skillet with tomatoes and remaining ingredients. Cover and simmer 20 minutes. Serve over hot cooked rice or noodles of choice. (Fat: less than 30% calories from fat)

— Chicken Cacciatore 'N Brown Rice —
(4 servings)

1-3/4 c. boned, skinless chicken (cooked)
1/2 c. whole-wheat flour
1/8 c. canola oil
1/4 c. fresh mushrooms (sliced)
1 medium green pepper (chopped)

3 cloves garlic (crushed)
1 pound tomatoes (chopped) or 2 cups canned
1 c. tomato puree
1 tsp. salt
1-1/2 c. brown rice

Cut chicken into bite-size pieces and coat with flour. Heat oil in large, heavy skillet and saute chicken pieces over low heat for 15 to 20 minutes, until they are lightly browned. Remove chicken from skillet and next saute mushrooms, green pepper, and garlic in the same skillet until tender. Blend in tomatoes, puree, and salt. Add chicken. Cover skillet tightly and simmer 30 to 40 minutes. Meanwhile, prepare rice. Serve each portion of chicken over 3/4 cup cooked rice. (Fat: approx. 30% calories from fat)

— Savory Chicken Squares —

Blend 3 ounces of low-fat cream cheese with 2 tablespoons of low-calorie margarine.

Add:
2 c. cooked chicken or turkey (skinless)
1/4 tsp. salt

1/8 tsp. pepper
2 T. skim milk
1 T. onion (chopped)

Mix all ingredients together. Separate an 8-ounce can of canned crescent rolls. Form into rectangular shapes by sealing 2 triangles together. Roll dough a little to make it thinner. Spoon 1/2 cup of chicken mixture into center of dough. Bring corners together and pinch to seal. Brush with melted margarine and sprinkle with Italian bread crumbs. Bake on baking sheet sprayed with nonstick cooking spray at 350 degrees for 20 to 25 minutes. Serve with a low-fat cream sauce. (See our Sauces section.) (Fat: 30% calories from fat)

— *Sherri Arrowwood, Greenville, SC*

— Easy Barbecued Chicken —
(6 servings)

3-1/2 pounds chicken pieces (skinless)   1 c. barbecue sauce (see our Sauces section)

Skin chicken pieces. Place them "skin" side down in a large, shallow baking pan. For easy cleaning, line pan with foil.

Baste chicken pieces liberally with barbecue sauce and place in oven. Bake at 350 degrees for 20 minutes, basting halfway through. Turn chicken pieces over and bake another 25 minutes, or until chicken is tender, basting occasionally. (Fat: less than 30% calories from fat)

— Martha's Barbecued Chicken —
(4 servings)

1 T. Worcestershire sauce
1/2 c. reduced-calorie catsup
2 T. brown sugar
1 T. lemon juice
2 T. reduced-salt soy sauce

1/2 tsp. ground ginger
2 garlic cloves (minced)
4 chicken breasts (skinned and trimmed of all fat)
Nonstick cooking spray

Combine first 7 ingredients and mix with a wire whisk. Place chicken in a shallow baking dish. Pour mixture over chicken, coating both sides.

Cover and marinate in refrigerator for 30 minutes or longer.

Grill chicken, brushing with marinade. Or bake at 350 degrees for 45 minutes, basting occasionally. (Fat: 25% calories from fat)   — *Martha Elson, Anchorage, AK*

— Crispy Baked Chicken —
(4 servings)

This is a good finger food and nice for picnics.

1 frying chicken (skinned and cut in pieces or use chicken breasts only)
1 c. corn flake crumbs

2 T. canola oil
1 c. skim milk
Seasoning of choice

Preheat oven to 400 degrees. Remove all skin from chicken. Rinse and dry thoroughly. Season. Coat each piece in oil and dip in milk. Shake to remove excess liquid and roll in crumbs. Let stand briefly so coating will adhere. Place chicken in an oiled baking pan. Line pan with foil for easy clean-up. Do not crowd — pieces should not touch. Bake 45 minutes or more. Crumbs will form a crisp "skin." (Fat: less than 30% calories from fat)

— *Mrs. Hazel McConnell, Alma, MI*

— Chicken Chow Mein —
(7 servings)

Nonstick cooking spray
1-1/2 c. onion (chopped)
1 c. celery (sliced)
1/2 c. green pepper (chopped)
1 can (14-ounce) Chinese-style vegetables (drained)

2 c. chicken (cooked and chopped)
1 can (4-ounce) sliced mushrooms (drained)
1/4 tsp. ground cumin
1/4 tsp. chicken-flavored bouillon granules
1 T. cornstarch
3 c. water

Coat a large skillet with nonstick cooking spray. Place over medium heat until hot. Add onion, celery, and green pepper. Cook, stirring constantly, 3 minutes or until vegetables are tender.

Stir in chicken, Chinese vegetables, mushrooms, and cumin. Cook over medium heat 1 minute.

Dissolve bouillon granules and cornstarch in water. Add to chicken and vegetable mixture. Continue to cook over medium heat, stirring constantly, until thickened and bubbly.

Serve over chow mein noodles or hot cooked rice that has been cooked without salt or fat. (Fat: less than 30% calories from fat)

— Chicken 'N Rainbow Peppers —
(3 to 4 servings)

2 T. flour
1 oven cooking bag (regular size)
1/4 c. water
2 tsp. basil leaves
2-3 pound roasting chicken breast
Salt and pepper

1 green pepper (cubed)
1 sweet red pepper (cubed)
1 sweet yellow pepper (cubed)
1 medium onion (quartered)
1 T. reduced-calorie margarine

Preheat oven to 350 degrees. Shake flour into cooking bag. Place in a 13x9x2-inch baking pan. Add water and basil. Squeeze bag to bland ingredients. Rinse chicken. Pat dry. Sprinkle chicken with salt and pepper. Place chicken in bag. Turn bag to coat with herbed mixture. Place peppers and onion in bag around chicken. Dot chicken and vegetables with margarine. Close bag with nylon tie. Make 6 half-inch slits in top. Bake 50 to 70 minutes or until tender. Let stand 10 minutes. Spoon vegetables over sliced, skinned chicken. (Fat: less than 30% calories from fat)

— Italian Baked Chicken —
(4 servings)

4 chicken breasts (boned and skinned)

1 bottle of low-fat Italian dressing

Put chicken in baking pan or dish. Sprinkle chicken with small amount of salt, pepper, and paprika. Cover chicken in low-fat Italian dressing. Cover and bake at 350 degrees for 1 hour and 15 minutes or until done. When done, spoon a little dressing over chicken before serving. (Fat: less than 30% calories from fat)

— Mrs. Joyce Morrow, Muncie, IN

— Creamed Chicken Casserole —
(6 servings)

4 chicken breasts (3-ounce) halves (skinned)
Nonstick cooking spray
1/4 tsp. salt
1/4 tsp. pepper
1/2 carton (8-ounce) plain, unsweetened,
    low-fat yogurt

1/2 c. skim milk
1/2 can (10-1/2-ounce) cream of chicken soup
    (undiluted) — use low-fat variety if
    possible
5 unsalted crackers (crushed)
1 tsp. reduced-calorie margarine (melted)

Combine chicken breast halves and water to cover in a medium saucepan. Cover and bring to a boil. Reduce heat and simmer 20 minutes or until chicken is done. Drain well. Remove chicken from bone. Coarsely chop chicken.

Place coarsely chopped chicken in a 1-quart casserole dish coated with cooking spray and sprinkle with salt and pepper. Combine cream of chicken soup, skim milk, and yogurt in a medium bowl, stirring until well blended. Pour soup mixture evenly over chicken.

Combine crushed crackers and melted margarine, stirring well. Sprinkle cracker mixture evenly over top of casserole. Bake at 350 degrees for 20 minutes or until thoroughly heated. (Fat: 30% calories from fat)

— Easy Baked Chicken —

Legs and short joints of chicken (leave skin on) — rinse and pat dry.
Sprinkle with following:

Rosemary

Garlic powder

Black pepper

Celery flakes

Paprika

Bake for 1 hour at 350 degrees in a cooking bag of choice. Be sure to punch several holes in bag. Remove skin before you eat to keep this recipe extremely low in fat. (Fat: less than 30% calories from fat)

— Chicken or Turkey Divan —
(6 servings)

2 packages (10-ounce) frozen broccoli or 2 bunches fresh broccoli (cut in pieces)

2-3 c. white meat of turkey or chicken (cooked, skinless, boneless)

Nonstick cooking spray

2 T. flour

1 tsp. chicken bouillon

1 can (12-ounce) evaporated skim milk

1 can (10-1/2-ounce) cream of chicken soup (low-fat variety if possible)

1/4 c. reduced-fat mayonnaise

1 c. plain nonfat yogurt

1/2 tsp. curry powder

1/2 c. low-fat Cheddar cheese (grated)

1/2 c. plain breadcrumbs

Layer broccoli and turkey or chicken in a 13x9x2-inch casserole sprayed with cooking spray.

In a bowl, combine flour and bouillon. Add small amount of evaporated milk, stirring to form a paste. Gradually add remaining milk, cream soup, mayonnaise, yogurt, and curry powder. Mix well. Pour over broccoli and meat.

Top with grated cheese and bread crumbs. Bake at 350 degrees for 25 to 30 minutes. (Fat: less than 30% calories from fat)

— Cornish Hens 'N Stuffing —
(8 servings)

Bake stuffing separately to hens. Serve 1/2 hen per person.

1/2 onion (finely chopped)

1/2 c. celery (chopped)

1-1/2 c. fresh mushrooms (chopped)

1/2 apple (grated or chopped)

1/4 c. dried apricots (chopped)

1/2 c. low-salt chicken broth (defatted)

3 c. whole-grain bread, cut into 1/2-inch cubes

2 T. toasted pecans (finely chopped)

1 package Butter Buds (optional)

1/2 tsp. freshly ground pepper

1/2 tsp. each dried rosemary and sage

4 Cornish hens

2 T. red currant jelly (melted)

In a nonstick skillet, combine onion, celery, mushrooms, apple, apricots, and 1/4 cup chicken broth. Cook over medium heat until onions are tender (about 4 minutes). Transfer to a large bowl. Add bread cubes, pecans, Butter Buds, pepper, rosemary, sage, and remaining chicken stock. Combine until all ingredients well moistened. Spoon into a medium baking dish and cover with foil. Set aside.   *(Continued)*

Preheat oven to 450 degrees. Tie the legs of each hen together. Place hens on rack in a roasting pan and bake for 10 minutes. Reduce heat to 350 degrees, remove hens and brush with currant jelly. Return hens to oven along with the dish of stuffing. Bake until the juices run clear when hens are pricked in the thighs and stuffing is heated through (about 30 to 40 minutes). Let hens set for 5 minutes before cutting in half lengthwise. Remove skin and serve with stuffing. (Fat: 30% calories from fat)

— Turkey Loaf Surprise —
(6 servings)
The surprise is that it looks and tastes so good.

1 T. canola oil	1-1/4 pounds ground turkey
2 tsp. garlic (minced)	1 egg white (lightly beaten)
1 c. celery (finely chopped)	1/2 tsp. salt
1/2 c. onion (chopped)	1/2 tsp. pepper
1-1/2 c. red sweet pepper (diced)	1/2 c. fresh bread crumbs
2-1/2 c. fresh mushrooms (thinly sliced)	1/2 c. fresh parsley (minced)

In a large nonstick skillet, heat oil briefly and saute garlic, celery, onions, and red pepper, stirring until vegetables are slightly softened (about 3 to 5 minutes).

Boil a kettle of water and preheat oven to 375 degrees.

Stir mushrooms into the red pepper mixture. Cover and cook until mushrooms start to give up their liquid. Remove cover and saute vegetables, stirring them until all liquid has evaporated. Remove vegetables from heat and set aside.

In a large bowl, combine turkey, egg white, salt, pepper, bread crumbs, and parsley. Add sauteed vegetables and mix well. Transfer turkey mixture to a lightly oiled loaf pan (approx. 8x4) and set the pan in a large shallow baking dish.

Place the pans in the preheated oven. Pour boiling water into outer pan to depth of 1 inch or so. Bake loaf for 1 hour and 15 minutes. Remove loaf pan from outer pan and from the oven. Let it stand for 15 minutes, then remove from pan for slicing. (Fat: 25% calories from fat)

— Chicken Fried Rice —
(4 servings)

3 chicken breast halves (boned and skinned)	Nonstick cooking spray
2 c. water	2 tsp. peanut oil
2 T. reduced-salt soy sauce	1/2 c. fresh mushrooms (finely chopped)
1 egg (lightly beaten)	1/4 c. green onions (thinly sliced)
1/2 tsp. pepper	2 c. long-grain rice, cooked without salt or fat

Combine chicken and water in a large saucepan. Bring to a boil. Cover, reduce heat, and simmer 30 minutes or until chicken is tender. Remove chicken. Reserve broth. Cut chicken into 3/4-inch pieces and set aside.

Skim and discard fat from broth, reserving 1/3 cup broth. Save remaining broth for other uses. Combine 1/3 cup reserved broth, soy sauce, egg, and pepper. Stir well. Set aside.

(Continued)

Coat a wok with cooking spray. Add oil. Heat at medium-high (375 degrees) until hot. Add mushrooms, onions. Stir-fry 3 minutes. Stir in rice and chicken. Cook, stirring frequently for 6 to 8 minutes or until thoroughly heated. Drizzle egg mixture over rice and chicken mixture, stirring constantly until eggs are cooked. Serve warm. (Fat: 25% calories from fat)

— Hawaiian Chicken —
(4 servings)

1 can (8-ounce) unsweetened pineapple slices
   (undrained)
1 T. sesame seeds (toasted)
3 T. honey

1/4 tsp. rubbed sage
4 chicken breast halves (skinned)
Nonstick cooking spray

Drain pineapple, reserving 3 tablespoons juice. Set aside. Combine reserved pineapple juice, sesame seed, honey, and sage in a small bowl. Mix well.

Place chicken, skinned side down, on rack of a broiler pan coated with nonstick cooking spray. Brush chicken with honey mixture. Broil 8 inches from heat for 25 minutes, basting often with honey mixture. Turn chicken. Broil an additional 15 minutes or until tender.

Baste pineapple slices with honey mixture and broil 5 minutes, turning once. Transfer chicken to serving platter. Cut pineapple slices in half and arrange on each chicken breast half. (Fat: 25% calories from fat)

— Lemon Chicken —
(14 servings)

1/3 c. lemon juice
1/4 c. reduced-salt soy sauce
1 clove garlic (minced)
1/2 tsp. salt

1/4 tsp. pepper
2 pounds chicken breast halves (skinned and
   boned)
Nonstick cooking spray

Combine first 5 ingredients in a shallow container. Mix well. Add chicken. Cover and marinate in refrigerator 2 to 3 hours, turning once. Drain and discard marinade.

Transfer chicken to rack of a shallow roasting pan coated with cooking spray. Bake at 325 degrees for 1 hour or until chicken is done. Cut into 2-ounce slices. (Fat: 20% calories from fat)

— Parmesan Baked Chicken —

1 fryer (2-1/2 to 3 pounds) — cut into serving
   pieces
1 tsp. salt
1/4 tsp. pepper
1/4 tsp. garlic salt
1/4 tsp. paprika

1/8 tsp. thyme
1/4 c. Parmesan cheese
1 T. minced parsley
1/3 c. fine bread crumbs
1/3 c. water
1 T. canola oil

(Continued)

Preheat oven to 350 degrees. In a paper bag, place seasonings, cheese, parsley, and crumbs. Coat chicken by shaking a few pieces at a time in the bag.

Coat shallow baking pan with cooking spray, pour in water, and arrange chicken pieces. Sprinkle chicken with oil and bake uncovered in oven for 45 minutes.

Lower oven heat to 325 degrees. Cover pan with foil and bake 15 minutes longer. Remove foil. Raise oven heat to 350 degrees and bake 10 minutes longer. (Fat: less than 30% calories from fat)

— Pan-Fried Chicken —
(4 servings)

2 whole chicken breasts (skinned, boned, halved)

Preheat a nonstick skillet over medium-high heat. Add chicken breasts and brown 10 minutes on each side. Reduce heat. Cook 15 to 20 minutes, turning occasionally. (Fat: 21% calories from fat)

— Chicken Rolls with Spinach Stuffing —
(8 servings)

1 small onion (chopped)
1/4 pound fresh mushrooms (chopped)
Nonstick cooking spray
1 package (10-ounce) frozen chopped
   spinach (thawed)
2 T. grated Parmesan cheese
1 T. chili sauce
1/2 tsp. dried whole basil
1/2 tsp. grated lemon rind

1/4 tsp. salt
8 chicken breast halves (skinned and boned)
1 can (16-ounce) whole tomatoes (drained
   and chopped)
1/3 c. onion (finely chopped)
1 clove garlic (crushed)
1/2 tsp. dried whole Italian herb seasoning
1/4 tsp. pepper
2 T. tomato sauce

Combine 1 chopped onion and mushrooms in a shallow 2-quart casserole dish coated with cooking spray. Cover with heavy-duty plastic wrap and microwave at high for 4 to 4-1/2 minutes or until vegetables are tender. Drain off liquid. Set aside.

Place spinach on paper towels and squeeze until barely moist. Add spinach, cheese, chili sauce, basil, lemon rind, and salt to onion mixture. Mix well. Set aside.

Place each chicken breast half between 2 sheets of heavy-duty plastic wrap. Flatten to 1/4-inch thickness, using a meat mallet or rolling pin. Place 1/4 cup spinach mixture in center of each chicken piece. Roll up lengthwise and secure with a wooden pick. Place rolls, seam side down, in a casserole dish recoated with cooking spray.

Combine tomatoes, 1/3 cup finely chopped onion, garlic, Italian herb seasoning, and pepper. Spoon evenly over chicken rolls. Cover with wax paper and microwave at high for 12 to 14 minutes or until chicken is done, rotating dish after 5 minutes and rearranging rolls so that uncooked portions are to outside of dish.

Transfer chicken to a warm platter. Stir 2 tablespoons tomato sauce into liquid in dish. Cover and microwave at high for 1-1/2 to 2 minutes or until thoroughly heated. Pour over chicken. Serve immediately. (Fat: 20% calories from fat)

— Roast Chicken —
(4 servings)

1 roasting chicken (about 3 to 4 pounds)
Powdered rosemary
Black pepper

1 large yellow onion (quartered)
3 cloves garlic

Wipe inside of chicken with damp paper towel. Wash outside with cold water. Rub outside of bird and inside cavity with generous amounts of rosemary and black pepper. Put onions and garlic inside cavity. Skewer neck skin to back. Tuck wing tips behind shoulder joints. Place chicken breast side up in a shallow roasting pan. Roast at 375 degrees for 60 to 75 minutes. Let stand 10 minutes before slicing. Remove skin and fat before serving. (Fat: 22% calories from fat)

— Chicken Enchiladas —
(6 servings)

4 chicken breasts (skinless and poached)

Sauce:
2 cans reduced-fat cream of mushroom soup
1 onion (chopped)
1 can (7-ounce) green chiles (diced)

1 can (12-ounce) evaporated skim milk
8 ounces nonfat Cheddar cheese (grated)
7-ounce bag baked corn tortilla chips

Topping: 1 c. reduced- or nonfat Cheddar cheese (grated)
Preheat oven to 350 degrees. Shred poached chicken and set aside. In a large saucepan, heat all ingredients for sauce. Set aside.

Spray a 13x9-inch pan with cooking spray. Line the bottom with 1/3-bag tortilla chips. Layer with 1/3 of shredded chicken and sauce. Repeat layering twice. Sprinkle with cheese. Bake for 30 to 45 minutes or until cheese is bubbling. Serve hot. (Fat: 30% calories from fat)

7

Soups, Sandwiches, & Snacks

INTRODUCTION TO SOUPS

What Low-Fat Means —
What is your greatest food concern? According to the Food Marketing Institute, 46% of Americans said their biggest worry was the fat content. This figure is up 29% from just a year ago. I say, "Right on!" I believe this SHOULD be our biggest worry.

How can you quickly tell if something is low in fat? Keep in mind that a low-fat food will not have over 3 grams of fat per 100 calories. For example, if calories per serving are 100 but the food has 6 grams of fat, that food is too high in fat.

Why Is Fat So Fattening? —
First, remember that a gram of fat has 9 calories, whereas a gram of protein or carbohydrates has only 4 calories per gram. Right off, you can see that fat is twice as heavy in calories as protein or carbohydrates. There is a greater worry when it comes to fat, however. For example, fat found in meat is ready to go right into your fat cells for storage. If you eat 100 calories of a pure fat such as butter, your body automatically stores 97 of them for fat. Only three calories are used.

Not so with carbohydrates, because they have to go through many body processes before storage. Your body will burn carbohydrates rather than store them. If you eat 100 calories of a carbohydrate such as spaghetti, your body will burn up 23 calories just getting it ready for storage.

Reducing the amount of fat you eat can help you lose weight and that's without any other changes in your diet. Reducing fat will help keep weight off. So where other diets fail, it has been proven that people who switch to a low-fat way of eating, coupled with regular exercise, keep their weight off.

Every recipe in this book is low in fat. Some foods get less than 30% of their calories from fat. Others less than 20% calories from fat. The foods very low in fat get only 10% or less of their calories from fat. Keep in mind when you use regular mayonnaise or cheese instead of nonfat or low-fat varieties, you are greatly increasing the calories coming from fat.

It is so important to cut the amount of meat you are eating when you switch to a low-fat diet. When you prepare your plate, have only small servings of meat. Have lots of vegetables, fruits, and whole-grain bread, but eat only small portions of meat. Meat should be eaten once a day or less. Many days, I have no meat at all.

How Much Is Enough? —

How many fat grams can you have in a day and still be eating the low-fat way? Some health experts will tell you that you can have more fat grams than I feel is good. For example, they will tell you that if you weigh 100 pounds, you can divide your weight by two to get the number of fat grams you can have — in this case, 50. This is all with the assumption you have an active life style.

However, I believe this is too much. I weigh 105 pounds and I try to have not over 20 fat grams per day. I do this by having, most days, cereal with sliced banana or nonfat yogurt with a raisin bagel for breakfast; vegetable or some other low-fat soup with pita bread and fruit for lunch; then maybe spaghetti with tomato sauce, bread, and fruit for dinner. Having meals like this put me way under my 20 grams of fat for the day. Now some days, I will have foods that carry me over the 20 grams, but I strive to stay within the 20 grams most days. I lead a very active life, exercising an average of 1-1/2 hours each day.

Dr. Castelli of the famous Framington Heart Study, advises that no individual should consume more than 30 fat grams per day.

Foods That Benefit —

So often we hear about foods that are bad for us. Following are some foods that do good things for our bodies. I know you'll want know about them.

— Potassium cuts stroke risk. Eating some of the following foods can reduce your risk of death by stroke: cantaloupe, avocado, baked potato, skim milk, dried apricots, lima beans, salmon, spinach, beet greens, almonds, peanuts.

— Cinnamon can increase and even triple insulin activity. Eating cinnamon even in small amounts can boost your insulin. Cloves, tumeric, and bay leaves also boost insulin production, although not as much as cinnamon. Adding 1/8 teaspoon of cinnamon, for example, to cereal will increase insulin efficiency.

— Eating yogurt helps stomach problems of all kinds: upset stomachs, infections, diarrhea, and ulcers. It may also boost immunity and reduce risk of colon cancer.

— Eating dried beans — legumes — can lower blood cholesterol. Eating a cup of cooked beans like navy or pinto or even canned beans every day decreases blood cholesterol an average of 19%.

— Garlic and onions help prevent cancer. In tests, animals that had garlic and onion oils rubbed into their skin were not as likely to develop skin cancer. Animals exposed to cancer-causing agents and then fed garlic compounds did not develop colon cancer in 75% of the cases studied.

— Pineapples help guard against osteoporosis. Manganese and calcium also are a help against this crippling bone disease.

— Carrots, pumpkins, and sweet potatoes help slow down the process of clogging the arteries. In a major 10-year study of over 22,000 doctors, it was discovered that beta carotene (present in vegetables deep orange in color) cuts the risk of heart attacks dramatically.

— Foods high in beta carotene may also cut your chances of lung cancer. Studies show that smokers and former smokers who consume the most beta carotene foods are only half as likely to develop lung cancer as those who skimp on such foods.

Nourishing the Spirit —

Just as the body must have proper food to survive, so must our spirits have food from God's Word. We can eat the best diet and yet be unhappy and unfulfilled if we are not also feeding our spirits from the Scripture.

> All the labour of man is for his mouth, and yet the appetite is not filled (Eccles. 6:7).

We are incomplete if we have not met Jesus and let Him fill our lives with His spirit and His Word.

Viewers Write —

Dear Beverly,

 . . . I appreciate your show for so many reasons. Your exercises are effective, but your approach is gentle and encouraging. I'm not up to your speed yet, but I can see improvement. Because I'm firming up, people have asked me if I've lost weight. (I haven't yet.)

Your diet tips are so helpful. I've used the starvation technique for years to keep my size down, but my body has not been maintained. I'm so very grateful to you for helping me take good care of this wonderful body God has given me. I have only a few pounds to lose, but I don't mind waiting this time to take the pounds off properly.

Your suggestion to "sip" the extra water has been a great encouragement and has made that project "do-able" for me. I had been one of those people who took her 8 ounces like medicine, and I always gave up.

And finally, I appreciate your spiritual encouragement and the fact that you share the gospel so honestly and openly . . .

Also —

Dear Beverly,

 . . . You are so right, Beverly, "energy creates energy." I must have my "fix" as you put it, each day. I am 54 and have just retired from teaching. Through your wonderful encouragement and gentle manner, I have lost 25 pounds and my doctor is so pleased my cholesterol is now 210. It was over 300. I now have more time for my daily walk and I "sip" my water all day long.

Dear one, you probably have no idea how many lives you have helped. If folks out there really desire to feel the best that they can, then all they need to do is follow your excellent, common-sense advice . . . Thank you, too, for the spiritual food . . .

Hints for Soup —

— When making soup with homemade stock, chill the stock before making the soup so fat can easily be removed.

— If oil is called for, use safflower, olive, or canola. Corn oil can also be used.

— Avoid animal fats like butter and lard. When a recipe calls for butter, use reduced-calorie margarine instead.

— When a recipe calls for cooking vegetables in oil, generally a few teaspoons will do the job. If not, add water for extra moisture.

— When adding meat to a soup, cook the meat on a rack first to allow-fat to drip off. Then add to soup.

— For cream soups, use evaporated skim milk in place of cream.

— Save leftover grains, such as rice, for use in soups. This adds nutrition and flavor.

— For protein and fiber, add beans to soups.

— Pastas also make a good addition to most soups.

— Small cubes of tofu will add protein to soups.

— Experiment with varied spices to add spark to soups.

— Imitation butter granules will add a buttery flavor when needed.

— Always use non or low-fat cheeses.

SOUPS

— Mushroom-Barley Soup —
(4 servings)

1-1/2 c. onion (chopped)
1/2 pound mushrooms (sliced)
3 c. water
1/4 c. parsley (chopped)

1 c. carrots (sliced)
4 c. low-sodium beef broth
1/2 c. barley (rinsed and drained)
1/4 tsp. black pepper

Over medium-high heat, bring all ingredients to a boil in a large pot. Lower heat and simmer partly covered for 40 minutes until barley is tender. (Fat: less than 20% calories from fat)

— Sharon Armour, Mililani, HI

— Chicken Soup —
(4 servings)

1/3 c. chicken meat (boneless and skinless)
2/3 c. onion (chopped)
1 T. canola oil
4 c. defatted chicken stock
1 c. canned tomatoes
1 c. okra (cut up)

2 T. parsley (chopped)
1/3 c. brown rice
1 tsp. salt
1/4 tsp. pepper
1 tsp. Worcestershire sauce

Boil chicken in 4 cups water. Cool and reserve the stock. Cut into bite-size pieces.

Saute the onion in oil and add stock, vegetables, rice, seasonings, and chicken. Stir well. Simmer 45 minutes over medium heat. (Fat: less than 30% calories from fat)

— Peel-A-Pound Soup —

Small head of cabbage (chopped)
1 to 2 cans tomatoes
1 medium onion (chopped)

1 green pepper (chopped)
3 to 4 stalks celery (chopped)

Put all the above in large pot. Cover with water and bring to a boil. Simmer until tender. Can add a package of dry onion soup mix, parsley, and garlic salt for more flavor. (Fat: less than 20% calories from fat)

— Ann Buel, Fairfax, VA

— Onion Potato Soup —
(7 servings)

1 T. reduced-calorie margarine
2-1/2 c. green onions (chopped)
2 T. flour
6 c. chicken stock or broth (defatted and
   divided)

1-3/4 c. potatoes (peeled and cut into 1/2-inch
   pieces)
1/4 tsp. white pepper
1 T. dried dill weed (finely chopped)
1/4 c. nonfat, plain yogurt
Salt to taste

In a large saucepan over medium heat, melt margarine. Add green onions and cook, stirring until soft (about 5 minutes). Stir in flour and cook, stirring until smooth (about 2 minutes). Gradually stir in 3 cups stock or broth until mixed smoothly into flour mixture. Add potatoes, white pepper, and dill. Bring mixture to boil over medium-high heat. Reduce heat and simmer for 12 minutes or until potatoes are tender. Stir frequently to prevent potatoes form sticking to bottom of pan. Using a measuring cup, scoop up about 1/2 cup vegetables and liquid and transfer mixture to a blender. Add 1 cup more stock or broth and the yogurt. Blend until thoroughly pureed (about 30 seconds). Return puree to pot. Add remaining 2 cups of stock or broth, stirring until hot, but not boiling (about 5 minutes). Stir in salt and serve. (Fat: 22% calories from fat)

— Vegetable Minestrone —
(6 servings)

2 tsp. olive oil
1 medium onion (finely chopped))
1 garlic clove (minced)
4 c. vegetable stock (or 2 vegetable bouillon
   cubes with 4 c. water — divided)
15 ounces tomato sauce
2 c. garbanzo beans (cooked) or one 15-ounce
   can garbanzo beans(drained)
1 large celery stalk (diced)
1 medium carrot (thinly sliced)
1 large potato (peeled and cubed)

1 medium zucchini (diced)
1/4 c. fresh parsley (chopped)
1 tsp. dried basil leaves
1/2 tsp. dried marjoram leaves
1/4 tsp. dried thyme leaves
1/8 tsp. ground celery seeds
1/4 tsp. black pepper
1/2 c. small pasta seashells or macaroni
   (uncooked)
Salt to taste

(Continued)

In a Dutch oven or large pan, combine olive oil, onion, garlic, and 3 tablespoons vegetable stock. Cook on medium high, stirring frequently for 5 to 6 minutes or until onion is tender. If liquid begins to evaporate, add a bit more stock. Add remaining vegetable stock, tomato sauce, garbanzo beans, celery, carrot, potato, and zucchini. Stir well. Add parsley, basil, marjoram, thyme, celery seeds, and pepper. Mix well. Bring to boil. Lower heat and simmer about 15 minutes. Bring soup to boil again. Add pasta. Reduce heat to simmer, stirring occasionally, for 15 to 20 more minutes or until vegetables and pasta are tender. Salt to taste. (Fat: 14% calories from fat)

— California Chicken 'N Rice Soup —
(4 servings)

3 chicken breast halves (skinless)
4 c. water
1 can (14-ounce) low-salt chicken stock
1 onion (chopped)
3 carrots (sliced)
2-1/2 c. converted rice (cooked)

3 T. lime juice
1/8 tsp. ground cayenne pepper
1 small avocado (cubed)
2 tomatoes (cubed)
3 T. fresh coriander (minced)
4 ounces low-fat cheese (cubed)

In a 4-quart pot over medium heat, bring chicken, water, stock, and onion to a boil. Reduce heat and simmer for 25 minutes. Add carrots and simmer for 20 minutes.

Remove chicken from pot and set aside until cool enough to touch. Remove bones and cut into bite-size pieces.

Return chicken to pot. Stir in rice, lime juice, and pepper. Heat for 5 minutes, but don't boil. Stir in avocado, tomatoes, and coriander. Heat thoroughly.

Divide cheese among 4 soup bowls. Add soup and serve. (Fat: 24% calories from fat)

— Microwave Potato Chowder —
(6 servings)

1 T. low-calorie margarine
1 c. onions (chopped)
1 c. red or green bell peppers (diced)
2 pounds (6 medium) potatoes (diced)
3 c. chicken broth (defatted)
2 tsp. dried thyme leaves
2 bay leaves

1 c. skim milk
1 package (10-ounces) frozen corn (thawed and drained)
1/4 c. parsley (chopped)
1/8 tsp. cayenne pepper
Salt and pepper to taste

In microwave, melt margarine in 2-1/2-to 3-quart microwave-safe dish on high for 1 minute. Add onions and bell peppers. Microwave on high for 3 minutes. Stir in potatoes, broth, thyme, and bay leaves. Cover and cook on high for 20 minutes. Remove and discard bay leaves. Remove 4 cups cooked potato with slotted spoon and put in blender. Add milk and puree until smooth. Return mixture to dish. Stir in corn, parsley, and cayenne. Season with salt and pepper. Heat on high for 3 minutes. (Fat: less than 30% calories from fat)

— Beefy Grains Soup —
(6 servings)

2 c. dry green split peas (uncooked)
1 c. pearl barley (uncooked)
2 c. macaroni (uncooked)

2 c. lentils (uncooked)
1-1/2 c. rice (uncooked)

Combine all ingredients. Package by 1-1/3 cups in airtight containers. Label and use in following recipe:

6 c. water
1-1/3 c. of the above soup mix
1 tsp. salt
2 carrots (sliced)
1 onion (chopped)

2 stalks celery (chopped)
1-1/2 c. cabbage (shredded)
1 can (15-ounce) tomato sauce
1 can (24-ounce) tomato juice
2 c. cooked extra-lean ground beef

Put water, soup mix, and salt in large Dutch oven. Bring to boil.
Cover and simmer for 1 hour. Add other ingredients. Simmer for 30 minutes or until vegetables are tender. (Fat: 30% calories from fat)

— Okra Gumbo —
(6-8 servings)

1/2 c. water
2 T. canola oil
3 dozen medium okra
2 large onions (chopped)

4 large or 6 small tomatoes (peeled and
  chopped)
1/3 c. fresh parsley (chopped)
Salt and pepper to taste

In large frying pan, combine water, oil, okra, and onions. Simmer at least 20 minutes. Add tomatoes, parsley, salt, and pepper. Cook until thickened somewhat and tender. (Fat: 20% calories from fat)

— Ryland's Lentil Soup —
(6-8 servings)

1 small can of tomatoes
1 bag (12-ounce) of lentils (2 c.)
1 small can of spinach (drained)
9 c. water
1 medium onion (chopped)

1 stalk celery (chopped)
1 carrot (grated)
Salt and pepper to taste
1-1/4 tsp. thyme
1 bay leaf

Put lentils in colander and rinse. Then in a pot bring 9 cups water and lentils to a boil. Lower heat and cook for 1 hour. Add onions, celery, carrots, and seasonings. Continue cooking until vegetables are tender. Stir frequently during cooking. (Fat: less than 10% calories from fat)

— *Ryland Chesser, Anderson, SC*

— Easy Vegetable Soup —

In crock pot, put 2 cans of prepared vegetable soup. (Place cans in refrigerator for a while prior to opening to allow fat to harden for easy removal.) Rinse out cans, fill with water, and add to pot.

Then add the following:

1/4 tsp. each of oregano, basil herbs, and garlic juice
2 to 3 bay leaves (remove after cooking)
2 to 3 beef bouillon cubes (no salt needed, cubes are salty enough)

Dash of red pepper (optional)
Dash black pepper
1 to 2 cans tomato paste
1 quart frozen vegetables (I start them in the microwave first and add them to the pot.)

Combine all ingredients and cook for 6 to 8 hours in crock pot. Add water if needed. (Fat: less than 30% calories from fat)

— Mary Alice Stevens, Springhill, LA

— Navy Bean Soup —
(11 servings)

1 package (16-ounce) dried navy beans
2 quarts boiling water
1 tsp. salt
1-1/2 c. onion (diced)

1/4 c. celery (diced)
1 T. reduced-calorie margarine (melted)
2 c. canned stewed tomatoes

Soak beans in boiling water in Dutch oven for 30 minutes. Stir in salt. Cover and bring to boil. Reduce heat and simmer 2 hours.

Saute diced onion and celery in melted margarine until tender. Add sauteed vegetables and tomatoes to bean mixture. Stir well.

Simmer, uncovered for 1 hour or until beans are tender. Serve hot. (Fat: less than 10% calories from fat)

— Ryland's Vegetable Macaroni Soup —

1 can (19-ounce) vegetable soup (we use Progresso brand)
1 can (15-ounce) peas and carrots
1 can (15-ounce) stewed tomatoes
2 c. macaroni (cook elbow macaroni in boiling water for 8 min. before adding to soup)

1/2 tsp. of the following seasonings:
Basil leaves
Tarragon
Bay leaves
Celery flakes
Crushed rosemary

Combine all ingredients and simmer 15 to 20 minutes on low heat. (Fat: Trace)

— Ryland Chesser, Anderson, SC

— Carrot Soup —
(6 servings)

2 T. canola oil
1 c. onions (chopped)
3 c. carrots (chopped)
4 c. water
3 packets instant chicken-flavored broth mix

2 tsp. tomato paste
1 ounce white or brown rice (uncooked)
1-1/2 c. evaporated skim milk
Salt and pepper to taste

Heat oil in a large saucepan over medium heat. Add onions and cook until tender, adding water as needed.

Add carrots, water, broth mix, tomato paste, and rice. Reduce heat to low, cover, and simmer for 30 to 40 minutes, until rice and carrots are tender.

Pour soup through a strainer into another saucepan. Place about 1/2 cup of the vegetables back in the broth. Place remaining vegetables in blender and blend until smooth. Add to broth.

Stir in milk, salt, and pepper. Heat, stirring frequently until heated thoroughly. (Fat: less than 30% calories from fat)

— Creamy Potato Soup —
(9 servings)

4 medium red potatoes (peeled and cubed)
1 small onion (chopped)
4 green onions (chopped)
1 clove garlic (minced)

2 cans (10-1/2 ounce) no-salt chicken broth
  (defatted and undiluted)
1 c. skim milk
1/2 tsp. salt
1/8 tsp. white pepper

Combine potatoes, onion, green onions, garlic, and broth in a heavy, 3-quart saucepan.

Cover and simmer for 20 minutes or until potatoes are tender. Process potato mixture in batches in container of blender or food processor until smooth.

Combine pureed mixture with milk and remaining ingredients. Stir well.

Reheat soup to serving temperature or cover and refrigerate until thoroughly chilled. (Fat: less than 10% calories from fat)

— Bean Soup —
(4 servings)

12 ounces beans of choice (cooked)
2 c. evaporated skim milk
Salt and pepper to taste

1/8 tsp. garlic powder
1/8 tsp. dried thyme

In a blender container, combine all ingredients. Blend until smooth. Pour mixture into small saucepan. Heat, stirring frequently, until hot. Add water as desired for thinner consistency. (Fat: less than 10% calories from fat)

— Vegetable-Cheese Soup —
(6 servings)

1 package (10-ounce) frozen, mixed
   vegetables (thawed)
1 small onion (diced)
2 T. all-purpose flour
1 tsp. dried whole Italian herb seasoning
1/4 tsp. salt
1/8 tsp. pepper

1 tsp. chicken-flavored bouillon granules
1 c. water
1 c. skim milk
1/4 c. low-fat American cheese or Alpine
   Lace nonfat cheese (shredded)
2 tsp. Dijon mustard

Combine thawed mixed vegetable and diced onion in a medium saucepan. Combine flour, Italian herb seasoning, salt, and pepper. Stir well. Add to vegetables and stir to coat well.

Dissolve bouillon granules in water and milk. Add to saucepan and bring to boil.

Cook, stirring constantly, for 5 minutes or until mixture is thickened and bubbly.

Reduce heat to low and add cheese and mustard. Stir to blend. Serve immediately. (Fat: less than 20% calories from fat)

— Fresh Garden Soup —
(10 servings)

6 c. water
2 c. tomato juice
1 c. potato (peeled and diced)
1 c. onion (chopped)
1 c. whole kernel corn
1 c. lima beans (cooked and drained)

3/4 c. chicken (cooked and chopped)
1/2 c. carrots (sliced)
1/2 c. celery (chopped)
2 T. chicken-flavored bouillon granules
1 tsp. garlic powder
1-1/2 tsp. Worcestershire sauce

Combine all ingredients in a large Dutch oven. Cover and bring to boil. Reduce heat and simmer for 45 minutes to 1 hour. Serve hot. (Fat: less than 10% calories from fat)

— Broccoli Soup —
(15 servings)

1-1/2 c. water
1 package (10-ounce) frozen chopped
   broccoli (thawed)
1 package (10-ounce) frozen cauliflower
   (thawed)
1/3 c. onion (chopped)

2 tsp. chicken-flavored bouillon granules
1/4 tsp. ground mace
1 T. cornstarch
3 c. skim milk (divided)
1/2 tsp. salt
1/8 tsp. pepper

Combine water, broccoli, cauliflower, onion, and bouillon granules in small Dutch oven. Cover and bring to boil. Cook for 5 to 8 minutes or until vegetables are tender. Do not drain. Stir in mace.

Process vegetable mixture in batches in container of blender until mixture is smooth. Return mixture to Dutch oven.

Dissolve cornstarch in 1/2 cup milk. Stir into vegetable mixture. Add remaining 2-1/2 cups milk, salt, and pepper to vegetable mixture. Stir well. Cook over medium heat, stirring frequently, until mixture is thickened and bubbly. (Fat: less than 10% calories from fat)

— Onion Soup —
(4 servings)

1 T. reduced-calorie margarine
1 medium onion (thinly sliced)
5-1/2 c. water

1 T. plus 2 tsp. beef-flavored bouillon
   granules
1/2 tsp. Worcestershire sauce

Melt margarine in a large saucepan over low heat. Add onion. Cover and cook over low heat for 20 minutes or until onion is lightly browned, stirring occasionally.

Add water, bouillon granules, and Worcestershire sauce. Stir well.

Cover and bring to a boil. Reduce heat and simmer for 10 minutes. Serve hot. (Fat: less than 10% calories from fat)

— Zucchini Soup with Herbs —
(4 servings)

5 c. zucchini (chopped)
1 large potato (peeled and cubed)
1 c. water
3 green onions (thinly sliced)
1 T. reduced-calorie margarine (melted)

1/2 c. water
1-1/2 tsp. dried whole tarragon
1/2 tsp. chicken-flavored bouillon granules
1/2 c. skim milk

Combine zucchini, potato, and 1 cup water in a small Dutch oven. Cover and bring to a boil. Boil for 10 minutes or until crisp-tender. Do not drain.

Saute onions in margarine until tender. Add to zucchini and potato. Add 1/2 cup water, tarragon, and bouillon granules, stirring to blend. Add skim milk and cook over medium heat until thoroughly heated. (Fat: less than 20% calories from fat)

— Chicken 'N Corn Soup —
(4 servings)

1 can (1-pound) cream-style corn
1-1/2 c. water
1 package instant chicken-flavored broth mix

1 c. cooked noodles
4 ounces skinless chicken (cooked and cubed)
Salt and pepper to taste

In medium saucepan, combine all ingredients. Heat over medium-low heat, stirring frequently, until soup boils.(Fat: less than 20% calories from fat)

— Vegetarian Chowder —
(6 servings)

2 T. olive oil
1 c. onions (chopped)
1/2 c. carrots (chopped)
1 c. celery (chopped)
2 cloves garlic (minced)
9 ounces potato (cubed)
1 can (1-pound) tomatoes

2 c. water
1 small bay leaf
1 tsp. dried thyme
1/2 tsp. dried basil
Salt and pepper to taste
1-1/2 c. macaroni (cooked)

(Continued)

Heat oil in a large saucepan over medium heat. Add onions, carrots, celery, and garlic. Cook, stirring frequently, for 10 minutes. Add small amounts of water, if necessary, to prevent drying.

Add remaining ingredients, except macaroni. Reduce heat to low. Cover and simmer for 40 minutes. Add macaroni. Heat through. Remove and discard bay leaf before serving. (Fat: less than 30% calories from fat)

— Lima Bean Soup —
(4 servings)

1 package (10-ounce) frozen lima beans
 (thawed)
2 c. water
2 packets instant chicken-flavored broth mix
1 T. plus 1 tsp. reduced-calorie margarine
1 tsp. curry powder

1 T. minced onion flakes
1 small bay leaf
Salt and pepper to taste
1/2 c. evaporated skim milk
1 T. dried chives

In a medium saucepan, combine beans, water, broth mix, margarine, curry powder, onion flakes, bay leaf, and pepper. Bring to a boil over medium heat. Reduce heat to low. Cover and simmer until beans are tender (about 20 minutes). Remove and discard bay leaf.

Place soup mixture in a blender and blend until smooth. Return to saucepan.

Stir in milk. Heat, stirring until heated thoroughly. Do not boil. Spoon soup into individual serving bowls. Garnish with chives. (Fat: less than 30% calories from fat)

— English Pea Soup —
(8 servings)

1 c. split peas (uncooked)
6 c. water
1 c. onions (chopped)
1/2 c. celery (chopped)

1/2 c. carrots (chopped)
1 clove garlic (minced)
1/2 tsp. dried thyme
Salt and pepper to taste

Place peas and water in a large saucepan over medium heat. Bring to boil. Add remaining ingredients. Reduce heat to low. Cover and simmer until peas are soft (about 2 hours). Stir occasionally while cooking. For a thicker soup, mash cooked peas with fork or potato masher. (Fat: less than 10% calories from fat)

— Quick Beef Soup —
(8 servings)

1/2 pound lean ground chuck
2 cans (8-ounce) tomato sauce
2 c. carrots (sliced)

1/4 c. onion (chopped)
1 jar (2-1/2-ounce) sliced mushrooms
2 c. water

Cook ground chuck in a large nonstick skillet over medium heat until browned, stirring to crumble. Drain and pat dry with paper towels. Wipe pan drippings from skillet with paper towel.

Return ground chuck to skillet. Add tomato sauce, sliced carrots, chopped onion, and undrained sliced mushrooms. Stir in water.

Cover and bring to boil. Reduce heat and simmer 30 to 35 minutes or until carrots are tender, stirring occasionally. Serve hot. (Fat: less than 10% calories from fat)

— Bayou Gumbo —
(makes 16 cups)

1/4 c. all-purpose flour
1 c. green pepper (chopped)
1-3/4 c. celery (chopped)
1-1/2 c. onion (chopped)
2 c. water (divided)
1-3/4 tsp. chicken-flavored bouillon granules
2 cans (16-ounce) no-salt tomatoes (undrained and chopped)
3-1/2 c. no-salt tomato juice
1 pound okra (sliced)
3 T. fresh parsley (chopped)

3 c. (chopped, cooked) turkey breast (skinned before cooking)
1 bay leaf
1/2 tsp. garlic powder
1/2 tsp. hot sauce
1/4 tsp. black pepper
1/4 tsp. whole thyme
1-1/2 pounds medium shrimp (peeled and deveined)
1 can (12-ounce) fresh oysters (drained)

Place flour in shallow baking dish. Bake at 400 degrees for 12 to 14 minutes or until browned, stirring every 4 minutes. Set aside.

Combine green pepper, celery, onion, 1/3 cup water, and bouillon granules in a large Dutch oven. Cook over medium heat 10 to 12 minutes or until vegetables are tender. Stir in flour. Gradually stir in remaining 1-2/3 cup water, tomatoes, and next 9 ingredients. Cover. Reduce heat and simmer for 45 minutes.

Add shrimp and oysters. Simmer for 10 to 15 minutes or until shrimp are done and oysters begin to curl. Discard bay leaf. (Fat: 30% calories from fat)

— Traditional Chicken 'N Rice Soup —
(makes 2 quarts)

2 quarts chicken stock (defatted)
1/4 c. carrots (chopped)
1 c. celery (chopped)

1 small onion (chopped)
1/4 c. raw brown rice

Put chicken stock and vegetables into a 4-quart saucepan. Simmer until vegetables are about half done (about 15 minutes). Then add rice and continue cooking until rice is tender (about 10 minutes). (Fat: 30% calories from fat)

— Beef Minestrone —
(makes 12 cups)

1/2 pound fresh green beans
Nonstick cooking spray
3/4 pound lean ground chuck
1/2 c. onion (minced)
2 cloves garlic (minced)
4 c. water
2 cans (14-1/2-ounce) no-salt stewed tomatoes (undrained)
1 tsp. beef-flavored bouillon granules

1/4 tsp. salt
2 c. shredded cabbage
1 can (19-ounce) cannellini beans (drained)
1-1/2 c. zucchini (diced)
4 ounces vermicelli (uncooked and broken into 2-inch pieces)
1/2 c. grated Parmesan cheese
1/4 c. fresh basil (minced)

(Continued)

Wash green beans. Remove strings. Cut into 1-inch pieces. Set aside. Coat a Dutch oven with cooking spray. Place over medium heat until hot. Add ground chuck, onion, and garlic. Cook until meat is browned, stirring to crumble. Drain and pat dry with paper towels. Wipe drippings from pan with a paper towel.

Return meat to Dutch oven. Add green beans, water, tomatoes, granules, and salt. Bring to boil. Cover, reduce heat, and simmer for 15 minutes until tender. Sprinkle each serving with 2 teaspoons Parmesan cheese and 1 teaspoon basil. (Fat: 25% calories from fat)

— Light Mushroom Soup —
(makes 4 cups)

Nonstick cooking spray
1/2 pound fresh mushrooms (sliced)
1 shallot (chopped)
4 c. water

1 T. beef-flavored bouillon granules
1/8 tsp. garlic powder
1/8 tsp. pepper

Coat a large nonstick skillet with cooking spray. Place over medium-high heat until hot. Add mushrooms and shallot and saute until tender. Set aside.

Combine water, beef bouillon, garlic powder, and pepper in a large saucepan. Bring to a boil. Add mushroom mixture. Reduce heat and simmer for 5 minutes until completely heated. (Fat: less than 20% calories from fat)

— All-Fresh Veggie Soup —
(makes 12 cups)

1/2 pound fresh green beans
1 can (46-ounce) no-salt tomato juice
2-1/2 c. tomatoes (peeled and chopped)
2 c. cabbage (finely shredded)
1-1/2 c. fresh okra (sliced)
2 c. potatoes (peeled and cubed)
1 c. carrots (sliced)
1/2 c. onion (chopped)

1/2 c. pearl barley (uncooked)
1 tsp. fresh oregano (minced)
1-1/2 tsp. hot sauce
1/2 tsp. salt
1/2 tsp. pepper
1/2 c. fresh corn kernels (about 1 ear of fresh corn)

Wash beans and remove strings. Cut into 1-inch pieces.

Combine beans, tomato juice, and next 11 ingredients in a large Dutch oven. Bring to a boil. Cover, reduce heat, and simmer 45 minutes. Stir in corn kernels. Cover and cook an additional 15 minutes or until vegetables are tender, stirring occasionally. (Fat: less than 20% calories from fat)

— Chili Lite —
(8 servings)

2 medium onions (chopped)
1 green pepper (chopped)
1 T. canola oil
1 pound extra-lean ground beef
1 can (15-ounce) tomato sauce

Water
1 tsp. chili powder
1/2 tsp. salt
Pepper to taste
2 cans (16-ounce) kidney beans (undrained)

(Continued)

In a large, nonstick skillet, saute onions and green pepper in oil until onions are tender and clear-looking. With a slotted spoon, remove onion and pepper and set aside. Drain fat from skillet and wipe clean.

Add ground beef to skillet and cook, stirring to break up. Continue cooking until done. Place meat in strainer and drain off fat. Rinse meat under hot water.

Again, wipe skillet clean. Place tomato sauce in skillet. Fill tomato sauce can with water and stir into sauce. Add onions, peppers, ground meat, and seasonings. Bring to boil, lower heat, and simmer uncovered for 10 minutes.

Add kidney beans and liquid and cook, covered, an additional 20 minutes. (Fat: 16% calories from fat)

— Fast 'N Easy Chili —
(4 servings)

1 pound ground turkey
1 can (8-ounce) tomato sauce
1 T. chili powder

1-1/2 c. water
1 envelope onion soup mix
1-1/2 cans kidney beans (drained)

In a 2-quart casserole, cook turkey in microwave on high for 4 minutes. Drain. Add other ingredients. Cover and cook 10 minutes on high, stirring once. Let stand, covered, for 5 minutes. (Cooking times will vary depending on your microwave.) (Fat: 30% calories from fat)
— *Sharon Armour, Mililani, HI*

INTRODUCTION TO SANDWICHES AND SNACKS

Tips for Weight Control —

As I write this book, I am 50 years old. Many of you have read my book, *Your Health Coach,* and you know my testimony — how at the age of 27 I was in very poor health. How I battled against putting on weight by starving myself and all the problems that go with that. I am thankful God showed me a better way and through life-style changes (eating the healthy, low-fat way, and embracing exercise) I turned my health around. Today I help thousands of people do the same.

Whether therefore ye eat, or drink or whatsoever you do, do all to the glory of God (1 Cor. 10:31).

Even though the recipes in this book are low in fat, let me share some tips that I use to control my weight. Whenever I am having a food (for instance the Traditional Lasagna in the Grains section under Pastas) I do not have as large a serving as I think I can eat. Instead, I always have a small serving along with a salad or some steamed vegetables, like broccoli, a serving of high-fiber bread and skim milk. I leave room for fresh fruit for dessert. You can follow a similar routine with all the foods in this book — especially when you want to lose some weight.

Remember, eat small servings supplemented with complex carbohydrate foods such as bread, steamed vegetables, and fruits. Why? You become full by the weight of food in your stomach. So, at each meal be sure to eat foods that weigh something. For example, fruit contains a lot of water and is quite filling.

I told myself a long time ago, "If you don't want to look like a big mac, don't eat a big mac!" Think of yourself as a special creation of God Almighty, uniquely made by Him.

> What? know ye not that your body is the temple of the Holy Ghost which is in you, which ye have of God, and ye are not your own?
>
> For ye are bought with a price: therefore glorify God in your body, and in your spirit, which are God's (1 Cor. 6:20).
>
> There hath no temptation taken you but such as is common to man: but God is faithful, who will not suffer you to be tempted above that ye are able; but will with the temptation also make a way to escape, that ye may be able to bear it (1 Cor. 10:13).

You need three meals a day because regular biological rhythms and hunger patterns are established when you eat three meals a day. When you skip meals, you interfere with your body's delicate system of letting you know when you are hungry and then when you are full. Skipping meals leads to binging and overeating. Never go longer than 5 hours between meals. Remember to sip water throughout the day and do have eight to ten glasses a day. When you do this, cravings for food will disappear. Once you train yourself to have that much water, your body will automatically crave water.

One thing you must do to lose weight and keep weight off is eat breakfast. If you do not eat breakfast, health experts say, you slow your body's metabolism by as much as 5% plus you increase your chance of having a heart attack. If you are not hungry and cannot stand the thought of breakfast, try eating dinner no later than 6 p.m. and see if you aren't hungry the next morning. If you do this and still are not hungry, plan to have some fruit or a bagel a little later in the morning. Eating breakfast is just a habit that needs to be cultivated. Once you begin changing the way you eat, you will find you are hungry and ready for breakfast in the morning.

A TV Viewer Writes —

> Dear Beverly,
>
> Just had to write and let you know how much I appreciate your program . . . I've been watching and participating for a few months.
>
> I am 46 years old, married with two children . . . On my birthday in June, I weighed 260 pounds and was plagued with almost constant migraine headaches, diarrhea, exhaustion, insomnia, borderline severe depression, anxiety attacks, and more. Also, I had no self-esteem.
>
> I have been a Christian for 25 years, but after a number of years of both financial and physical problems, I felt as though God didn't care about me. On the last day of August, I began counseling sessions with a professional counselor from our church. After listening to a condensed version of my history and current problems, he asked me some (what I thought) were strange questions: Did I drink water? Walk or exercise daily? Sit outside in the sun (not

sun bathing)? How much sleep did I get? What and how much did I eat? Did I take vitamins?

I had already decided to keep a diet journal — not to diet — listing the foods eaten and keeping the calories from 1,200 to 1,500 daily.

All that was many weeks ago. I began eating nutritionally-sound meals of primarily complex carbohydrates, fresh fruits, vegetables, limiting fat intake, and eliminating junk foods. I also began to walk 30 minutes daily, drink water, get adequate sleep, take vitamin and mineral supplements, and get out in the sun for 30 minutes or so daily. About 15 weeks ago, I began exercising with you three to five times a week.

I have lost 51 pounds, 6 dress sizes, and am no longer a victim of migraines or any other physical and emotional problems. I am off a number of prescribed heavy-duty medications that were not helping but were causing serious side effects.

Please note — the change in my life style was for my physical well being, not to lose weight. I truly did not believe that I was capable of losing weight. I had been unable to lose weight for over 15 years, though I was faithful to numerous types of diets . . . I even tried extremely low-calorie diets of 800 calories or less and yet gained weight.

I want to say that from the first day until now, I have not felt hungry, deprived, or tempted. Before, by day two of a diet, I was craving chocolate intensely and watching the clock to see when I could eat again. I follow and adhere to all the nutrition tips and instructions you give us.

Every time I step on the scales, I am surprised to see more weight loss. And every time I look in a full-length mirror, I can't believe those are my thighs.

I appreciate the sweet spirit you exhibit and the reinforcement of sound nutrition and health habits . . . Spiritually speaking, my thinking has been renewed and my communion with the Lord has been restored.

What a joy to hear such good news from this dear lady! God is no respecter of persons — what He's done for others, He will do for you. So many of our health and spiritual problems are directly and indirectly tied to our diet and exercise habits. If you are experiencing failure in your life style today, take a look at your eating and exercise habits. This precious lady's letter is not unusual. I constantly hear from people who have found renewal through proper diet and exercise.

Lunch Tips —

— Remember, a high-fat lunch will leave you feeling sluggish; while a low-fat lunch gives you more energy.

— Many lunch meats, such as bologna and salami, are extremely high in saturated fats and sodium.

— Always include whole-grain bread or pita bread and fresh fruit in your lunch.

— Drop the idea that lunch means sandwiches. Buy some plastic containers that will fit into a lunch bag and pack good-for-you foods.

— A salad adds vitamins and fiber to your lunch and will help you feel satisfied.

— Keep a bottle of your favorite reduced-calorie dressing with you.

— When eating from a salad bar, avoid everything but the fresh fruits and vegetables. Forget the potato salad, macaroni salad, and other fat-laden "salads."

— In a fast food restaurant, try a baked potato instead or a burger. Ask for it dry with margarine on the side so you can control the amount of fat you eat.

— Freezing low-fat dishes at home and warming small portions of them in a microwave at lunchtime is a great idea.

Tips for Packing Lunches —

— Pack a whole-grain muffin instead of a cupcake.

— Save small containers from low-fat yogurt and use them later for packing such items as fruit salad or cottage cheese. Then discard them.

— Let children help pack their lunches using these containers.

— Help children cut and wrap their favorite fresh fruits and vegetables. They will be more likely to eat them this way.

— Give your children a variety when it comes to sandwich fillings. Try peanut butter with raisins, bananas, or chopped apples, for example.

— For children who resist whole-grain bread, make a sandwich with one slice each of white and whole-grain. Or begin buying the new white bread that has all the fiber and nutrition of whole-grain bread.

— Fresh or dried fruit is good for dessert.

— Whole-wheat pretzels or butter or oil-free popcorn fill the bill for munchies.

— Core an apple and fill the center with peanut butter.

SANDWICHES AND SNACKS

— Ryland's Pita Veggie Pocket Sandwich —

1 small green pepper (chopped)
1 medium onion (sliced)
1 small jar mushrooms (drained)

Nonstick cooking spray
1/2 T. light soy sauce

In a cast-iron skillet sprayed with cooking spray, stir-fry the above ingredients for about 5 to 6 minutes until tender. Add soy sauce. Stir and set aside.

In a salad bowl, toss the following ingredients:

1/2 tsp. garlic powder
Pinch of tarragon

1/2 head of lettuce (chopped)
1 tomato (chopped)

Add a low-fat salad dressing of choice. Add skillet ingredients and toss. Stuff 5 pita sandwiches with this mixture.

(For variety, you may use low-fat cheeses or lean, low-fat cooked meats such as turkey or chicken. Just remember, fat grams will increase with use of cheese or meat.) (Fat: 1 gram per sandwich when made without meat or cheese)   — *Ryland Chesser, Anderson, SC*

— Lean and Tasty Beef Sandwich —

2 slices pumpernickel rye bread
Mustard of choice
2 ounces lean roast beef (thinly sliced)

3 fresh mushrooms (sliced)
1 ripe tomato (sliced)

Spread bread with mustard. Layer each bread slice with beef mushrooms and tomato. Note: rump roast is the leanest cut of beef. (Fat: 21% calories from fat)

— Sliced Turkey in Pita —

1 pita (pocket bread)
1/2 tsp. mustard
2 ounces roast turkey breast

Lettuce
2 ripe tomato slices
1 thin slice onion

Spread pita pocket with mustard. Stuff with turkey, lettuce, tomato and onion. (Fat: 14% calories from fat)

— Seasoned Turkey Burgers —
(6 servings)

1 pound ground turkey
1/2 c. dried bread crumbs (whole-grain if
  possible)
3 T. onion (finely chopped)
2 T. ketchup
1 T. lemon juice

1 tsp. Worcestershire sauce
1 tsp. soy sauce
1/2 tsp. paprika
1/4 tsp. hot pepper sauce
Pepper to taste

Combine all ingredients and shape mixture into 6 patties. Fry, broil, or grill the burgers until done. Serve with fresh lettuce, tomatoes, and whole-grain buns. Or serve plain with salad on the side. (Fat: 25% calories from fat)

— Pita and Turkey —
(4 servings)

1/4 pound ground raw turkey
1/2 small onion (chopped)
1/4 green pepper (chopped)
1 small garlic clove (minced)
2 T. plus 2 tsp. salt-reduced tomato sauce
1/2 tsp. chili powder

1/4 tsp. ground cumin
Pepper to taste
2 large whole-wheat pita breads (cut in half)
2 c. lettuce (shredded)
1 small tomato (chopped)
1 scallion (thinly sliced)

Lightly coat skillet with nonstick cooking spray and place over moderately high heat. Add turkey, onion, bell pepper, and garlic. Cook until vegetables are limp (about 3 minutes). Stir in tomato sauce, chili powder, cumin, and pepper. Simmer for 10 minutes or until slightly thickened. Remove from heat and let cool slightly, then toss with lettuce, tomato, and green onion. Spoon into warmed pita breads. (Fat: less than 25% calories from fat)

— Lean Beef Burrito —
(8 servings)

1 pound low-fat ground beef
8 flour tortillas (10-inch size)

Sauce:
8 ounces no-salt tomato sauce
1/4 tsp. garlic

4 ounces part-skim American cheese (shredded)
1/4 c. scallions (chopped)

1/2 tsp. cumin
1 T. lemon juice
1 T. sugar

Brown and drain ground beef. Combine sauce ingredients and pour over beef, stirring to mix. Place 1/2 cup of beef mixture in each tortilla, fold and place seam side down on a baking sheet. Top with cheese and scallions. Bake 15 minutes at 350 degrees. Serve with lettuce and tomatoes. (Fat: 26% calories from fat)

— Healthy Pizza —
(8 servings)

1 package pizza crust mix (ready to bake
   according to package directions)
2 c. mushrooms (sliced)
1-1/2 c. carrots (shredded)
1 c. zucchini (finely sliced)
1/2 c. onion (chopped)
1 T. canola oil
8 ounces no-salt tomato sauce

1/2 tsp. garlic
1/2 tsp. fennel
1 tsp. basil
1/2 tsp. oregano
1 tsp. brown sugar
1 c. part-skim mozzarella cheese
1/2 c. Parmesan cheese

Preheat oven to 425 degrees. Spray a 14-inch pizza crisper pan with cooking spray. Press prepared crust onto pan and bake 14 to 16 minutes. Meanwhile, saute mushrooms, carrots, zucchini, and onion in oil over medium heat for 3 minutes. When crust is prebaked, sprinkle with vegetables, sauce, seasonings, sugar, and cheese. Bake for 15 more minutes. Remove from oven. Cool slightly before serving. (Fat: 29% calories from fat)

— Mexican Cheeseburgers —
(4 servings)

1 pound low-fat ground beef
1/2 tsp. cumin
1/8 tsp. pepper
4 flour tortillas (warmed)

1/2 c. tomato (chopped)
1/2 c. lettuce (chopped)
1/2 c. part-skim Cheddar cheese (shredded)

Combine ground beef, cumin, and pepper. Mix lightly. Form into 4 patties. Place on a broiler pan or outdoor grill, 3 to 4 inches from heat. Broil to desired doneness, turning once. Top half of each tortilla with equal portions of tomato, lettuce, and cheese. Place burger on top, fold, and serve. (Fat: 29% calories from fat)

— DeBitha's Pizza —
(makes 2 pizzas)

Dough:
4-2/3 c. all-purpose flour
1/2 tsp. pepper
2 T. olive oil

1-1/2 envelopes yeast
1/2 tsp. salt
1-1/8 c. warm water

Mix all ingredients well and knead until dough is smooth. Place in large, olive-oiled bowl. Cover with dish towel and leave in warm, draft-free place for 2 hours to rise. (Dough will double in bulk.) Punch dough into thickness desired for pizza. May use immediately or wrap tightly in plastic and freeze for future use.

Sauce:
2 iron skillets (10-inch)
1 large can Italian tomatoes
1 T. oregano
1 chicken breast (cooked, thinly sliced)
1 T. olive oil

1 T. basil
Salt and pepper to taste
1 large green pepper or red pepper (thinly sliced)
1 small can tomato paste
5 cloves garlic (crushed)

Rub half of oil in pans and set aside. Use remainder of oil to fry garlic over low heat until cooked. Do not burn. Add tomatoes and paste. Heat for few minutes. Then add basil, oregano, salt, and pepper. Cook over medium heat for 10 to 15 minutes. While sauce is cooking, stretch dough carefully over bottom of iron pans and up the sides 2 inches. Spoon small amount of sauce over each dough, covering entire surface. Add chicken and peppers. Cover with more sauce, filling almost to top of dough. Cheese is not necessary, but if you want some, use a nonfat variety. Bake in preheated oven at 475 degrees for about 40 minutes or until crust pulls away from edges of pan and is golden brown. Crust will be very crisp, so cut each pizza into 4 pieces after cooling about 5 minutes. (Fat: 30% calories from fat)   — DeBitha Harrelson, Elba, AL

— Vegetable Pizza with Oat Bran Crust —
(4 servings)

1 c. oat bran cereal (uncooked)
1 c. all-purpose flour
1 tsp. baking powder
3/4 c. skim milk
3 T. canola oil
1 can (8-ounce) low-sodium tomato sauce

1 c. sliced mushrooms
1 medium green, red pepper combination (cut into rings)
1/2 c. onion (chopped)
1-1/4 c. part-skim mozzarella cheese (shredded)
1/2 tsp. Italian seasoning (crushed)

Combine oat bran, flour, and baking powder. Add milk and oil. Mix well. Let stand 10 minutes. Heat oven to 425 degrees. Lightly spray 12-inch pizza pan with nonstick cooking spray. With lightly oiled fingers, pat dough out evenly. Shape edge to form rim. Bake 18 to 20 minutes. Spread tomato sauce evenly over partially-baked crust. Top with vegetables, sprinkle with cheese and seasonings. Bake an additional 12 to 15 minutes or until golden brown. (Fat: 30% calories from fat)
          — Evelyn Harrison, Lafayette, IN

— Tuna-Cheese Sandwiches —
(2 servings)

1 can (6-1/2-ounce) low-salt tuna packed in
   water (drained)
1-1/2 ounces low-fat Cheddar cheese
   (shredded)
1/8 tsp. pepper
1 T. green onions (thinly sliced)

2 T. plain, nonfat yogurt
2 tsp. pimento (diced)
1 tsp. mustard
1/4 tsp. low-salt Worcestershire sauce
4 slices whole-wheat bread
Nonstick cooking spray

Combine tuna and next 7 ingredients. Stir well. Spread tuna mixture evenly over 2 slices of bread. Top with remaining bread slices. Transfer sandwiches to a griddle coated with cooking spray. Cook until bread is lightly browned and cheese is melted. (Fat: 25% calories from fat)

— Cucumber/Watercress Party Sandwiches —
(12 servings)

1 medium cucumber (peeled and cut into 12
   1/8-inch slices)
1/4 c. nonfat sour cream
1 ounce "lite" cream cheese (softened)

3/4 tsp. dried whole chervil
1/4 tsp. onion powder
8 slices bread of choice
1/4 c. (generous) fresh watercress (minced)

Press cucumber slices between layers of paper towels to remove excess moisture. Set aside. Combine sour cream, cheese, chervil, and onion powder. Stir until smooth. Set aside.

Remove crust from bread. Cut three 1-1/2 inch rounds from each bread slice. Spread 1/2 teaspoon reserved sour cream mixture on 12 bread rounds. Place a cucumber slice on top of sour cream mixture. Top with 12 remaining bread rounds. Frost sides of sandwiches with remaining sour cream mixture. Roll sides of sandwiches in minced watercress. (Fat: 25% calories from fat)

— Tasty Peanut-Apple Spread —
(makes 1-1/4 cups)

1/4 c. part-skim ricotta cheese
3 T. creamy peanut butter
2 T. unsweetened apple juice

1/2 tsp. vanilla extract
1/4 tsp. lemon juice
1 small apple shredded (approx. 1 c.)

Combine ricotta cheese, peanut butter, apple juice, vanilla, and lemon juice in a small bowl. Beat at low speed with an electric mixer until smooth.

Add shredded apple. Mix well. Serve at room temperature with sliced apples, sliced pears, rice cakes, or graham crackers. (Fat: 30% calories from fat)

— Open-Faced Beef Sandwiches —
(makes 2)

2 slices pumpernickel rye bread
2 ounces lean roast beef (thinly sliced)
3 fresh mushrooms (sliced)

1 ripe tomato (sliced)
Mustard

Spread bread with mustard. Layer each bread slice with beef, mushrooms, and tomato. (Fat: 21% calories from fat)

8

Vegetables

INTRODUCTION TO VEGETABLES

For so many people the answer to their weight and eating problems lie in learning moderation and self-control. For many, help lies in just restructuring a life that has gone out of control.

A Viewer Writes —

> Dear Beverly,
> ... I decided to exercise with you and now I haven't been able to stop. I've tried lots of other exercise shows but I never stuck to any of them and here it is two months later and I have been exercising with you every day!
> I used to be a compulsive overeater. I am 35 years old and I thought I never could get it under control, but since exercising with you and following your helpful nutrition suggestions and tips — it's like a wonderful miracle. I finally feel free of that awful obsession ... if you knew how I was just a few short months ago, you wouldn't believe it. Overeating is a disease as bad as alcoholism. It's just as self-destructing. I was a food-aholic, stuffing anything and everything into my mouth all the time. Instead of waking up with a hangover, I would wake up so sick to my stomach! I was always depressed and irritable.
> But now I feel free of that obsession. I still have my moments but I'm kinder to myself and say its OK and go on and little by little, I'm getting away from that way of life. You're helping me learn about a new, healthier way of life. I drink the water, skim milk, walk, read labels, look for fat content of food, and for the first time in a very long while, I can see a bright light at the end of the tunnel ... I lost 15 pounds and have a way to go but I feel confident about getting it off through the positive changes in my life."

Food Abuse: Bulimia and Anorexia —

Bulimia and anorexia, binging and starving, are not pleasant topics, but so many have problems with this. Eating disorders affect 1% of those between the ages of 12 and 25.

Symptoms are developing at even younger ages. It's not unusual for an 11-year-old to become anorexic or bulimic, especially when she is maturing faster than her peers. Also, these eating disorders are most common among females.

Why does this happen? Experts say it is society's glorification of the fashionable slim body combined with peer pressure at school that often causes these unhealthy fears of food. Now we are discovering that parents' attitudes toward eating also play a major role in the development of these problems.

Studies conducted of girls with eating disorders showed that their mothers often also had the same problem. A mother's concern with dieting and weight just made the issue more critical to the daughter. It was discovered that many mothers thought their daughters should lose weight and even rated their daughters less attractive when they considered them overweight.

Eating disorders can be brought on by parents comparing one child to another. Or by a parent constantly nagging a child to eat. One anorexic young girl whose father had been constantly demanding that she eat, suddenly began eating when her dad left town on an extended business trip.

Instead of comparing or criticizing our children, we should praise them for all their good points. And if a child truly is overweight, lead her, by example, into an exercise program she can enjoy and cook the low-fat way.

Do you praise your child? Do you encourage exercise? Do you take time to prepare healthy, low-fat meals? Do you set an example of moderation and self-control without preaching about it?

> But covet earnestly the best gifts: and yet shew I unto you a more excellent way (1 Cor. 12:31).

God does have a better way for us. We have to pray and seek His way in our lives and be open to the leading of the Holy Spirit who indwells every believer.

Water: Essential to Healthy Living —

Just as the cheapest foods like potatoes, carrots, rice, and dried beans are often the most healthful, so is the cheapest drink — water. Without water we would die in a few days even though we can live for weeks without food. More than half the weight of the human body is water. Water is the basis for all body fluids, including digestive juices, blood, urine, lymph, and perspiration. All cell processes and all organ functions depend on it.

Water is essential as a lubricant: as the basis for saliva, mucous secretions throughout the body and the fluids that bathe the joints. Water is needed to keep food moving through the intestinal tract and to eliminate wastes. It helps prevent constipation and regulate body temperature.

Under average circumstances, your body loses and needs to replace 2 to 3 quarts of water every day. If you are exercising or doing physical work in the heat, the loss will be much greater. We get some water from the foods we eat, especially from fruits and vegetables, most of which are 85-96% water. Some water is produced as a by-product of metabolism. Six to 8 glasses of liquid, including juices, milk, and soups, are needed to make up the balance. Alcoholic and caffeinated beverages like coffee, tea, and colas do not fulfill the demands of the body for water.

In fact, they increase urine production.

While juices and milk are good for you, nothing meets the need of the body like water. Water is quite possibly the single most important factor in losing weight and keeping it off. Although too many of us take it for granted, water is essential to permanent weight loss.

Water suppresses the appetite naturally and helps the body metabolize stored fat. Studies show that a decrease in water intake will result in an increase in fat deposits on the body. An increase in water leads to a decrease in fat. Why? Because the kidneys do not function properly without adequate water. If they don't work right, then the liver has to deal with more trash. Since one function of the liver is to convert fat into energy for the body, it is essential that the liver not have to help out the kidneys. The liver needs to be free to take care of fat properly; otherwise, fat will be stored and weight loss will stop.

Water is a good diuretic. Fluid retention will greatly decrease when the body is getting proper amounts of water. The less water you drink, the more fluids your body will retain in preparation for survival. It will begin to hold on to every drop of fluid. Diuretics are a temporary solution to fluid problems, because as soon as you are off them, the fluid retention starts again because the body is receiving inadequate water. Also diuretics force out essential nutrients along with the fluids. Give your body plenty of water and the fluid retention will decrease or cease.

Excess salt will also contribute to fluid retention. The more salt you eat, the more water your body uses to deal with it. To get rid of unnecessary salt, drink plenty of water.

An overweight person needs even more water than a thin person. Since more fat must be dealt with in the overweight body, more water is needed to handle the load.

Water helps maintain good muscle tone by giving muscles ability to contract and preventing dehydration. Water reduces sagging skin problems that usually follow weight loss.

Of course, water relieves constipation. If a body is getting too little water, it siphons off what it needs from internal sources like the colon. So water is essential to proper removal of wastes from the body.

Cold water is absorbed more quickly by the body than warm.

Drinking 6 to 8 glasses of water a day can mean a breakthrough for you in weight control and weight loss.

Tips for Great Tasting Vegetables —

— Cook vegetables just until they are tender, yet crisp, if you want maximum taste and nutrition.

— Steaming fresh and frozen vegetables in a rack over boiling water will help preserve flavor and freshness.

— Almost all canned vegetables contain salt.

— Leaving skin and peeling on vegetables makes them more fiber-rich.

— Use spices instead of fats to enhance flavor in vegetables.

— Use polyunsaturated oils such as safflower, canola, sunflower, corn, or soybean when cooking vegetables.

— Always use reduced-calorie margarine instead of butter. However, be aware that low-calorie "tub"-style margarines have a high water content.

— When sauteing vegetables use a small amount of oil or margarine in a nonstick skillet or with nonstick cooking spray. Then add water or broth to prevent drying.

— When making a cream sauce, always use evaporated skim milk in place of cream.

— When using cheeses, always choose low-fat or nonfat varieties.

— A very small amount of soy sauce on vegetables gives them a good taste.

— Onion powder adds flavor to cooked green vegetables such as green beans.

— Imitation butter granules add flavor when butter is needed.

Don't Throw Away the Best Part —

No matter how you try, cooking of any kind destroys nutrients to some degree or other. The amount lost depends on how fresh the food was at the start and how it was handled and stored before you bought it. Also the length of cooking time, the temperature of cooking, and exposure to air and water will determine how many nutrients are destroyed. Vitamin C and the B vitamins are most easily destroyed by cooking. Other vitamins will cook out into the water.

When your mother told you to eat all your vegetables, she was telling you right. Vegetables are full of good things and nutritionists and doctors everywhere are now proclaiming the various health benefits of different vegetables. Here are some suggestions to help you prepare vegetables and fruits as nutritiously as possible:

— Cook for as short a time as possible. Microwaving, steaming, and stir-frying are good methods. If cooking in a pot, use a lid to cut cooking time.

— Eat vegetables raw when possible. When not possible, try to cook them whole and with the peeling.

— Never soak fruits or vegetables.

— When boiling vegetables, use as little water as possible. Place them in the water only when it is at a full boil. This helps reduce cooking time. Preserve the water that you cooked the vegetables in for making soups, sauces, and gravies. This way you still get the nutrients.

— Don't leave cooked food standing for long periods at room temperature. Rather, cook foods as close to serving time as possible.

— Shop frequently for fresh produce and don't buy a lot at a time. If the produce looks wilted or discolored, buy frozen. Frozen fruits and vegetables retain more Vitamin C than fresh produce that has been mishandled or has sat in the store for days.

Cooking Methods and What They Do —

— Microwaving: This method is best for preserving nutrients in vegetables because the cooking time is so short and usually little or no water is needed. There is also little or no nutritional loss when reheating leftovers.

— Steaming: Here too, the cooking time is short and nutrients are retained well. Generally vegetables lose 50% less minerals through steaming than through boiling.

— Boiling: If you must boil vegetables, use as little water as possible and don't put food in pot until water is at a full boil. Cover pot to speed cooking. For example, green beans lose 72% of their Vitamin C when french cut and boiled, but lose only 46% when cooked whole.

— Baking and Roasting: The higher the temperature and the longer the cooking time, the more nutrients lost. For example, baked potatoes lose 60% of Vitamin C if left standing for 1 hour but only 20% if eaten right after cooking.

— Frying: Frying at high temperature destroys nutrients. Stir-frying is quicker and less destructive to vitamins and minerals. For example, french fried potatoes lose up to 90% of their Vitamin C.

Suggested Cooking Times and Seasoning for Vegetables —

— Broccoli (1 bunch): cook 5 to 8 minutes; season with ginger, soy sauce.

— Brussels Sprouts (1 pound): 10 minutes in microwave to 20 minutes when steaming; season with dill, rosemary, lemon juice.

— Cabbage (1 pound): 6 minutes microwave to 14 minutes steamed; season with caraway seed, dill.

— Carrots (1 pound): 6 minutes in microwave to 12 minutes steamed; season with basil, parsley, dill.

— Cauliflower (1-1/4 to 1-1/2 pounds): Microwave 10 minutes to 18 minutes steamed; season with chives, dill, nutmeg.

— Greens (1 bunch): 8 minutes microwave to 15 minutes boiled; season with lemon juice, oregano.

— Potatoes (16 ounces): 12 minutes microwave to 30 minutes steamed or boiled; season with caraway seed.

— Spinach (1 Pound): 7 minutes microwave to 5 minutes steamed; season with basil, nutmeg, oregano.

— Summer squash (1 pound): 7 minutes microwave to 12 minutes steamed; season with basil, oregano, parsley.

— Sweet Potatoes (16 ounces): 12 minutes microwave to 35 minutes steamed; season with lemon or orange juice.

— Turnips (1 pound): 9 minutes microwave to 35 minutes steamed; season with basil, caraway seed.

— Winter squash (3 pounds): 12 minutes microwave or steamed; season with allspice, cardamom.

Green, Non-Starchy Vegetables

— Stir-Fried Vegetables —
(2-3 servings)

3 T. sesame oil
4 broccoli florets
1 small zucchini (sliced)
1 small yellow squash (sliced)
6 fresh mushroom caps (sliced)
1 small carrot (sliced)

4 cherry tomatoes
1/2 c. white or red cabbage (finely sliced)
1/2 c. fresh spinach (chopped)
1/2 c. scallions (sliced)
3 T. soy sauce

In very hot nonstick skillet or wok, combine sesame oil and all vegetables. Toss and cook for one minute, stirring constantly. Add soy sauce, tossing until well blended. May want to serve over rice. (Fat: 25% calories from fat)

— *Sherri Arrowwood, Greenville, SC*

— Glazed Carrots —
(6 servings)

1 medium bunch carrots (peeled)
1/8 c. reduced-calorie margarine
1/3 c. firmly-packed brown sugar

1 tsp. nutmeg
3 to 4 T. fresh orange juice

Slice carrots diagonally. Steam slightly until tender but crisp. Saute in margarine. Add brown sugar, nutmeg, and orange juice. Cook and stir until brown sugar melts and carrots are glazed. Serve immediately. (Fat: 25% calories from fat)

— Fried Okra —
(4 servings)

1 pound okra
1/2 c. corn meal
1/2 tsp. salt

1/4 tsp. pepper
2 T. canola oil

Slice okra into 1/2-inch rounds. In a paper bag, combine corn meal, salt, and pepper. Add okra and shake. Fry in hot oil until okra is browned. Drain on paper towels. (Fat: 30% calories from fat)

— Green Beans 'N Tomatoes —
(8 servings)

1 pound fresh green beans
1 red pepper (cut into 1/2-inch strips)
1/2 c. red onion (chopped)

1 can (16-ounce) plum tomatoes (chopped)
1/4 tsp. black pepper

Wash green beans. Remove ends and strings. In a medium saucepan, combine ingredients and heat to boiling but do not boil. Cover. Reduce heat and simmer 10 to 30 minutes until beans are tender. (Fat: 7% calories from fat)

— Green Beans 'N Lemon —
(4 servings)

1 pound fresh green beans
1/4 c. fresh lemon juice

1/4 tsp. black pepper
1/2 tsp. or less salt

Wash beans. Remove ends and strings. In a covered vegetable steamer basket over boiling water, steam beans 5 to 15 minutes until tender. Do not overcook. Combine lemon juice, black pepper, and salt. Pour over hot beans. (Fat: 4% calories from fat)

— Zucchini 'N Tomatoes —
(6 servings)

1 can (16-ounce) plum tomatoes (diced)
1/2 medium yellow onion (chopped)
2 cloves garlic (minced)

3 small zucchini (sliced 1/2-inch thick)
2 T. fresh parsley (chopped)
1/2 tsp. dried basil

In a medium saucepan, simmer tomatoes, onion, and garlic 30 to 45 minutes. Add sliced zucchini. Simmer 15 to 20 minutes until zucchini is beginning to soften but is still crisp. Sprinkle with parsley and basil. (Fat: 6% calories from fat)

— Green Beans 'N New Potatoes —
(6-8 servings)

2 pounds fresh green beans
2 T. canola oil
1 large onion (chopped)
1-1/2 T. Worcestershire sauce

Salt to taste
6 to 8 new potatoes (unpeeled)
Tabasco to taste

Wash and snap beans. In large pot, combine all ingredients and cover with water. Simmer until beans and potatoes are tender. (Fat: 30% calories from fat)

— Microwave Squash Toss —
(6 servings)

3 small yellow squash (cut into 1/2-inch slices)
2 medium zucchini (cut into 1/2-inch slices)
1 jar (2-ounce) sliced pimento (drained)
1/2 tsp. dried Italian seasoning

1/4 tsp. salt
1/4 tsp. garlic powder
3 T. water
2 tsps. reduced-calorie margarine

Combine yellow squash, zucchini, pimento, Italian seasoning, salt, and garlic powder in a 2-1/2-quart casserole. Add water and dot with margarine. Cover with heavy-duty plastic wrap and vent. Microwave on high for 8 to 10 minutes until vegetables are tender. Stir at 3-minutes intervals. Let stand, covered, for 2 minutes. (Fat: less than 30 calories per 1/2-cup serving)

— New Orleans Zucchini —
(4 servings)

3 zucchinis (sliced thick)
1 onion (chopped)
2 garlic cloves (minced)
1 can (8-ounce) tomato sauce

1/2 tsp. dill weed
1/4 tsp. rosemary (crushed)
1/4 tsp. thyme

Combine all ingredients in a skillet or large saucepan. Cover and cook over low heat 10 to 15 minutes or until crisp but tender. (Fat: 20% calories from fat)

— *Martha Elson, Anchorage, AK*

— Stuffed Cabbage —
(4 servings)

8 large cabbage leaves
2 c. boiling water
12 ounces lean ground beef
1 onion (sliced)
1 T. low-calorie margarine
2 T. chopped onion
1/3 c. brown rice

1/2 tsp. salt
Dash of pepper
3 T. warm water
1 T. lemon juice
1 T. brown sugar
1 c. tomato sauce
2 c. cold water

Rinse cabbage leaves and cut off heavy stems. Blanch cabbage in 2 cups boiling water until just soft. Remove leaves, pat dry, and set aside.

Brown beef. Saute onion in margarine.

(Continued)

In a separate bowl, mix beef, chopped onion, rice, salt, and pepper, and 3 tablespoons water.

Place 2 heaping tablespoons of beef mixture in center of each leaf. Tuck sides in and roll up, enclosing mixture. Secure with toothpick.

Put sauteed sliced onion in a saucepan, add lemon juice, brown sugar, tomato sauce, and 2 cups water. Stir. Place cabbage rolls in sauce, folded side down. Cover and cook over low heat for 1 to 1-1/2 hours or until rolls are firm. Baste occasionally and add water if necessary. (Fat: 20% calories from fat)

— Squash Casserole —
(20 servings)

3 pounds yellow squash (sliced)
1 onion (chopped)
2 carrots (peeled and sliced)
2 cans cream of chicken soup
2 c. nonfat yogurt

1 jar (2-ounce) pimentos
2 c. chicken broth
1 package herb-seasoned stuffing
Nonstick cooking spray

Preheat oven to 350 degrees. Steam squash, onion, and carrots until tender. Drain. Combine soup, yogurt, and pimentos in large mixing bowl. Stir in cooked vegetables. In large skillet, heat 1 cup broth. Turn off heat and stir in stuffing mix. Add remaining chicken broth and toss stuffing lightly until moist. Coat a 9x13-inch casserole dish with nonstick cooking spray. Layer squash mixture, alternating stuffing. Bake, uncovered, 30 to 35 minutes, until bubbly. (Fat: 18% calories from fat)

— Broccoli Casserole —

1-1/2 c. water
1/8 c. low-calorie margarine
1 package (6-ounce) cornbread stove top
   stuffing mix
2 packages (10-ounce) chopped broccoli
2 T. self-rising flour
1 tsp. chicken bouillon

3/4 c. skim milk
1 package (3-ounce) low-fat cream cheese
1/4 tsp. salt
4 green onions (sliced)
1 c. nonfat Cheddar cheese (shredded)
Paprika

Combine water, margarine, and package of stuffing seasoning. Bring to boil and remove from heat. Stir in bread crumbs. Spoon inside baking dish coated with margarine.

Cook broccoli and drain. Place broccoli inside bread crumb well.

Melt 2 tablespoons margarine in saucepan. Add flour and stir smooth. Cook 1 minute stirring constantly. Add bouillon, milk, and cook over medium heat until thick. Add cream cheese and salt. Stir in onion. Pour over broccoli. Sprinkle with cheese and paprika.

Cover and bake at 350 degrees for 35 minutes. Remove cover and bake 10 more minutes. (Fat: 30% calories from fat)   — *Sherri Arrowwood, Greenville, SC*

— Vegetarian Pizza —
(6 servings)

Nonstick cooking spray
1/2 c. onion (chopped)
1 clove garlic (minced)
4 c. tomatoes (seeded and chopped)
3 T. red wine vinegar
2 T. fresh basil (minced)
1/2 tsp. dried whole oregano
1/4 tsp. pepper

3 (6-inch) whole-wheat pita bread rounds
1 c. (4 ounces) low-fat process American cheese or Alpin Lace fat-free yellow cheese (shredded)
1 medium green pepper (chopped)
1 small zucchini (thinly sliced)
3 ounces fresh mushrooms (thinly sliced)
2 T. Parmesan cheese (grated)

Coat a large, heavy skillet with cooking spray. Place over medium heat until hot. Add onion and garlic and saute until tender.

Add chopped tomatoes, vinegar, basil, oregano, and pepper to skillet. Bring to boil. Reduce heat and simmer, uncovered, 20 minutes or until sauce reduces by 1/3. Stir occasionally. Remove tomato sauce from heat. Set aside.

Cut a slit around edge of each bread round. Carefully split apart. Place split bread rounds on a baking sheet. Bake at 450 degrees for 5 minutes or until bread rounds begin to brown. Spread 1/4 cup tomato mixture evenly over each toasted round. Sprinkle shredded cheese equally over each round.

Arrange vegetables on top of cheese. Sprinkle with Parmesan cheese.

Bake at 450 degrees for 10 minutes or until cheese melts and vegetables are tender. (Fat: 25% calories from fat)

— Mushrooms and Peas —
(4 servings)

2 tsp. reduced-calorie margarine
1 c. mushrooms (sliced)
1 package (10-ounce) frozen peas (thawed)

1/8 tsp. garlic powder
1/8 tsp. dried thyme
1/4 c. water

Melt margarine in a small saucepan over medium heat. Add mushrooms and cook, stirring 2 minutes.

Add peas, spices, and water. Cover and cook 10 to 12 minutes until tender. (Fat: less than 30% calories from fat)

— Oriental Cabbage —
(6 servings)

1 T. sesame oil
1 c. onions (sliced)
6 c. cabbage (shredded to 1/4-inch thickness)
1 T. soy sauce

1/8 tsp. garlic powder
1/4 tsp. ground ginger
1 packet instant beef-flavored broth mix
2 T. water

Heat oil in a large nonstick skillet over medium heat. Add onions and cook until tender (about 5 minutes). Reduce heat to low. Add cabbage.

In a small bowl, combine remaining ingredients. Pour over cabbage. Cook, covered, until cabbage is tender (about 20 minutes). Stir occasionally while cooking. (Fat: 30% calories from fat)

— Chinese Spinach —
(4 servings)

1 package (10-ounce) frozen chopped
    spinach (thawed and drained)
1 can (4-ounce) mushroom pieces (drained)
1 T. plus 1 tsp. reduced-calorie margarine
1/2 packet instant chicken-flavored broth mix

2 T. soy sauce
1/8 tsp. garlic powder
2 T. green onion (chopped — green part only)
1/2 tsp. sugar (or equivalent sweetener)
Dash ground ginger

Combine all ingredients in a large nonstick skillet. Heat, stirring frequently, until hot. (Fat: less than 30% calories from fat)

— Broccoli 'N Cheese Casserole —

1 pound fresh broccoli
1 c. water
1/2 tsp. salt
1/4 c. onion (chopped)
1/4 c. celery (chopped)
1/4 pound fresh mushrooms (sliced)
2 tsp. reduced-calorie margarine (melted)
1 can (8-ounce) sliced water chestnuts

1/2 c. (2 ounces) nonfat Alpin Lace yellow
    cheese (shredded and divided)
1/2 can (10-3/4-ounce reduced-calorie cream
    of mushroom soup (undiluted)
1/2 c. skim milk
1/8 tsp. garlic powder
1/8 tsp. pepper
Nonstick cooking spray

Trim off large leaves of broccoli. Remove tough ends of lower stalks. Wash thoroughly. Cut into 1-inch pieces.

Bring water to boil in large saucepan. Add broccoli and salt. Cover, reduce heat, and simmer 5 minutes or until tender. Drain liquid and set broccoli aside.

Saute onion, celery, and mushrooms in margarine in saucepan until tender. Combine broccoli, sauteed vegetables, and drained water chestnuts in a large bowl. Set aside.

Combine 1/4 cup cheese, soup, and milk in saucepan. Cook over low heat, stirring constantly until cheese melts. Stir in garlic powder and pepper. Pour over broccoli mixture, tossing lightly to coat.

Spoon mixture into 2-quart casserole coated with cooking spray. Bake at 350 degrees for 25 minutes. Sprinkle with remaining 1/4 cup cheese. Bake an additional 5 minutes or until cheese melts. (Fat: 25% calories from fat)

— Carrot Casserole —
(6 servings)

2 c. carrots (cooked and mashed)
2 T. (1/2 ounce) low-fat American cheese or
    Alpin Lace nonfat cheese (shredded)
1 egg or egg substitute (beaten)

1/4 c. skim milk
1/2 tsp. salt
1/8 tsp. pepper
Nonstick cooking spray

Combine all ingredients, except cooking spray. Stir well. Pour mixture into a 1-1/2-quart casserole dish coated with cooking spray.

Bake at 325 degrees for 40 minutes or until thoroughly heated. (Fat: less than 10% calories from fat)

— Cauliflower Casserole —
(10 servings)

1 medium cauliflower (cut into flowerets)
Nonstick cooking spray
1/2 tsp. salt
1/8 tsp. pepper

1/2 c. plain, nonfat yogurt
2 T. (1/2-ounce) low-fat American cheese or
    Alpine Lace nonfat cheese (shredded)
1 tsp. sesame seeds (toasted)

Cook cauliflower in boiling water to cover in a medium saucepan for 8 minutes or until tender. Drain well.

Place half of cauliflower in a 1-quart casserole dish coated with cooking spray. Sprinkle with salt and pepper. Top with half each of yogurt, and cheese.

Repeat layers with remaining cauliflower, yogurt and cheese. Sprinkle with sesame seeds and bake at 350 degrees for 20 minutes or so. (Fat: less than 30% calories from fat)

— Fresh Tomato and Zucchini —

2 T. onion (chopped)
1-1/2 c. zucchini (cubed)
1 tomato (cut up)

1 T. canola oil
Basil, salt, and pepper to taste

Saute onion and zucchini in oil. Stir for 1 minute or so. When getting a bit soft, add tomato. Stir and add basil, salt, and pepper to taste. Remove from heat before tomato gets too soft. Other spices that could be used are garlic powder, oregano. Serve hot and sprinkle with Parmesan cheese. (Fat: 20% calories from fat)
        — *Stephanie M. Tobin, Saskatoon, Canada*

— Pan-Fried Zucchini —

2 T. onion (chopped)
1 tsp. canola oil
1 qt. zucchini (grated)

Chopped dill and basil to taste
Salt and pepper to taste

In frying pan, saute onion in oil. With coarse grater, grate zucchini into pan. Sprinkle with chopped dill, basil, salt, and pepper to taste. Stir until cooked crisp but tender (about 5 minutes). (Fat: 20% calories from fat)
        — *Stephanie M. Tobin, Saskatoon, Canada*

— Simply Asparagus —
(4 servings)

1/2 pound fresh asparagus (trimmed)
2 T. water

1 fresh lemon (cut in wedges)

Wash and trim asparagus. In a nonstick skillet, heat water to boiling. Add asparagus spears. Cover tightly and steam over medium-high heat for 3 to 5 minutes until asparagus is crisp-tender. Shake occasionally. Serve with lemon. (Fat: Trace)

— Zucchini Casserole —
(8 servings)

4 medium zucchini (sliced)
3/4 c. carrot (shredded)
1/2 c. onion (chopped)

1/2 c. water
1/2 c. plain, low-fat yogurt
Nonstick cooking spray

Cook zucchini in boiling water in medium saucepan 5 minutes or until crisp-tender. Drain well and set aside.

Combine carrot, onion, and 1/2 cup water in a large saucepan. Cover and bring to boil. Reduce heat. Simmer 10 minutes or until crisp-tender. Drain off liquid.

Add yogurt and zucchini to saucepan. Stir gently.

Spoon mixture into a 1-1/2-quart casserole dish coated with cooking spray. Bake at 350 degrees for 30 to 40 minutes or until thoroughly heated. (Fat: less than 10% calories from fat)

— Broccoli Casserole —

2 T. flour
1/2 c. nonfat milk
1/4 c. onion (chopped)
Nonstick cooking spray

8 ounces low-fat Cheddar cheese (grated)
3 c. broccoli (finely chopped)
6 egg whites (beaten)
3 large sheets phyllo dough

(Phyllo dough is fat free. By coating the layers of the dough with nonstick cooking spray instead of melted butter, you can create a low-fat pastry. This dough can also be used in other recipes as a substitute for high-fat crusts or toppings.)

Preheat oven to 325 degrees. Coat a shallow 1-1/2-quart casserole dish with nonstick cooking spray. Set aside.

Stir flour into nonfat milk until it dissolves. Spray frying pan with nonstick cooking spray and saute onion. Add milk mixture, stirring constantly until thickened. Blend in cheese. When cheese melts, add broccoli. Pour into casserole dish. Add egg whites and mix gently.

Cut sheets of phyllo dough in half. Top casserole mixture, alternating one piece of phyllo dough with one spray of nonstick cooking spray to create 6 layers. Bake 35 to 45 minutes. (Fat: 23% calories from fat)

— Summer Squash Casserole —
(8 servings)

1 pound yellow squash
1/2 c. onion (chopped)
2 jars (4-ounce) diced pimento (drained)
1/4 c. green pepper (chopped)
1 egg or egg substitute
2 T. fat-free mayonnaise

1 tsp. salt
Nonstick cooking spray
2 T. cracker crumbs
1/4 c. (1-ounce) low-fat process American cheese or Alpine Lace nonfat cheese (shredded)

Cook squash in boiling water in medium saucepan 15 minutes or until tender. Drain and mash.

Combine chopped onion, pimento, green peppers, egg, mayonnaise, and salt in medium bowl. Stir well. Stir in squash.

(Continued)

Spoon squash mixture into a 2-quart casserole dish coated with cooking spray. Sprinkle with cracker crumbs.

Bake at 325 degrees for 30 minutes. Top with cheese during the last 5 minutes of baking time. (Fat: less than 30% calories from fat)

— Asparagus Casserole —
(8 servings)

1 package (10-ounce) frozen asparagus spears
1/2 can (10-3/4-ounce) reduced-calorie cream
   of mushroom soup (undiluted)
1 can (8-ounce) sliced water chestnuts
   (drained)

1/2 c. skim milk
1/2 c. (2-ounces) low-fat process American
   cheese or Alpine Lace fat-free cheese
   (shredded)
Nonstick cooking spray

Cook asparagus according to package directions, omitting fat and salt. Drain and set aside.

Combine soup and milk, stirring until blended. Layer half each of water chestnuts, asparagus, soup mixture, and cheese in a 1-1/2-quart casserole dish coated with cooking spray.

Repeat layers with remaining chestnuts, asparagus, soup mixture, and cheese.

Bake at 325 degrees for 20 minutes or until thoroughly heated. (Fat: 30% calories from fat)

— Easy Stir-Fry Vegetables —
(8 servings)

Nonstick cooking spray
1 clove garlic (crushed)
1 T. low-sodium soy sauce
3 c. cabbage (shredded)
2 c. broccoli flowerets
1 c. carrots (sliced)
1 c. green onions (sliced)

2 c. fresh mushrooms (sliced)
1 package (6-ounce) frozen snow pea pods
   (partially thawed)
1 T. cornstarch
2 tsp. chicken-flavored bouillon granules
1 c. water

Coat a wok or large skillet with cooking spray. Heat at medium for 2 minutes.

Add garlic and soy sauce. Stir-fry 3 minutes.

Add cabbage, broccoli, carrot, and green onions. Stir-fry 3 to 4 minutes or until vegetables are crisp-tender.

Add mushrooms and snow peas. Stir-fry 1 to 2 minutes. Combine cornstarch, bouillon granules, and water, stirring to dissolve. Pour over vegetables and stir-fry until thickened and bubbly. (Fat: less than 10% calories from fat)

— Baked Okra —
(8 servings)

3 c. fresh okra (sliced)
Nonstick cooking spray
1 c. onion (chopped)
1 c. tomato (chopped)

1 c. green pepper (chopped)
1/2 tsp. salt
1/8 tsp. pepper

Spread okra in a 13x9x2-inch baking dish coated with cooking spray. Layer tomato and remaining ingredients over okra. Cover loosely with aluminum foil. Bake at 400 degrees for 1 hour or until okra is tender, stirring occasionally. (Fat: less than 10% calories from fat)

— Stuffed Tomatoes —
(8 servings)

8 medium tomatoes
1 package (10-ounce) frozen, chopped
   spinach (thawed)
2 tsp. reduced-calorie margarine
2 T. all-purpose flour

1/2 tsp. salt
1/2 tsp. dry mustard
1/4 tsp. Worcestershire sauce
2 T. soft bread crumbs
Nonstick cooking spray

Cut tops from tomatoes. Scoop out pulp, leaving shells intact. Chop and preserve pulp. Invert tomato shells on paper towels. Drain 10 minutes.

Cook spinach according to package directions, omitting salt and fat. Drain well.

Melt margarine in medium saucepan over low heat. Add flour, salt, mustard, and Worcestershire sauce, stirring until smooth. Cook 1 minute, stirring constantly. Stir in spinach and tomato pulp. Remove from heat.

Spoon spinach mixture into tomato shells. Top with bread crumbs and place in a shallow baking dish coated with nonstick cooking spray.

Bake at 400 degrees for 15 minutes or until mixture is thoroughly heated and bread crumbs are browned. (Fat: less than 10% calories from fat)

— Vegetable Burritos —
(15 servings)

Nonstick cooking spray
1 c. onion (sliced)
1 c. fresh mushrooms (sliced)
2 cloves garlic (minced)
4 c. zucchini (sliced)
1-1/2 c. carrots (thinly sliced)
1 c. green pepper (sliced)
2 c. tomatoes (chopped)
1/4 c. ripe olives (chopped)
1 T. seeded jalapeno pepper (minced)

2 cans (4-ounce) green chiles (chopped and
   drained)
1 tsp. chili powder
1/4 tsp. salt
1/2 tsp. dried whole oregano
1/2 tsp. ground cumin
1 c. (4-ounce) shredded Alpine Lace nonfat
   Cheddar cheese (shredded)
15 (6-inch) warm flour tortillas

Coat a large Dutch oven with cooking spray. Place over medium-high heat until hot. Add onion, mushrooms, and garlic. Saute until vegetables are tender and all liquid absorbed. Add zucchini and next 5 ingredients. Saute, stirring constantly, about 10 minutes or until vegetables are crisp-tender. Drain vegetables and green chilies and next 6 ingredients. Stir well.

Spoon 1/3 cup vegetable mixer onto each tortilla and fold over edges. Serve immediately. (Tortillas may be warmed by wrapping tightly in aluminum foil. Bake at 350 degrees for about 15 minutes.) (Fat: less than 30% calories from fat)

— A. Krueger, Tulsa OK

Starchy Vegetables

Tips for Starchy Vegetables —

Starchy vegetables include white potatoes, sweet potatoes, yams, corn, peas, and all varieties of winter squash.

— These vegetables are higher in carbohydrates, protein, and calories than other vegetables.

— Many weight-watching groups view one serving of a starchy vegetable as being equivalent to one serving of bread.

— Potato skins are rich in nutrients and fiber and should be left on the potato if possible.

— Store potatoes of all types in a cool, dark place with good ventilation. Higher temperatures cause sprouting and refrigeration turns some of the starch to sugar.

— Make several holes in a potato before baking it. This allows steam to escape and will prevent the potatoes from "exploding" all over the oven.

— Many spices go well with potatoes. Some are dried chives, oregano, dill weed, and basil. For example, top a baked potato with dried chives, imitation bacon bits, and any low-fat cheese for a real, low-fat taste treat. Or try topping your potato with your favorite pasta sauce, salsa, low-fat yogurt, and steamed vegetables.

— Yams are a sweet potato variety with reddish skin and orange flesh. They are sweet and very moist.

— Sweet potatoes taste great sprinkled with or mashed with ground cinnamon, nutmeg, cloves, ginger, or allspice.

— Sweet potatoes also blend well with fruits such as apples, pineapple, and oranges.

— Winter squash is more easily peeled after cooking. Before cooking, cut squash in half and remove seeds and stringy material.

— Squash halves make pretty holders for many fillings and stuffings.

— To bake a squash, place halves, cut-side down, in a shallow baking pan. Cover with foil and bake in a 400-degree oven for 30 to 45 minutes until tender.

— Squash can also be cooked by cutting in cubes and boiled in about 1 inch of water until tender. This takes about 15 minutes.

— Winter squash goes well with such spices as cinnamon, nutmeg, cloves, ginger, and allspice.

— When buying fresh peas, choose full, bright green pods. Store, unshelled, in refrigerator.

— Cook fresh peas, covered, in 1 inch of boiling water with 2 or 3 empty pods for 8 to 10 minutes, until tender.

— Spices that blend well with peas are basil, thyme, rosemary, sage, marjoram, and mint.

— Adding onions to peas while cooking also enhances flavor.

— Spices that go well with corn include curry, chili powder, nutmeg, or rosemary.

— Corn blends well with others vegetables such as onions, green and red peppers, and pimento.

— Also delicious with corn are cream sauces made with evaporated skim milk or cheese sauces made with nonfat cheeses.

— To cook moist baked potatoes and sweet potatoes in the microwave, wash potatoes and leave slightly wet. Wrap in microwave plastic wrap and prick through the wrap and into the potato lightly with a fork several times. Place in microwave for about 10 minutes. When done, take out of microwave and wrap in aluminum foil for about 5 to 10 minutes. Potatoes will be moist and delicious. (Note: Leave potatoes in plastic wrap when you place them in the foil.)

Potato Facts —

Do you remember those diets that advocated eating the steak but skipping the potato? That was before the public was made aware of the fact that they were overdosing on proteins and neglecting their most important energy source: complex carbohydrates.

Now potatoes and pasta are part of every health-conscience, low-calorie diet as long as their toppings remain low in fat too. Just one pat of butter can contain more calories than the whole potato.

Potatoes are rich in nutrients. For example, a medium Idaho russet baking potato with the peeling has as much protein as half an egg; as much vitamin C as 4 ounces of tomato juice; more potassium than a banana; and twice the fiber of comparable servings of rice and pasta.

For tasty mashed potatoes, start with baking potatoes because they cook up fluffy. Cook peeled potato chunks in as little water as possible. Save the cooking water and use it to supplement skim milk when mashing. This adds lost nutrients back into the mixture and helps cut fat. To add flavor try a dash of olive or sesame oil or crushed garlic. Low-fat buttermilk is an excellent addition because it has the texture of heavy cream and the taste of sour cream.

Pureed potatoes are a healthy substitute for fatty thickeners in soups and casseroles.

— Potatoes in Hollandaise Sauce —
(makes 2 cups)

2 medium russet baking potatoes (baked)	1-1/2 T. fresh lemon juice
1 c. evaporated skim milk	1/2 tsp. dry mustard
1 T. butter-flavored granules	1/4 tsp. ground tumeric
1 T. onion powder	1/8 tsp. white pepper
1 tsp. chicken bouillon granules	

Prepare after potatoes are baked. Allow potatoes to cool. Cut in half and scoop potato from skins.

In blender, combine remaining ingredients except scooped-out potato. Process until smooth. Gradually add potato, blending smooth. Transfer to a small saucepan and heat through.

Serving Suggestion: Top a hot baked potato with steamed vegetables then drizzle hollandaise sauce over this. This sauce is also good over broccoli, asparagus, and grilled salmon. (Fat: 20% calories from fat)

— Potato Cream Sauce —
(makes 2 cups)

1 small russet baking potato (peeled and diced)
1/2 c. water
1 T. butter-flavored granules
1 T. onion powder

1 tsp. chicken bouillon granules
1/2 to 1 c. evaporated skim milk
1/8 tsp. white pepper

In small saucepan, combine potato and water. Bring to boil, cover and simmer until potato is tender.

Using electric hand mixer, blend potatoes until smooth. Stir in 1/2 cup milk along with remaining seasonings. Blend until smooth, adding additional milk to reach a cream sauce consistency.

This can be used as a base for cream soups, casseroles, and scalloped potatoes.

— Mashed Potatoes —
(4 servings)

5 baking potatoes (peeled and diced)
1/4 c. defatted chicken broth
1/2 white onion (diced)

1-1/2 T. fresh basil
1/4 c. nonfat dry milk
1/8 tsp. white pepper

Steam potatoes until tender. Mash potatoes with chicken broth using potato masher or food processor. Add remaining ingredients. Stir to blend. Serve hot. (Fat: 30% calories from fat)

— Stuffed Potato Meal —
(8 servings — 1/2 potato each)

1 T. onion (chopped)
1/2 c. mushrooms (sliced)
1 T. canola oil
2 T. flour
1 c. skim milk

2 c. broccoli (steamed and chopped)
1-1/2 c. cooked chicken (skinless and cubed)
Pepper to taste
4 baking potatoes (baked)

Saute onions and mushrooms in oil in large pan. Add flour and stir to mix. Stir in milk. Add chicken and broccoli and continue to cook over moderate heat for 2 or more minutes. Add pepper. Place on opened baked potato. (Fat: 25% calories from fat)

— Twice-Baked Potatoes —
(8 servings)

4 small baking potatoes (1-1/4 pounds)
1/4 c. skim milk
2 T. low- or nonfat sour cream
2 T. fresh chives (chopped)
1/4 tsp. salt

1/4 tsp. pepper
2 egg whites
1/3 c. nonfat Cheddar cheese (shredded)
1/8 tsp. paprika

Wash potatoes. Bake at 400 degrees for 1 hour or until tender. Allow potatoes to cool completely. Cut in half lengthwise and scoop out pulp, leaving 1/8-inch thick peeling shells. Combine potato pulp, milk, sour cream, chives, salt, and pepper in a bowl. Mash with a potato masher until smooth. Set aside.

(Continued)

Beat egg whites (at room temperature) until stiff peaks form. Fold into potato mixture. Spoon potato mixture into shells. Place on ungreased baking sheet. Sprinkle 1 tablespoon cheese over each serving. Sprinkle paprika over this. Bake at 375 degrees for 15 minutes until thoroughly heated. (Fat: 20% calories from fat)

— Fryless Fries —
(4 servings)

Cut 1 pound of large red or white potatoes in fry-size strips. Soak them in cold water until water no longer turns cloudy. This removes excess starch.

Drain them and pat dry on paper towels to remove as much moisture as possible.

Place them in a single layer on a baking sheet and sprinkle them with black pepper. Bake in a 400-degree oven for approximately 20 minutes, turning occasionally until golden brown. (Fat: 20% calories from fat)

— Sweet Potatoes 'N Apples —
(6 servings)

1-1/2 pounds sweet potatoes	3 tart apples
2 T. reduced-calorie margarine	Cinnamon
1 T. sugar	Sugar substitute
Dash salt	

Peel and cut potatoes into 1/4-inch slices. Put into large skillet. Cover with water (about 1 cup). Dot with margarine. Sprinkle with salt and sugar.

Cover, bring to boil, and cook over medium heat for 20 minutes. Wash and slice apples. Spread over potatoes. Sprinkle with cinnamon. Cover and cook 10 minutes longer.

Remove cover and cook until sauce is absorbed (about 5 minutes). Sprinkle with sweetener and stir gently. (Fat: 25% calories from fat)

— Glazed Sweet Potatoes —
(8 servings)

3 pounds sweet potatoes (peeled and cut crosswise into 1/2-inch slices)	1 tsp. butter-flavored granules
	1/4 to 1/2 tsp. cinnamon
1/3 c. orange juice concentrate (thawed)	

Preheat oven to 350 degrees. Arrange sweet potatoes in a single layer in two large, shallow baking dishes. Mix orange juice concentrate, 1/3 cup water, butter granules, and cinnamon. Pour over sweet potatoes. Cover dishes tightly with foil and bake until tender (about 30 minutes). (Fat: 1 gram per serving)

— Sweet Fried Corn —
(4 servings)

Nonstick cooking spray	1/4 tsp. salt
3 c. fresh corn (cut from cob)	3 T. reduced-calorie maple syrup
1/2 c. onion (chopped)	3 T. skim milk
1/8 tsp. ground cinnamon	

(Continued)

Coat large nonstick skillet with cooking spray. Place over medium-high heat until hot. Add corn and onion and saute 5 minutes. Combine cinnamon and remaining ingredients. Add to corn in skillet and cook over medium heat 20 minutes, stirring frequently. (Fat: less than 20% calories from fat)

— Traditional Candied Sweet Potatoes —
(4 servings)

2 large sweet potatoes	1 T. reduced-calorie margarine
3 T. brown sugar	1 T. unsweetened orange juice

Wash sweet potatoes and pat dry. Prick each potato several times with a fork. Arrange sweet potatoes 1 inch apart on a layer of paper towels in the microwave oven. Microwave, uncovered, at high for 8 to 10 minutes or until sweet potatoes are tender, turning and rearranging potatoes after 4 minutes. Let potatoes stand 5 minutes.

Peel sweet potatoes and cut into 1/2-inch slices. Combine brown sugar and margarine in a 2-quart casserole. Microwave, uncovered, at high for 1 to 1-1/2 minutes or until sugar and margarine melt, stirring after 1 minute. Stir in orange juice. Add sweet potato slices and toss gently. Cover with wax paper and microwave at high for 1 to 2 minutes or until potatoes are thoroughly heated. Toss gently before serving. (Fat: less than 25% calories from fat)

— Zesty Garden Corn —
(4 servings)

3/4 c. fresh corn	1 tsp. sugar
3/4 c. fresh okra (sliced)	1/2 tsp. salt
1/3 c. green pepper (chopped)	1/8 tsp. pepper
1 small onion (chopped)	1 medium tomato (chopped)
1 T. water	1/8 tsp. hot sauce
1 tsp. reduced-calorie margarine	

Combine corn, okra, green pepper, onion, water, margarine, sugar, salt, and pepper in a 1-quart baking dish. Toss well. Cover with wax paper and microwave on high for 8 to 10 minutes, stirring at 3-minute intervals. Add chopped tomato and hot sauce. Cover and microwave on high for 1-1/2 to 2 minutes until mixture is thoroughly heated. (Fat: less than 20% calories from fat)

— Microwave Corn on the Cob —
(6 servings)

6 ears of fresh corn	1 tsp. dried salad herbs
2 T. reduced-calorie margarine (softened)	

Pull back husks from corn, leaving them attached at base of cob. Remove silks. Rinse corn and pat dry. Pull husks up over corn. Rinse corn husks. Do not drain. Arrange corn on paper towels in microwave oven. Cover with wax paper. Microwave on high for 16 to 18 minutes, rearranging after 8 minutes. Let stand 5 minutes. Remove husks.

Combine margarine and salad herbs. Spread 1 teaspoon margarine mixture over each ear of corn. (Fat: less than 25% calories from fat)

— Roast Potatoes —
(4 servings)

4 new potatoes (scrubbed and halved)
2 tsps. olive oil
Garlic powder

Powdered rosemary
Black pepper
1/4 c. water

Brush potatoes with olive oil. Sprinkle with garlic powder, rosemary and black pepper. Arrange cut side up in shallow roasting pan. Pour 1/4 cup water in bottom of pan. Roast at 375 degrees for 40 to 60 minutes or until tender. (Fat: 16% calories from fat)

— Pan-Fried Potatoes —
(4 servings)

1-1/2 T. olive oil
3 large baking potatoes (unpeeled and diced)

Black pepper to taste

In a nonstick skillet, heat oil. Add potatoes. Cook over medium heat, stirring frequently for about 10 to 15 minutes. Cover, cook 20 to 30 minutes, turning frequently. Remove lid. Cook 10 to 15 minutes or until browned. Sprinkle with black pepper. (Fat: 30% calories from fat)

— Oven French Fries —
(6 servings)

4 medium potatoes

1 T. oil

Peel potatoes and cut into long strips about 1/2 inch wide. Dry strips on paper towels. Toss in a bowl with oil as if making a salad. When strips are thoroughly coated with oil, spread them in a single layer on a baking sheet and place in a 475-degree oven for 35 minutes. Turn strips periodically to brown on all sides. If a crispier, browner potato is desired, place under broiler for about 2 minutes. (Fat: less than 20% calories from fat)

— *Mrs. Hazel McConnell, Alam, MI*

— Squash-Corn Casserole —
(6 servings)

4 c. yellow summer squash (sliced)
1/2 c. onions (chopped)
1 c. canned corn (drained)
1 egg or egg substitute (slightly beaten)

Pepper to taste
1 tsp. grated Parmesan cheese
3/4 ounce wheat germ

Steam squash and onions over boiling water until tender (about 10 minutes). Drain. Place in a blender and process a few seconds (until chopped).

Set aside 1 teaspoon each of the Parmesan cheese and the wheat germ to use as topping.

In a large bowl, combine squash mixture with remaining ingredients. Mix well. Pour into a 1-quart baking dish sprayed with a nonstick cooking spray.

Sprinkle with reserved topping. Bake, uncovered, 35 minutes until firm. (Fat: 20% calories from fat)

— Butternut Squash with Marmalade Sauce —
(4 servings)

2 c. butternut squash (unpeeled and cubed)
1 T. cornstarch
1/2 c. water

2 T. reduced-calorie orange marmalade
1/8 tsp. ground cinnamon

Cook squash in a small amount of boiling water in a covered saucepan until tender (about 15 minutes). Drain and peel squash. Set aside in a covered serving dish to keep warm.

In a small saucepan, combine remaining ingredients, stirring to dissolve cornstarch. Bring to a boil over medium heat, stirring constantly. Boil 1 minute, stirring. Add more water if a thinner sauce is desired. Spoon sauce over squash to serve. (Fat: less than 10% calories from fat)

— Dilled Potatoes —
(4 servings)

2 c. potatoes (unpeeled and cubed)
1 generous T. reduced-calorie margarine
1/4 c. green onions (sliced — green part only)
1/2 c. plain, nonfat yogurt

2 T. skim milk
Salt and pepper to taste
1/2 tsp. dill weed

Cook potatoes in boiling water in a covered saucepan until tender (about 15 minutes). Drain. Set aside in a covered serving dish to keep warm.

Melt margarine in a small nonstick skillet over medium heat. Add onions and cook until tender (about 5 minutes). Reduce heat to low. Stir in remaining ingredients. Cook, stirring until mixture is hot. Do not boil. Spoon sauce over potatoes to serve. (Fat: less than 30% calories from fat)

— Sweet Potatoes in Brown Sugar —
(4 servings)

2 T. plus 2 tsp. reduced-calorie margarine
1 T. firmly-packed brown sugar (or sweetener equivalent)

12 ounces sweet potatoes (peeled, cooked, and sliced 1/2-inch thick)
Ground cinnamon

Melt margarine in a large nonstick skillet over low heat. Stir in brown sugar. Add sweet potatoes. Sprinkle with cinnamon.
Cook, turning potatoes occasionally until hot. (Fat: 30% calories from fat)

— Broccoli-Cheese Stuffed Potatoes —
(8 servings)

4 or 5 large baking potatoes (cooked and split open for stuffing)
1 can (11-ounce) condensed Cheddar cheese soup

2 T. plain, nonfat yogurt
1/2 tsp. Dijon-style mustard
1 c. cooked broccoli flowerets
Chopped tomato

In a saucepan over medium heat, stir soup, yogurt, and mustard. Stir in broccoli. Heat thoroughly. Spoon over potatoes. Top with chopped tomatoes. (Fat: less than 28% calories from fat)

— Tangy Twice-Baked Potatoes —
(4 servings)

2 large baking potatoes
1 c. nonfat cottage cheese
1 tsp. horseradish

2 T. green onion (sliced)
Dash of pepper

Cut potatoes in half, lengthwise. Scoop out centers, leaving 1/8-inch shell. Mash potatoes with cottage cheese and horseradish. Stir in green onions and dash of pepper. Spoon potatoes into shells. Bake at 350 degrees for 30 minutes or in microwave 9 minutes for each potato. (Fat: less than 20% calories from fat)

— Creamy Mashed Potatoes —

Bake desired amount of potatoes, giving one per person, at 375 degrees for 1 hour. Wrap some unpeeled garlic cloves or small onions in foil (1 per every 2 potatoes) and roast them with the potatoes in the oven.

If microwaving, prick potatoes with a fork and microwave at full power 6 to 8 minutes for 2 potatoes; 10 to 12 minutes for 4 potatoes. Turn once during cooking. Let stand 1 minute before removing.

Slice potatoes in half and scoop out flesh. Mash with fork or potato masher. Squeeze garlic or onion out of their skins and mash them in with potatoes.

For a rich, smooth texture, whip some evaporated skim milk. Add a few grindings of black pepper. Mix in with potatoes and serve as is or garnish with snipped chives, minced parsley, or a dollop of nonfat, plain yogurt. (Fat: less than 20% calories from fat)

— Apple-Stuffed Butternut Squash —
(8 servings)

1 medium butternut squash
1/2 c. water
1 c. apple (unpeeled, finely chopped)
1/4 c. onion (chopped)
2 tsp. reduced-calorie margarine (melted)
1/2 c. nonfat or low-fat cottage cheese

1/4 tsp. salt
1/8 tsp. ground cinnamon
1/8 tsp. ground ginger
1/8 tsp. pepper
1/2 tsp. apple pie spice

Cut squash in half lengthwise and remove seeds. Place halves, cut side down, in a 12x8x2-inch baking dish. Pour water around squash and bake at 350 degrees for 45 minutes or until tender.

Saute apple and onion in margarine in a large skillet until onion is tender. Stir in cottage cheese, salt, cinnamon, ginger, and pepper. Set aside.

Carefully scoop out squash pulp, leaving shells intact. Chop pulp.

Add chopped pulp to apple mixture in skillet. Stir well. Spoon mixture into squash shells and sprinkle with apple pie spice.

Bake at 375 degrees for 15 minutes or until thoroughly heated. (Fat: less than 10% calories from fat)

— Baked Squash —
(6 servings)

2 pounds yellow squash
1 T. beef-flavored bouillon granules
1 c. hot water

1 tsp. reduced-calorie margarine (melted)
1/2 tsp. dried whole rosemary (crushed)

Cut yellow squash in half lengthwise. Place squash halves, cut side down, in a large, shallow baking dish.

Dissolve bouillon granules in hot water and pour bouillon around squash in baking dish. Bake, uncovered, at 350 degrees for 20 minutes.

Combine melted margarine and crushed rosemary, stirring well, turn squash and baste with margarine mixture. Bake, uncovered, an additional 15 minutes or until squash is tender. (Fat: less than 20% calories from fat)

— Potato Casserole —
(4 servings)

12 ounces potatoes (unpeeled, coarsely shredded)
1/2 c. onions (coarsely grated)
2/3 c. nonfat dry milk
1/8 tsp. garlic powder

1/4 tsp. salt
1/8 tsp. pepper
2 T. water
1 T. all-purpose flour

Preheat oven to 375 degrees.

In a large bowl, combine all ingredients. Mix well. Place in a 9-inch pie plate sprayed with nonstick cooking spray. Press mixture down gently with back of spoon.

Bake, uncovered, 30 minutes until lightly browned. (Fat: less than 10% calories from fat)

— Sweet Potato 'N Orange —
(4 servings)

12 ounces sweet potatoes (peeled and sliced 1/4-inch thick)
2 small oranges (peeled and sectioned)
1/4 c. orange juice (unsweetened)

1 T. honey
3/4 ounce wheat germ
1/4 tsp. ground cinnamon
4 tsp. reduced-calorie margarine

Preheat oven to 375 degrees. Place half the sweet potato slices in the bottom of a 1-quart baking dish that has been sprayed with a nonstick cooking spray. Top with half of the orange sections.

Top with remaining sweet potatoes and oranges.

In a small bowl, combine orange juice and honey. Pour over casserole. Sprinkle with wheat germ and cinnamon. Dot with margarine.

Bake, covered, 30 minutes or until sweet potatoes are tender. Uncover and bake 10 more minutes. (Fat: 25% calories from fat)

— Corn 'N Okra —
(8 servings)

1 can (16-ounce) whole tomatoes (undrained, chopped)
1 can (16-ounce) whole-kernel corn (undrained)

1-1/2 c. fresh okra (sliced)
1/2 c. onion (chopped)
1/2 c. celery (chopped)
1/4 c. green pepper (chopped)

Combine all ingredients in a large skillet. Stir well.

Cover and bring to a boil. Reduce heat and simmer 15 to 20 minutes. (Fat: less than 10% calories from fat)

9

MENUS & COOKING HELPS

Training Your Children —

Never make the mistake of thinking your eating, exercising, drinking, and smoking habits will not be passed on to your children. Children notice everything their parents say and do, and from an early age begin adopting the behavior of their parents. Yes, when they grow up, they live and think a lot like us.

If we are not careful about the way we eat and exercise or the habits we indulge in, our children won't be either.

> Train up a child in the way he should go; and when he is old, he will not depart from it (Prov. 22:6).

When you choose regular exercise and low-fat eating as a life style, so will your children.

A Viewer Writes —

> Dear Beverly,
> . . . God has been moving in my life in a tremendous way. He has brought me through some tough emotional struggles and (has) begun to show me areas in my life that need attention. In the midst of all of this, I found your program and was hooked from day #1.
> God is so good! He has worked in my life in not only the spiritual and mental areas, but also the physical — through your show. I have two small children and HAD 10 extra pounds from pregnancy. That extra weight is now gone as well as the tired and worn-out feeling I carried for (almost 4 years).
> I didn't start exercising to lose weight, but to feel better. Each day as we'd exercise together, you'd talk about nutrition and fat. Then God began to speak to me about my diet. My eating habits were awful. Then I began to think about my kids who were eating the same way . . . I decided to do something about it. Things aren't perfect yet, but I've begun to cut out many of the fatty foods in our diet. I bought lots of fruit and vegetables. I've been drinking lots of water too. And wouldn't you know it — my body has started to crave the good things

now. Praise God we're on our way to a healthier life!

Thank you so much for more ministry as an encourager . . . and for all the good information you provide.

Active Parents = Active Kids —

Invest in your child's future — set an example of healthy living for them.

Walk instead of drive to the bank when possible. Or take the stairs instead of the elevator. How about playing tennis on weekends instead of a movie? When you do this, parents, you are making the best investment of your time and in the future of your children. By example, you can teach your child to care about his health.

A study done of 100 four to seven year olds and their parents, showed that the children of active parents were found to be nearly 6 times more active than the children of inactive parents. Genetics does play a role somewhat in this. However, even though we cannot change our genes, we can change what we do with them. Parents who walk for exercise, garden regularly, jog, or go to the spa may be encouraging their children to develop a life-time of good habits.

Your energetic and health-conscious example is of more value to your child than savings bonds and IRAs. Research has shown that many children who are inactive up to the junior high age become inactive adults and prime candidates for heart disease and a number of other serious illnesses. I have always said that being a parent is a heavy responsibility. We must teach our children a healthy way of life. Health is not a matter of chance. It comes only as a result of a consistently healthy life style. Let's purpose to bring honor to the Lord by how we live and eat.

> I beseech you brethren by the mercies of God that you present your bodies a living sacrifice, holy acceptable unto God, which is your reasonable service (Rom. 12:1).

Children and Cholesterol —

High cholesterol as a child leads to high cholesterol as an adult, in most cases, and along with it a greater risk of heart disease.

How can we predict which children most likely have high cholesterol? Would it be those who do not exercise regularly? What about a high-fat diet? Or being overweight? Or a family history of high cholesterol? All of these factors could point to a child at risk.

But the single best indicator of high cholesterol in children is the amount of time they spend watching television. A recent survey of 1,000 children at the University of California at Irvine, showed that children watching 2 to 4 hours of TV each day were twice as likely to have high cholesterol as those watching less. It also found that those watching more than 4 hours of television more than quadrupled their chances of having high cholesterol.

No Short Cuts to Good Health —

A famous doctor once said that he found most people coming to him want a prescription for medication or surgery to fix their problems instead of embracing a healthy life style of low-fat eating and regular exercise.

We have a natural pharmacy right inside us, if we will listen to our own bodies and eat healthy, drink water, and exercise. For example, when we go for a walk, our brain produces a natural tranquilizer that makes us feel better, think better, and deal better with our problems.

If we treat our bodies right, they will protect us from illness much better than any medication a doctor could prescribe. The wise person seeks to prevent illness.

Guide to Herbs and Spices —

Following is a guide to the use of herbs and spices that can add to the flavor of your food thus enabling you to cut back on any fats you may be using for flavor.

If you have never used a great variety of herbs and spices, try using one at a time with some of your favorite foods.

Using herbs is also a good way to get used to using less salt. In fact, you can make your own seasoning blend to serve as a salt substitute. To do this, combine 1 part salt with 5 parts herbs, using an assortment of different herbs. For example, try 1/4 teaspoon salt with 1/4 teaspoon each of basil, thyme, dill weed, celery seed, and dried parsley. Or experiment with your own combinations.

Following are some herbs and spices and the foods whose flavor they enhance:

— Green vegetables: tarragon, dill, carroway seeds, chicken stock.

— Dried beans: crushed red pepper, small amount of salt, black pepper and a couple of drops of tobasco (after cooking).

— Allspice: meats, fish, gravies, relishes, and tomato sauce.

— Anise: fruit.

— Basil: green beans, onions, peas, potatoes, summer squash, tomatoes, lamb, beef, shellfish, eggs, sauces.

— Bay leaves: artichokes, beets, carrots, onions, white potatoes, tomatoes, meats, fish, soups and stews, sauces, gravies.

— Caraway seeds: asparagus, beets, cabbage, carrots, cauliflower, coleslaw, onions, potatoes, sauerkraut, turnips, beef, pork, noodles, cheese dishes.

— Cardamom: melon, sweet potatoes.

— Cayenne pepper: sauces, curries.

— Celery seed: cabbage, carrots, cauliflower, corn, lima beans, potatoes, tomatoes, turnips, salad dressings, beef, fish dishes, sauces, soups, stews, cheese.

— Chervil: carrots, peas, salads, summer squash, tomatoes, salad dressings, poultry, fish, eggs.

— Chili powder: corn, eggplant, onions, beef, pork, chili con carne, stews, shellfish, sauces, egg dishes.

— Chives: carrots, corn, sauces, salads, soups.

— Cinnamon: stewed fruits, apple or pineapple dishes, sweet potatoes, winter squash, toast.

— Cloves: baked beans, sweet potatoes, winter squash, pork and ham roasts.

— Cumin: cabbage, rice, sauerkraut, chili con carne, ground beef dishes, cottage or Cheddar cheese.

— Curry powder: carrots, cauliflower, green beans, onions, tomatoes, pork and lamb, shellfish, fish, poultry, sauces for eggs and meats.

— Dill seed: cabbage, carrots, cauliflower, peas, potatoes, spinach, tomato dishes, turnips, salads, lamb, cheese.

— Dill weed: vegetables, salads, poultry, soups.

— Ginger: applesauce, melon, baked beans, carrots, onions, sweet potatoes, poultry, summer and winter squash, beef, veal, ham, lamb, teriyaki sauce.

— Mace: carrots, potatoes, spinach, summer squash, beef, veal, fruits, sauces.

— Marjoram: asparagus, carrots, eggplant, greens, green beans, lima beans, peas, spinach, summer squash, lamb, pork, poultry, fish, stews, sauces.

— Mustard: asparagus, broccoli, brussels sprouts, cabbage, cauliflower, green beans, onions, peas, potatoes, summer squash, meats, poultry.

— Mustard seed: salads, curries, pickles, ham, corned beef, relishes.

— Nutmeg: beets, brussels sprouts, carrots, cabbage, cauliflower, greens, green beans, onions, spinach, sweet potatoes, winter squash, sauces.

— Oregano: baked beans, broccoli, cabbage, cauliflower, green beans, lima beans, onions, peas, potatoes, spinach, tomatoes, turnips, beef, pork, veal, poultry, fish, pizza, chili con carne, Italian sauces, stews.

— Paprika: salad dressings, shellfish, fish, gravies, eggs.

— Parsley flakes: all vegetables, soups, sauces, salads, stews, potatoes, eggs.

— Pepper: most vegetables, meats, salads.

— Poppy seed: salads, noodles.

— Rosemary: mushrooms, peas, potatoes, spinach, tomatoes, vegetable salads, beef, lamb, pork, veal, poultry, stews, cheese, eggs.

— Sage: eggplant, onions, peas, tomato dishes, salads, pork, veal, poultry, ham, cheese.

— Sesame seed: asparagus, green beans, potatoes, tomatoes, spinach.

— Tarragon: asparagus, beets, cabbage, carrots, cauliflower, mushrooms, tomatoes, salads, macaroni, and vegetable combinations, beef, poultry, pork.

— Thyme: artichokes, beets, carrots, eggplant, green beans, mushrooms, peas, tomatoes, pork, veal, poultry, cheese and fish dishes, stuffings.

— Tumeric: mustards and curries, chicken.

Seasoning Hints for Good Cooking

Seafood:

For flavoring seafood, try dill weed and lemon peel on baked or broiled fish. Or for a Chinese flavor, marinate seafood in a small amount of low-salt soy sauce and sprinkle with garlic powder and ginger. Tomatoes, onion flakes, garlic powder, basil, and oregano will add an Italian flavor when combined and poured over fish or shrimp.

Before baking, sprinkle fish with thyme and pepper, for a simple, tasty dish.

Poultry:

A combination of chopped tomatoes, onion, and green peppers along with garlic and oregano poured over chicken and baked makes a great dish.

Saute turkey cutlets in a nonstick skillet with a small amount of oil. Sprinkle with garlic powder and poultry seasoning.

Combine nonfat mayonnaise with Dijon mustard and spread on chicken. Then sprinkle with rosemary and bake. Easy, low in fat, and goes well with a number of side dishes.

Beef and Pork:

Steaks marinated in low-salt soy sauce, sherry extract, garlic powder, and ginger are wonderful on the grill.

Lemon or lime juice with garlic powder and rosemary makes a good marinade for beef or pork.

Add curry powder and minced onion flakes to meat loaf to give it added zing.

Try baking pork chops with Dijon mustard spread over them and sprinkled with rosemary or dill weed.

Egg Options —

Scramble eggs in a nonstick skillet and flavor with a little oregano and garlic powder.

Make a delicious crepe by folding a scrambled egg over sliced apples that have been cooked in a nonstick skillet with cinnamon.

Add spark and lower the calories in egg salad by seasoning with dill weed and using nonfat mayonnaise.

Fruits —

For apple dessert, slice and cook 4 apples in a saucepan or microwave until tender. Season them with 1/4 teaspoon vanilla extract, 1/4 teaspoon each of cinnamon and nutmeg, and sweetener to taste. This works well with pears too.

Enhance grapefruit halves by sprinkling them with cinnamon and a small amount of brown sugar. Broil until bubbly.

Easy fruit medley dessert happens when you saute fresh sliced peaches, apples, and pineapple in a nonstick skillet with cinnamon, nutmeg, and a few drops of vanilla.

Vegetables —

Spruce up carrots with cinnamon and orange peel as they cook.

Lemon peel and pepper add flavor to any vegetable.

Pumpkin pie spice is delicious on cooked squash.

When sauteing zucchini, season with dill weed, salt, and pepper.

Dress up cabbage by cooking it with tomatoes, onions, green pepper, cumin, and garlic.

Grain Tricks —

Mix leftover cooked grains (such as rice) with vanilla extract and cinnamon, reheat and serve.

Oriental rice is easy. Just cook with low-salt soy sauce, ginger, and garlic powder.

An easy pudding can be made from leftover rice by placing rice in a blender with crushed pineapple and coconut extract to taste.

Dairy Dishes —

Add cinnamon and vanilla to nonfat cottage cheese or plain yogurt.

Yogurt is a good base for salad dressing. To 1 cup plain, nonfat yogurt, add 1/2 teaspoon each of oregano and dill weed, 1/8 teaspoon garlic powder, and 1 tablespoon minced onion flakes. Tastes great.

This cottage cheese salad dressing is wonderful. Place nonfat cottage cheese in blender and mix with 2 tablespoons ketchup, 2 teaspoons pickle relish, 1 tablespoon finely minced green pepper and 1 teaspoon minced onion flakes.

A great dip for vegetables can be made by mixing 1 packet of instant beef-flavored broth mix, 1 tablespoon minced onion flakes, and 1 cup plain, nonfat yogurt.

Low-Fat Snacks —

Spread small amount of reduced-calorie margarine on whole-wheat toast. Sprinkle with cinnamon and sweetener for delicious cinnamon toast.

Give air-popped popcorn more flavor by spraying it with nonstick cooking spray and sprinkling on your favorite spice.

Food Staples and Their Fat Grams and Calories
(Information from *Eat for Healthy Food Guide*, Giant Foods, Inc., 1991.)

Food	Serving Size	Fat Grams per serving	Calories
Flour: All-purpose and self-rising	1 cup	4	400
Sugar: granulated, dark, and light brown	1 tsp.	0	16
Sugar Substitutes: Equal	1 packet	0	4
	1 tablet	0	0
Sweet 'N Low	1/10 tsp.	0	2
	1 packet	0	4
Butter: Land O' Lakes	1 T.	11	100
Margarines: Blue Bonnet	1 T.	11	100
Substitutes: Butter Buds or Molly McButter	1/2 T	0	4
Oils: Corn, olive, peanut, sunflower, vegetable	1 T	14	120
Shortening: Crisco	1 T.	12	110
Mazola, Pam	1 spray	1	2

Recipe Modifications —

Following is a chart showing you how to reduce calories and fat in some of your favorite recipes by making a few standard changes.

Instead of:	Change to:	Benefits:	Calories saved:
Oil dressing on pasta salad	Reduce by 1/4 c.	Less fat	600
Untrimmed steak	Trimmed steak	Less fat	55 per ounce
Cereal with 3 tsp. refined sugar	Cereal without sugar added	Less sugar	46

Instead of:	Change to:	Benefits:	Calories saved:
Buttered, salted popcorn	Plain popcorn	Less fat, less sodium	30 per c.
Salted peanuts	Unsalted	Less sodium	
Mayonnaise in dressing	Yogurt in dressing nonfat mayo	Less fat	480 per 1/3 c.
Mayonnaise in dressing	Buttermilk in dressing	Less fat	500 per 1/3 c.
1 bouillon cube	1 c. home made chicken stock	Less sodium (685 mg)	
Regular soy sauce	Reduced-sodium soy sauce	Less sodium (1,900 mg. per T.)	
Cream	Plain, nonfat yogurt	Less fat	720 per c.
Sour Cream	Plain, nonfat yogurt	Less fat	360 per c.
Full-fat cheese	Part-skim cheese (& less than called for)	Less fat	10-25 per ounce
Ground round in tacos	Diced chicken in tacos	Less fat	300 per pound
Bologna	Sliced chicken	Less fat	40 per ounce
Cream in soup	Evaporated skim milk in soup	Less fat	
Whole milk	Nonfat milk	Less fat	60 per c.
Frying in oil	Nonstick skillet	Less fat	125 per T. of oil
2 Eggs	1 egg and 1 egg white	Less cholesterol	60
Mayonnaise	Mustard	Less fat	95 per T.
Oil-packed tuna	Water-packed tuna	Less fat	220
Whole sandwich	Open-faced sandwich	Fewer calories	70-125 per slice
Butter/syrup on pancakes, waffles, French toast	Pureed berries	Less fat; less refined sugar	90/tsp. of butter 40/tsp. of syrup
Butter on toast	Dry toast or half the butter	Less fat	50-100
Chili with 1 pound ground beef	Chili with 1/2 pound ground beef	Less fat	400

Instead of:	*Change to:*	*Benefits:*	*Calories saved:*
Grapefruit juice (8 ounce)	1/2 Grapefruit	Less sugar; more fiber	60
Oil dressing on green salads	Oil-free dressing or fresh lemons	Less fat	125 per T.

Liquid and Dry Measurements —

Dash = less than 1/8 teaspoon
3 teaspoons = 1 tablespoon
2 tablespoons = 1 liquid ounce
4 tablespoons = 1/4 cup
8 tablespoons = 1/2 cup
12 tablespoons = 3/4 cup
16 tablespoons = 1 cup

1 cup = 1/2 pint liquid
2 pints = 1 quart
4 quarts = 1 gallon
1 pound of flour = 4 cups
1 pound of sugar = 2 cups
1 pound of butter = 2 cups
1 stick of butter = 1/2 cup

A WEEK OF MENUS

In the following section, I have laid out menus for seven days, three meals a day with snacks. These are just suggestions to help you get started, if you are new at the low-fat way of eating. But I encourage you to develop your own menus of foods that you and your family like. You will have a greater tendency to stick with low-fat eating if you are eating what you like.

The reason I am including snacks is because I want to encourage you to eat moderately several times a day. Three small meals a day plus in-between-meal snacks, will prevent overeating and you will store less fat this way. Overeating at two or three huge meals a day triggers an enzyme that causes the body to store more fat calories. Smaller meals keeps the metabolism up and lessens fat storage.

Plan your meals and your mealtimes. This gives you a sense of control over your food. Skipping meals often leads to binging and overeating. Never skip a meal.

Recipes for most of these meals can be found in this cookbook. Enjoy!

Day One
Breakfast:
— Ravenel's Oatmeal
— 1 c. skim milk
— 1 c. orange juic
Snack:— Fresh fruit of choice
Lunch:
— 1 serving Turkey 'N Fruit Salad
— Pita bread
— 1 serving Fruity Fluff
— Water with lemon slice
Snack:— Raisin bagel with cup of juice
Dinner:
— Tossed salad with low- or nonfat dressing of choice
— Zucchini-Rice Supper (1 small serving)
— Skim milk
— Baked Pears 'N Cinnamon (1 serving)

Day Two

Breakfast:
— Whole grain cereal
— Sliced banana
— 1 c. skim milk
— 1 piece whole-wheat toast with fruit spread
— 1 cup juice of choice
Snack: — Fresh grapes
Lunch:
— Mushroom-Barley Soup or low-fat soup of choice
— Greens 'N Garlic Salad (or low-fat green salad of choice)
— Peaches with Yogurt
— Water with lemon slice
Snack: — Air-popped popcorn with juice
Dinner:
— Shrimp Creole
— Tossed salad with low- or nonfat dressing of choice
— Pita bread
— Light Citrus Fluff (1 serving)
— Water with lemon slice

Day Three

Breakfast:
— Egg 'N Muffin
— 1 c. skim milk
— Fresh fruit of choice
Snack:— Fresh fruit with a few pretzels
Lunch:
— Ryland's Pita Veggie Pocket Sandwich
— Skim milk
— Spiced Oatmeal Cookies (1 or 2)
Snack:— Approx. 1/2 cup or so of bite-size, fruit-filled shredded wheat with juice
Dinner:
— Ann's Fried Chicken (1 small serving)
— Green Beans 'N Lemon
— Mashed Potatoes (see our recipe)
— Cucumber Salad
— Beverly's Nonfat Cornbread (1 serving)
— Fruit Dessert (1 serving)
— Water with lemon slice

Day Four

Breakfast:
— Breakfast Shake
— 1 toasted whole-wheat bagel, lightly spread with reduced-calorie margarine
— 1 T. fruit spread
Snack: — Fresh apple
Lunch:
— Eight-Vegetable Salad
— Pita bread
— Skim milk
— Lemon Delights cookies (1 or 2)
Snack: — Piece of cantaloupe
Dinner:
— Beverly's Lasagna (1 small serving)
— Fresh green salad with low- or nonfat dressing
— Quick 'N Easy Rolls
— Microwave Lemon Pudding (1 serving)
— Water with lemon slice

Day Five

Breakfast:
— Yogurt with fresh fruit of choice
— 1 whole-wheat English muffin lightly spread with reduced-calorie margarine
— 1 T. fruit spread
— 1 c. juice of choice
Snack: — 1 rice cake spread with very small amount of Tasty Peanut-Apple Spread and cup of juice
Lunch: (This is a good lunch for Saturday when children are home.)
— Seasoned Turkey Burger
— Skim milk
— Fresh grapes or strawberries
Snack: — Carrot and celery sticks
Dinner:
— Oven-Fried Catfish
— Twice-Baked Potatoes
— Fish Fry Coleslaw
— Low-Fat Hush Puppies
— Fruit Dessert
— Water with lemon slice

Day Six

Breakfast:
— Pancakes, from any of our recipes, topped with a low-fat syrup or fruit spread
— Skim milk
— 1/2 grapefruit
Snack: — 1/2 c. or so of bite-size, fruit-filled shredded wheat with juice
Lunch:
— Peel-A-Pound Soup
— Pita bread or toasted whole-wheat bagel
— Six-Fruit Salad
— Skim milk
Snack: — Nonfat frozen yogurt
Dinner:
— Beef, Stir-Fried and Tasty
— Rice Side Dish
— Delicious Raspberry Tapioca
— Water with lemon slice

Day Seven

Breakfast:
— Low-fat muffin of choice from our recipes
— Fresh fruit of choice
— Skim milk
Snack: — Air-popped popcorn
Lunch:
— Easy Chicken Salad
— Carrot sticks
— Low-salt crackers (4)
— Strawberry 'N Fruit Sherbet
— Water with lemon
Snack: — Fresh fruit of choice
Dinner: (This makes a good holiday meal when you have guests.)
— Turkey Breast
— Traditional Candied Sweet Potatoes
— Sweet Fried Corn
— Green Beans 'N Lemon (or green vegetable of choice)
— No-Fat Biscuits
— Low-Fat Pumpkin Pie

Resources

The following publications have served as valuable resources in the development of this cookbook and in my study of nutrition and exercise over the years:

1. *American Health Magazine*
2. *Shape Magazine*
3. *Health*
4. *Aviation Medical Bulletin*
5. *The Health Letter*
6. *Prevention Magazine*
7. *Tufts University Diet and Nutrition Letter*
8. *Eat for Health Food Guide,* Giant Food, Inc., 1991

BEVERLY'S PRODUCTS

Below is a listing of items available for purchase from Beverly Exercise.

Book:

Your Health Coach, by Beverly Chesser with Gale R. Cox, Whitaker House. A general nutrition book which teaches low-fat eating and benefits of exercise. Cost — $15.

Videos:

Total Body Workout — A one-hour exercise tape (done in two, 30-minute segments) with exercises for the entire body. These ballet-type, stretching exercises are designed to shape the body, improve posture, and increase flexibility. Cost — $39.95.

Hip and Thigh Workout — A one-hour exercise tape (done in two, 30-minute segments) for the hip and thigh area (inner and outer thigh and derriere). These ballet-type, uplifting exercises will firm and shape the hips and thighs. Cost — $25.

Audio Cassettes:

Exercise Audio Cassette Tapes — Exact photo instructions included.

Total Body Workout — An exercise program for the entire body. Floor exercises only. Low impact. No aerobics. Cost — $8.95.

Hip and Thigh Workout — Hip and thigh exercises only. Floor exercises. Low impact. No aerobics. Cost — $8.95.

Nutrition Teaching Tapes — Beverly speaks on diet and exercise. These tapes are designed to teach proper nutrition and the benefits of exercise. Cost — $5 each. (When you order 8 at a time, they come in a binder. Cost for eight — $40.)

— Tape 1: Introduction to Health
— Tape 2: More on Eating Right
— Tape 3: Health Helpers
— Tape 4: Selficide (Eating Disorders)
— Tape 5: Food Abuse and Diet Pills
— Tape 6: Fighting Fat
— Tape 7: Where's the Fat?
— Tape 8: Lose the Fat
— Tape 9: Cholesterol
— Tape 10: Fiber and Starch
— Tape 11: Fat and Breast Cancer
— Tape 12: Mono Fats

— Tape 13: Diabetes
— Tape 14: Weight Loss
— Tape 15: Bad Fats
— Tape 16: High Blood Pressure & Cholesterol
— Tape 17: Sugar Abuse
— Tape 18: Water and Coffee
— Tape 19: Starvers, Stuffers and Skippers
— Tape 20: How Many Fat Grams
— Tape 21: Stress Relief
— Tape 22: Healthy Bones
— Tape 23: PMS
— Tape 24: HDL Cholesterol

For further information or to order, write or call:
Beverly Exercise
P.O. Box 5434
Anderson, SC 29623
(803) 225-5799 or (803) 224-2498

Index